WOMEN
WHO
MAKE
MOVIES

Sharon Smith

CINEMA STUDIES SERIES · LEWIS JACOBS, CONSULTING EDITOR

Hopkinson and Blake, New York

Published by Hopkinson and Blake
329 Fifth Avenue, New York, N. Y. 10016

ISBN: 0-911974-09-1 (cloth), 0-911974-12-1 (paper)
Library of Congress Catalog Card Number: 74-79562
Manufactured in the United States of America

PHOTO CREDITS

*Grateful acknowledgment is made to Honor Moore
for the photos of Mary Ellen Bute and Shirley
Clarke (p. 32), Susan Sontag (p. 17), Juleen
Compton (p. 176) and Donna Deitch (p. 287).
Also to Samuel H. Robbins (Amy Greenfield, p. 173),
Robert Gumpert (Barbara Kopple, p. 174), Nancy
Stark (Louva Irvine, p. 175), Joedy Nerini (Coni
Beeson, p. 218), Emil Ihrig (Rosalind Schneider,
p. 285), Kevin G. Kelly (Johanna Demetrakas,
p. 285), Mary Ellen Andrews (Maria Harriton,
p. 285) and Karl Bissinger (Naomi Levine, p. 287).*

The jacket photo of Miriam Weinstein is by Gisela Hoelcl.

To my parents, T Ella and Cammie Levi,
and my husband Randolph P. Huber

Foreword

The history of women filmmakers is a spotty one. Curiously, women made their greatest impact in the pioneering years, when they were conspicuously involved in every facet of filmmaking except camera work (the cameras were awesome in their bulk and weight). Those were the days, of course, when filmmaking was a free-wheeling affair, with dozens of little companies springing up out of the pavement to grind out one- and two-reelers as fast as the camera could record them. Costs were low then, and anyone with imagination and flair could play. But as the new industry prospered, sophisticated management (male) assumed control of both picture-making and distribution, unions began their rise, and the influence of women dropped sharply (as did the image of women on the screen itself). It was not until the late 1960s, with the increased use of 16mm films, that women began to appear again in significant numbers—as producers, directors, writers, editors, and even cinematographers. True, only a few have been involved in the big theatrical films, but the medium of film has now become a much more pervasive thing—and the great interest in art films, educational films, commercial films, and experimental films has created new opportunities for women, and they are responding

The purpose of this book is two-fold: (1) to present a history of women filmmakers, and (2) to identify the new women filmmakers. If, in the telling, the charge of discrimination recurs it is because discrimination has been, and to an unfortunate extent still is, intrinsic to the story of women who make films.

I am indebted to the hundreds of women filmmakers who patiently responded to my letters, gave interviews, and arranged special screenings of their films, and to the women of the Margaret Herrick Library at the Academy of Motion Picture Arts and Sciences for their invaluable assistance. My thanks also to Kristina Nordstrom, Andrea Staskowski and Veronica Ariessohn, who helped in many ways.

Sharon Smith
Hartland, Maine

Contents

FOREWORD

PART ONE
OVERVIEW
A Survey of Women Filmmakers
Worldwide Since 1896 / p. 1

First, Alice Guy Blaché / p. 2

The United States / p. 11

Around the World / p. 91

PART TWO
THE NEW FILMMAKERS
Women Who Are Making Movies
Outside of Hollywood / p. 145

PART THREE
DIRECTORY
A Listing of Women Filmmakers
Throughout the United States / p. 221

———

ORGANIZATIONS / p. 289

DISTRIBUTORS / p. 292

BIBLIOGRAPHY / p. 296

INDEX / p. 299

PART ONE

OVERVIEW

A SURVEY OF WOMEN FILMMAKERS
WORLDWIDE SINCE 1896

The work of women filmmakers in the eighty-year history of motion pictures has never been chronicled, and alas a good deal of the information of the early years is now beyond retrieving. Those were the years, of course, when moviemaking was considered too inconsequential an enterprise to warrant the attention of an archivist. Even sadder, the work of women in later years often went unrecorded for the reason that *women* were regarded as inconsequential. Be that as it may, the survey that follows makes it clear that women have contributed in substantial numbers to the art and industry of motion pictures, both here and abroad.

This compendium begins at the beginning, with a pioneering Frenchwoman whose name is all but unknown, even to the women walking in her footsteps.

First, Alice Guy Blache

First there was Alice Guy Blaché, who was born in Paris in 1873 and reared in an environment that accorded women most of the privileges of children and imbeciles. Yet she became one of the important pioneers in the development of the motion picture. She was one of the first to see the potential of the Lumière brothers' invention for casting moving images on a screen, and although the historical accounting is not clear, she may have been the first person to use the motion picture to tell a story.

Blaché began her career as a filmmaker in Paris in 1896 with the camera manufacturing firm of Léon Gaumont. Eleven years later she came to the United States, and here, free of the restrictions French society imposed on women, she was able to put her zest and inventiveness to full use. In 1910 she formed her own production company, and in 1912, after a modest beginning in Flushing, New York, built a larger studio in Fort Lee, New Jersey, where she began turning out films that contributed significantly to the growth of the motion picture industry.

By 1915 her reputation was firmly established. In "Who's Who in the Motion Picture World," a book published that year, she received this tribute: "Mme. Alice Blaché, president of the Solax Co., is probably the best known woman executive and producer in the motion picture world. She enjoys a unique distinction in the fact that she writes and directs practically all of her productions. She started the production of multiple reels in this country and to her the credit is due for many of the best known features produced in the early days of feature productions. Her recent and striking successes have been such well-known productions as *The Tigress, The Heart of a Painted Woman,* and *The Shooting of Dan McGrew.*"

In her Fort Lee studio—the town of Fort Lee, just across the Hudson from Manhattan, was then a center of film activity—she directed at least one multireel film a month and supervised all aspects of production. As head of the company she was free to do any kind of story that struck her fancy, and her fancy encompassed every film genre—romance, comedy, adventure, even science fiction. Some of her titles: *Falling Leaves, Face at the Window, The Rose of the Circus, The Sewer,* Poe's *The Pit and the Pendulum, In the Year 2000* (in which women ruled the world), *The Million Dollar Robbery, The Beasts of the Jungle, Shadows of the Moulin Rouge,* and *A Man and a Woman.*

A few years after establishing the Solax Company, Blaché began to feel the pressure of competition from the larger studios. She reorganized the Solax Company as the U.S. Amusement Company and, a short time later, as Popular Plays and Players. The competition was too much to cope with, however, and about 1919 she ceased her own productions and hired herself out to make films for Pathé and Metro. (Her major films for these studios included *The Great Adventure* and *Tarnished Reputation.*)

It was a time of great personal stress. Just when her company went into a decline, her marriage to Herbert Blaché, who had worked closely with her since the Gaumont days, came to an end. With her two American-born children, Reginald and Simone, she returned to France in 1922, and although she sought film jobs there, none was to be had for a woman of middle age, and she never made pictures again. In 1953, when she was eighty years old, the French government finally took notice of her achievements and conferred on her the Legion of Honor. In 1964, when her daughter, Simone,

retired from a career in the American diplomatic service, she
returned to the United States to spend her last days in
Simone's home in Mahwah, New Jersey. Four years later, at
the age of ninety-five, Alice Guy Blaché died. No newspaper
carried an obituary.

Unresolved to this day is the question of who actually
made the first film with a plot line. Blaché claimed that distinction, and actively campaigned for it, but film historians
generally have credited her countryman, George Méliès, or
the American, Edwin S. Porter. (The brilliant and innovative
Méliès also was ill rewarded for his many accomplishments.
He died in a home for destitute actors.)

The motion picture that Blaché insisted was the first filmed
narrative was also the first film she ever made. Titled *La Fée
aux choux* (*The Good Fairy in the Cabbage Patch*), and
based on the mythical French tale of where babies come
from, it shows a young husband and wife coming upon a cabbage patch where a fairy waits to present them with a child.
The film, which probably ran for about a minute, launched
her career.

An Interview With Her Daughter

In an interview in the fall of 1974, Simone Blaché spoke
about her mother's early years and how she came to make
La Fée aux choux:

"Mother was the youngest of four daughters. Her father
was a book publisher and his business for a time was quite
successful, but when he died the family was left in financial
difficulty. Mother, who was then sixteen years old, decided
she would try to learn a trade and earn some money, so she
went to a secretarial school and learned to be a typist and a
stenographer. It was something quite unusual because at the
time—the late 1880s—women were not supposed to work. She
worked in various places and then, when she was twenty-
three years old, she found a job with the Gaumont company,

which made all sorts of cameras. I remember Mother telling me that once some Turkish pasha came and ordered a solid gold camera, and it was made for him. Léon Gaumont himself had a very fertile and inventive mind, and he was interested in all sorts of inventions. He heard of the invention of the Lumière brothers, who had made a machine to make motion pictures, and he went to see how it worked. I don't think he got the Lumière camera, I think he made one of his own. Anyway, he and his associates began playing around with this instrument. They didn't know what to do with it, they just played around with it, taking pictures. Pictures of moving things, such as trains, races, parades, and things like that.

"Mother was very interested in it. She was a secretary at Gaumont, but also partly a saleslady. She was a little bit of everything in that company. One day while they were filming the arrival of a train at a station, she asked Gaumont if he would let her try something with the camera and he said 'What! What! What! All right, if you *want* to—it's a child's toy anyhow.' So that was the famous moment when she got together in a garden with some young friends of hers and put on film the fairy tale of how children are born in cabbages. I believe it was shown that same year—1896—at the International Exhibition in Paris."

The Gaumont company then went into the business of making motion pictures and Blaché became the company's main director. The first customers for Gaumont films, Simone Blaché recalled, were circus managers. "The films were shown as part of the circus entertainment," she said. "Mother got to know a very strange and interesting breed of people, lion tamers and all sorts of people like that."

Some of Blaché's earliest films for Gaumont were *Les Petits Voleurs du Bois-Vert* (*Little Thieves of Bois-Vert*), *La Momie* (*The Mummy*), *Le Courrier de Lyon* (*The Lyons Courier*), *Le Cake-Walk de la pendule* (*The Clock's Cakewalk*), *Le Gourmand effrayé* (*The Scared Glutton*), *Démenagement à la cloche de bois* (*Moving Out in the Night*), all one-reelers.

Gaumont set up a studio for her and she went on to more ambitious projects These included *La Esmeralda, Faust et Méphisto, Vendetta, L'Enfant de la barricade* (*The Child of the Barricade*), and *Passion du Christ*. *Passion du Christ*, made in 1906, is said to have required twenty-five sets and 300 extras. (French historians have wrongly attributed this film to Jasset, who had been hired by Blaché to assemble the large cast.)

Herbert Blaché was an Englishman who ran the Gaumont branch in London and later in Berlin. Alice Guy first met him on a visit to the Berlin office in 1906. A few months later, when she was directing a film in Arles in the south of France —a picture based on the French classic, "Mireille"—Herbert Blaché arrived to see how the work was going on. They married after a short time and almost directly left for the United States to operate a branch for Gaumont products in Cleveland. The year was 1907.

The Cleveland branch did poorly—Gaumont was still trying to push his ill-fated Chronophone—and the Blachés quickly closed it and moved to New York, where Mme. Blaché, still learning her first English words, formed her own film production company.

Despite the reputation she achieved in the United States, Blaché faced hard times when she went back to France after her divorce in 1922. With two children to support, she took up writing summaries of film stories for several pulp magazines. It paid a meager living.

The discrimination she encountered in France against working women came as a blow, especially after her experience in the United States. "Mother was really cherished in the United States," Simone Blaché said. "She used to say that people treated her so wonderfully here because she was a woman, because she was a woman in film. The situation in France was quite the reverse. She kept up her contacts with a number of people in the industry and went to see many pictures, but she was never able to get a film job again.

"The only reason she is remembered at all now is that she made great efforts to stake her claim, to say 'I was the first person that ever did this. Now you've got to pay attention. You've got to take notice. I am the one who did it.' Finally, she was given the Legion of Honor for meritorious service. It was a very great day in her life, of course."

Blaché had departed from the United States in 1922 in haste, leaving her affairs in disarray. In 1927, in an effort to establish her credentials, she came back to find the films she had made. "She had left everything here," her daughter said, "and she had nothing to prove what she had done. She went to the Library of Congress and many other places where she thought her films might have been saved, but she could not find any of them." It was only after her death that some of her films—early one-reelers—were found by the American Film Institute.

Some film historians refer to her as Alice Guy, others use the name Blaché. "Mother was known as Alice Guy only until her marriage," said Simone Blaché. "She worked in this country as Alice Blaché and because she had built her reputation with that name she kept it after her divorce. She referred to herself as Alice Guy Blaché. Father, incidentally, was of French descent and our name is pronounced blah-*shay*."

How would Simone Blaché describe her mother?

"She was a very dynamic and energetic person. Very self-reliant. She was somewhat shy, but she overcame that very well. She couldn't speak a word of English when she came here, but she overcame that as well. She was very generous and very warm. She had to love people and be loved by them. When her marriage broke apart I saw her almost on the point of committing suicide.

"In many respects she was a nineteenth-century person. She believed in the family. It was beyond her to understand life without the family structure. And yet she had strong feminist views. She was enthused by everything she saw and heard that was feminist in any way."

Fifty years ago, Alice Guy Blaché made the observation that filmmaking was more suited to women than to men. "It has long been a source of wonder to me," she wrote, "that many women have not seized upon the wonderful opportunities offered to them by the motion picture art to make their way to fame and fortune as directors of photodramas. Of all the arts there is probably none in which they can make such splendid use of talents so much more natural to a woman than to a man and so necessary to its perfection."

Alice Guy Blaché

In *The Passion*, made in Paris in 1906, Blaché used
elaborate sets of wood and plaster designed by Menessier.
She also experimented with close-ups.

In 1917, well-established now as a U.S. filmmaker,
Blaché (center) went to the Florida Everglades
to shoot *Spring of the Year*.

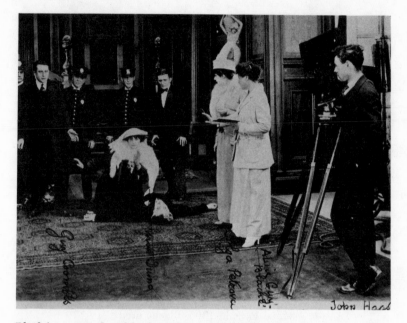

Blaché conceived and built sophisticated sets in her
Fort Lee studio. In this photo, obtained from her
daughter, Blaché identified some of the people involved
in a drama filmed in the late teens. From the left: Guy
Coombes, a prominent player of the time, Miss Dumo,
the international star Olga Petrova, director Blaché,
and cameraman John Haas.

In the United States

Lois Weber

The first American woman filmmaker was Lois Weber, whose bold themes brought her into constant conflict with distributors.

Weber, a pianist and musical comedy actress, began making motion pictures in 1913, and at first worked with her husband, the actor Phillips Smalley. She wrote, directed and produced half a dozen of their films, and also starred in them. In 1916 she formed Lois Weber Productions, leased a studio from Universal, staffed it with dozens of writers and technicians, and produced a long list of pictures based on her own screenplays. One of her first films under the banner of Lois Weber Productions was *Where Are My Children?* (1916), the story of an idealistic physician who advocates birth control. The hero is thrown in jail for his troubles while an unsavory colleague collects great wealth performing abortions. Weber's advocacy of birth control made her a figure of controversy, but she never backed away from this issue, and in fact made four more films on the subject. (The picture, incidentally, is said to have cost $12,000 and brought in more than $500,000. A magazine of the time described her as "the highest-salaried woman director in the world today," an observation of less than shattering impact since there were only a handful of women directors extant, but it demonstrated that Weber was attracting wide attention.) By 1920 she had directed more than seventy-five pictures. Most, however, were the one- and two-reelers that filled out the feature programs of the period.

Many of her films dealt frankly with marital problems. Typical of these was *What Do Men Want?* (1921), which tells of men who leave good wives for other women. In 1927, amid thickening clouds of controversy, she made *The Sensation Seekers*, the story of a minister's tempestuous romance with a wild society girl, and followed that with *Angel of Broadway*. The latter, a drama about a prostitute, was rejected by the major distributors, and Lois Weber was all but finished. Seven years later she made a final stab at directing for a small independent company named Pinnacle. This last film, *White Heat*, about marital infidelity and interracial love, also was turned down by the distributors.

Other Directors of the Early Years

There were more women directors in Hollywood during the teens and twenties than in any period since that time. One estimate has it that there were twenty-six between 1913 and 1927, but in a number of instances, particularly in the teens, actresses and screenwriters directed their own pictures anonymously, so a true compilation is impossible.

Directors known to have followed on the heels of Lois Weber were Elizabeth Pickett, whose credits have unfortunately found their way to oblivion, and Ida May Park, co-director with Joseph de Grasse of the short, *Simple Pool*. Park subsequently did fifteen more films, most of them in collaboration with de Grasse. They included *The Fires of Rebellion* (1917), *Broadway Love* (1918), *Amazing Wife* (1919), *The Butterfly Man* (1920) and *The Midlanders* (1920).

In 1913 also, the serial star Grace Cunard formed a close association with director Francis Ford and co-directed and co-wrote many of her serials, including *Broken Coin* (1915, twenty-two two-reel episodes), *Peg o' the Ring* (1916, fifteen episodes) and *The Purple Mask* (1916, sixteen episodes).

Cunard also directed on her own the short feature *The Campbells Are Coming* (1915), and wrote scenarios for several of Ford's films.

Ruth Ann Baldwin directed many films for Universal, including a short, *The Black Page* (1915), *The Butterfly* (1917) and *The Woman Who Could Not Pay* (1917). For Metro she directed *Broken Commandments* (1919) and *Puppets of Fate* (1921). Cleo Madison, an actress at Universal, produced and directed the one-reel *Liquid Dynamite* (1915), then stepped up to the two-reel *The King of Destiny* (also 1915), *Her Bitter Cup* (1916) and possibly *The Chalice of Sorrows* (though this 1916 film is generally credited to Rex Ingram). For Universal and Bluebird Photoplay, Elsie Jane Wilson directed *Dona Perfecta* (1915), *The Human Catos* (1916), *The Silent Lady* (1917), *New Love for Old* (1918) and *The Lure of Luxury* (1919). Mrs. George Randolph Chester (her first name has been lost in time) co-directed several films with her husband for Vitagraph. These included *The Wreck* (1917), *The Sins of the Mother* (1918), *Vengeance on Demand* (1919), *Slaves of Pride* (1920) and *The Sons of Wallingford* (1921). Gene Gauntier (nee Genevieve G. Ligget), was an assistant director at the Kalem Studio, where she wrote the scripts for the more than 500 films in which she starred. In 1920, Vera McCord directed *Good Bad Wife* and Beverly C. Rule directed *Mystery of Washington Square*. In 1921, Margery Wilson filmed *That Something*, and Ruth Jennings Bryan (later Ruth Bryan Owen) directed *Once Upon a Time*. In 1922 Mildred Webb co-directed *Where Is My Wandering Boy Tonight?*, and in 1923 Julia Crawford Ivers made *The White Flower*. May Tully directed *The Old Broken Bucket* (1921), *Our Mutual Friend* and *Kisses* (both 1922) and *That Old Gang of Mine* (1926). In 1925 Frances Nordstrom co-directed *Her Market Value*. Lillian Ducey wrote and directed several films, including *Upstairs and Down* (1919), *Enemies of Children* (1923), *The Worry* (1927) and *Behind Closed Doors* (1929). Jane Murfin, a writer of Broadway hits who was lured to Hollywood to do screenplays, co-directed *Flapper Wives* and *Love Master* in 1924. (Murfin also earned a fair measure of esteem for managing the silent screen career of a German shepherd named Strongheart, a heroic beast who was second in stardom only to the fabled Rin-Tin-Tin. In 1934, in a development for which Strongheart could take no credit, Murfin was appointed script supervisor at RKO.)

Lucille McVey (also known as Polly Drew) co-produced and directed with her husband, Sidney Drew, a series of one-reel comedies that came out almost every week in 1917. She was also a writer, costumer and set designer, and acted in most of their films. After Sidney Drew died in 1919, she continued her career as director, producer and actress, with films such as *Bunkered* (1919), the shorts *Emotional Mrs. Vaughan* and *Stimulating Mrs. Barton* (both 1920) and *Cousin Kate* (1921). About 1919 Gale Henry, another actress-turned-director, organized her own film company, Bull's Eye Film Corporation, and was turning out comedies.

Another pioneer in directing, producing, writing and photographing films—and an actress as well—was Nell Shipman (a transplanted Canadian who never lost her deep affection for her native country). *The Girl From God's Country* (1921), her most famous film, was shot in "the Great North Woods." She wrote, directed and starred in it. Other films she made were *The Black Wolf* (1917), *Baree, Son of Kazan* (1918), *The Golden Yukon* (1919), *Neptune's Daughter* (1922) and *Back to God's Country* (1927). "It warms our hearts and inspires our minds to know there is a generation of young and lively students who care about our beginnings, study the ring circles of our growth, and are ready themselves to contribute to the ever-present goal of film perfection." So wrote Nell Shipman. The time was around 1925. She could by then refer to herself as an "old trail-blazer."

Writer Frances Marion did many scripts for Douglas Fairbanks and Mary Pickford, but was dissatisfied with the way some of the pictures were directed. In 1921 Pickford permitted her to direct *The Love Light*. The following year she directed *Just Around the Corner*, and in 1924 she directed *The Song of Love*.

Other writers who tried their hand at directing included Anita Loos (who worked with Griffith), Elinor Glyn, Clara Beranger, Agnes Johnson, Dorothy Farnum, Marion Fairfax and Wanda Tuchock (who wrote for King Vidor and later directed *Daughters of America*).

The celebrated actress Mabel Normand is purported to have directed a number of shorts for Keystone in which she starred, usually with Chaplin. Actress Ruth Stonehouse also directed shorts during these early years and wrote some scripts as well.

Lillian Gish directed one film, *Remodeling Her Husband* (1920), starring her sister Dorothy and written by Elizabeth Carter. It concerns, it might be noted, a woman who leaves her unfaithful husband and goes to work for her father. Later, when the husband has been properly humbled, she leaves her job and takes him back. The film was successful, but Gish, a rather conservative person, preferred to devote her energies to acting, observing in her ladylike way that directing was "no career for a lady."

In 1922 Nazimova not only produced her grandiose adaptation of *Salome*, but also directed it, though she gave credit for the direction to her husband, Charles Bryant.

Mary Pickford is best known as an actress, of course, but she was a producer and a director as well. She formed the Artcraft production company within Famous Players, then in 1919 founded United Artists with D. W. Griffith, Charlie Chaplin and Douglas Fairbanks. Pickford did not take formal directing credits for her films because she felt that doing so would have impaired her "Little Mary" image, but her cinematographer, Charles Rosher, later confirmed that she had done a lot of her own directing. Said Rosher: "She knew everything there was to know about motion pictures."

Other prominent silent-era personalities who turned their hand to producing were Gloria Swanson, Clara Kimball Young, and Bessie Barriscale.

Writers and Editors of the Early Years

The most successful writer was Frances Marion, whose career extended into the forties and who is best remembered for *Stella Dallas, The Champ, Min and Bill, The Wind, Dinner at Eight* and *Camille.* In view of Marion's own success, the plot of her first screenplay has a certain irony. She described it in an article she wrote in 1924 for the American Magazine: "A young girl believes she is destined to become a great writer. She is so bent on having a career as a novelist that she refuses to marry the man who is in love with her and whom she, in fact, really loves. She has written her first novel, thinks it is wonderful, but tells her lover that if it fails she will give up her dreams of fame and marry him. . . . We would follow that with scenes showing that the book did fail, and that the girl, chastened by her experience, gladly accepted her lover."

Well-known writers of that period who worked in Hollywood included Elinor Glyn, who added countless innuendoes to one word with *It* (1926), starring Clara Bow; Rachel Crothers (*Nice People,* 1922); Agnes Johnson (*Forbidden Paradise,* 1924); and Bess Meredyth (*Wonder of Women,* 1928). Anita Loos (who had begun her long career in 1912 with *The New York Hat* for Griffith) wrote satires and helped to establish the success of dashing Douglas Fairbanks. Josephine Lovett won one of the first Academy Award nominations for *Our Dancing Daughters* (1928). June Mathis wrote the scenarios for *Four Horsemen of the Apocalypse* (1921), *Blood and Sand* (1922) and *Ben Hur* (1922), and by her writing helped develop the allure of Rudolph Valentino. An expert cutter, too, she was given the assignment of condensing Von Stroheim's famous *Greed* to manageable length and making it "commercial," a task she executed with a cold-heartedness that made Hollywood gasp. Lotta Woods wrote adventures, such as *Robin Hood* (1923) and *The Thief of Bagdad* (1925). Ethyl Kennedy, Beulah Marie Dix, Marion Fairfax and Lenore Coffee were also prominent screen writers at this time.

One of the most interesting of the early screenwriters was Ouida Bergere, a woman of many talents. First a vaudevillian, later a Broadway actress, Bergere also headed her own talent agency during World War I, managing Nazimova, Lionel Atwill, Adolphe Menjou and other stars. She wrote screenplays for the major studios from 1915 to 1935. Her credits included *Bella Donna* (1918), *Idols of Clay* (1920), *Cytherea* (1924), *Garden of Allah* (1927), and *Peter Ibbetson* (1935), an adaptation for which she also designed the costumes. The widow of actor Basil Bathbone, she died in 1974.

Hollywood's first woman film editor was Viola Lawrence, a now legendary veteran whose career spanned half a century. Lawrence started in motion pictures in 1912 as an errand girl at the Vitagraph Studios in Brooklyn, and after a while became an assistant editor. In 1915 she was assigned an O. Henry three-reeler as an editor, and the following year did a nine-reel "spectacular," *Within the Law*. With these credentials she moved to Hollywood, where she worked for several major studios, beginning with Universal, and some of the top directors including John Ford, Howard Hawks, Fred Niblo, Victor Fleming, Orson Welles and George Sidney. From 1925 to '27 she was supervising editor for Columbia. Her films in the twenties included *Awakening* (1928), *Queen Kelly* (1929), and Goldwyn's first sound picture, *Bulldog Drummond* (1929). Lawrence retired in 1961. Reviewing her career before her death in 1973, she said, "I loved films and I was happy. It was my life."

There were some women who edited film before Lawrence

—including Anna McKnight, who worked as early as 1911, and Mamie Wagner, who in 1914 cut *The Call of the North*, *The Squaw Man* and *The Virginian*—but none could challenge Lawrence's position as Hollywood's first full-fledged woman editor. Other important woman editors, however, were soon to make their mark as important members of the industry. These women, all of whom had long and distinguished careers, were Anne Bauchens, Irene Morra, Blanche Sewell, Eda Warren and Margaret Booth.

Anne Bauchens began a long association with Cecil B. DeMille in 1918 with the films *We Can't Have Everything* and *Till I Come Back To You*. In 1919 her credits included *Don't Change Your Husband*, *For Better For Worse* and *Male and Female*. In the twenties she worked on seventeen pictures, almost all of them for Paramount. Her career was to continue for two more decades.

Irene Morra, a native of New York, began working in Hollywood in 1913. Her first assignment was splicing D. W. Griffith's *Intolerance*. Some of her early credits in a fifty-year career were *High Society* (1927) and *Sunny Side Up* (1929), both for Fox. Blanche Sewell, who also got started in the teens, worked on her most important films in the thirties and forties.

Eda Warren got her first job in Hollywood in 1922 as a secretary, later became a script clerk, and began editing in the late 1920s. Her career extended well into the sixties. Her credits in the twenties include *Hula* (1927) and *Dangerous Curves* (1929), both for Paramount.

Both in terms of longevity and production, the most remarkable of all the women pioneers, however, is Margaret Booth, who began her career in 1919 and was still pursuing it with full vigor and creativity in 1974. Through her brother, an actor, Booth got her first job in 1919 working for D. W. Griffith, from whom she learned editing techniques. After a while (she can't remember the year), she joined Louis B. Mayer as an editor. Mayer became part of MGM in 1924 and she went along with him and worked as an editor until 1937, when she became supervising editor of all films at the MGM studios and the films in Europe in which MGM had an interest. She left MGM in 1968, and since that time has been closely associated with Ray Stark, working on all his productions.

Booth recalls that in the 1930s and early forties she and Dorothy Arzner were probably the two most influential women executives in Hollywood.

In the Thirties: Dorothy Arzner

The transition from silent pictures to sound pictures was surprisingly quick. In 1926 Warner Brothers introduced the first sound track and by 1929 sound films were predominant. Sound changed the industry, the art, even the craftsmen, including directors and writers. The improvisational methods of the teens and twenties gave way to planned scripts, rigid production schedules and careful budgets. The industry became big business. Films were far more expensive, and they were produced, packaged and marketed with a new sophistication that came with big financing and a tough new breed of executive interested only in the bottom line of the ledger. Small independent filmmakers, for whom many women had worked, were wiped out when the major studios took over, and the influence of women declined sharply.

The only important woman director in Hollywood when the movies made the change from silents to talkies was Dorothy Arzner, who in fact ranked as one of the industry's "Top Ten" directors of the period. Small, pretty, and soft-spoken, Hollywood's "lady director" proved early that she was a master of her craft and could handle not only the army of technicians at her command, but also the movies' strongest personalities. Of no small significance, considering the negative attitudes of studio executives, was the fact that she directed from a woman's point of view, blunted though it was by years of studio intransigence. Exercising a strong independence, she sought to undo the stereotypes of women characters as scheming witches or lightheaded husband-chasers, depicting them when the story permitted as persons of intelligence, humor and humanity. Her choice of stars—and in many cases their choice of her—often reflected this. Clara Bow, Claudette Colbert, Katharine Hepburn, Ruth Chatterton, Sylvia Sidney, and Rosalind Russell were all personalities of independent spirit, and in Arzner they found a kindred soul. She was the only director who worked with all of them.

Arzner was born in San Francisco in 1900, and grew up in Los Angeles, where her father owned the Hoffman Cafe, a restaurant popular with Hollywood's pioneers. Within its dark-paneled walls, D. W. Griffith, Charlie Chaplin, Mack Sennett, Erich von Stroheim, Hal Roach and many others who shaped the industry gathered frequently for dinner and often talked until the small hours. Although it was in this ambience that Dorothy Arzner was raised, she enrolled at the University of Southern California with medicine as her goal. When the United States went into World War I, however, she volunteered as an ambulance driver. Back home after the war, she got a job in the story department at Paramount—as a typist. She rose to script supervisor, and later, under the tutelage of Nan Hernon, became an editor. Soon she was in charge of the Editing Department at Realart, a Paramount subsidiary. Her work here was as prodigious as it was creative. In a single year she edited thirty-two features, and her distinctive style of cutting, exemplified by her editing of the bullfight sequence in Valentino's Blood and Sand (1922), established her as one of the leading editors of the entire silent era. After cutting James Cruze's The Covered Wagon (1924), she worked closely with Cruze on all aspects of the epic Old Ironsides (1925), which she wrote and edited and even helped shoot. She was now ready, she felt, for a film of her own and she persisted until she got one.

Arzner's first assignment as director was *Fashions for Women* (1927), starring Esther Ralston. She was handed the story—a French farce in which a cigarette girl impersonates a famous beauty—and told to make a script out of it and be ready to shoot in two weeks. Not only did she get the picture going on time, she brought it in ahead of schedule (and in the process established her trademark of luxuriously-decorated interiors). The headline of a newspaper review hailed it as a "Triumph for Star and Woman Director," and in London the International Festival of Women's Films awarded her its first prize for directing. In the same year she directed the comedy *Ten Modern Commandments*, again starring Esther Ralston in a story of chorus girls and their hi-jinks, and followed it with a similar lark, *Get Your Man*, with Clara Bow. In 1928, she did *Manhattan Cocktail* with Nancy Carroll, an innovative film that had a theme song, score and special effects, but no dialogue. (Her use of theme music, which became another characteristic of her work, was widely adopted by others.) The British magazine Close-Up observed that "in her so far brief career as a director, she has already won an established reputation and a following of discriminating admirers."

After urging Paramount to get into sound and color, Arzner was assigned to make the studio's first sound film in 1929. *Wild Party*, with the strong-willed Clara Bow and Fredric March, was a zany, highly-styled romp about flappers and emancipated co-eds who swoop down on local speakeasies and nearby men's colleges. Francine Parker, who visited Arzner in her home near Palm Desert for an article in the summer 1973 issue of Action, says of this film: "As is usual for Arzner, the relationships between women are intriguingly explored, adding depth to our understanding of the relationships between women and men. The romance between Clara Bow, the student, and her professor, Fredric March, is delicate and touching—more so contrasted against the film's background of near high-camp."

In *Wild Party*, incidentally, Arzner improvised the first use of an overhead mike when she removed a microphone from its stand and attached it to a fishpole. Thus was solved the problem of actors having to ease over to the sides of the set where the stationary mikes stood.

In 1930 she directed Ruth Chatterton in two films that elevated the actress to "First Lady of the Screen," in the language of the press. The first, which also starred Clive Brook, was *Sarah and Son*, the story of a woman's attempts to locate and retrieve her missing son, who had been given to a wealthy family by her husband. It broke box-office records at the Paramount Theater in New York. The second, *Anybody's Woman*, was the romantic tale of a chorus girl arrested for indecent exposure and the lawyer who defended her. In the same year she directed *Paramount on Parade*, the annual hoopla of the studio's stars parading gaily across the screen.

Then came: *Honor Among Lovers* (1931, with Claudette Colbert and Fredric March), *Working Girls* (1931, with Paul Lukas and Frances Dee), *Merrily We Go to Hell* (1932, with Sylvia Sidney and Fredric March), *Christopher Strong* (1933, for RKO, with Colin Clive and Katharine Hepburn in her first major role), *Nana* (1934, for United Artists, with Anna Sten), *Craig's Wife* (1936, for Columbia, with Rosalind Russell), *The Bride Wore Red* (1937, for MGM, with Joan Crawford and Franchot Tone), *Dance, Girl, Dance* (1940, for RKO, with Maureen O'Hara and Louis Hayward) and *First Comes Courage* (1943, for Columbia, with Merle Oberon and Brian Aherne).

Arzner's favorite film is *Craig's Wife*, based on the play by George Kelly, who complained about it. Although Arzner used Kelly's words and shot the film in the sequence of the play, Kelly felt the interpretation was so different that it was not his play at all. (He did think the film was well done, however.) The Rosalind Russell characterization of Harriet Craig, who drives away her husband and friends in her anxiety to ensure her material security, is brittle and tense, but calculated to evoke understanding. Viewed today, however, the neurotic Harriet Craig might raise some hackles.

In *The Bride Wore Red*, Joan Crawford is a cabaret girl who poses as a society woman and wins the affections of a millionaire. Her trick is exposed and she must return to her former life, her consolation prize the faithful Franchot Tone. A reviewer for The Times called it "a woman's picture, smoldering with its heroine's indecision and consumed with talk of love and fashion." The wartime picture *First Comes Courage* was something else. Set in Nazi-occupied Norway, it tells of a woman (Merle Oberon) who is reviled by her village for bedding down with a German officer. But she is actually a spy for the Allies. Later, when she has a chance to flee the Nazis with the man she really loves, she stays on to fight. This time the Times reviewer complimented Arzner for her "crisp cutting, swift tempo, sinuous camera work, exquisite lighting, effective gestures, and a brilliantly handled chase sequence at the end." The reviewer added that "the significance of her achievement lies not so much in the quality of her work as in the fact that she was able to do it at all."

This is the way Francine Parker sums up her work: "The humanistic aspect of Arzner is the essence of her art; even her peripheral characters are brush-stroked in with startling detail. Her concentration is mainly on actors and their varying rhythms and colors. The stark reality combines with a certain lyricism which she evokes from their performances. She is a master of comic business, as in the hilarious opening of *Anybody's Woman* and the wedding ring sequence in *Merrily We Go to Hell*. Sometimes a farcical sequence will go on and on, becoming unbearably funny until one realizes the human pain it juxtaposes; sometimes there are passing interludes or one-line zingers, provoking postponed chuckles. Her flair for the zany, both structurally and visually, however, is combined with an extraordinary realization of techni-

cal detail in establishing illusions of special backgrounds
and milieus. . . . As did Lois Weber and Alice Guy Blaché
before her, Dorothy Arzner believes that 'woman's dramatic
sense is invaluable to the motion picture industry.'"

And yet there was always the problem of being a woman
in a man's world. In a 1972 article in Saturday Review, Marjorie Rosen quotes her: "The only hope for me was to tap
my own creative center enough to hope to make successes
with each picture. I knew that if I failed in that, I did not
have the kind of fraternity men had for one another to support them."

Marking a widespread revival of interest in her work, the
Directors Guild of America on January 25, 1975, held "A
Tribute to Dorothy Arzner" in Los Angeles. The hall was
packed with a thousand admirers lucky to get in.

Only a few other women directors managed to survive the
pressures of the 1930s, and their roles were distinctly minor
ones. Marjorie Gaffney, a writer and assistant director,
worked on *Middle Watch* (1930) and *Conflict* (1936).
Vyvyan Donner, who had had an active career in the twenties—as a writer, producer, director, and distributor of silent
films—worked on newsreels for Fox Movietone News. Grace
Elliot directed a number of shorts in 1931, including *The
Three Racketeers, Ten Thousand and Broke, The Devil's
Marriage, Man About Town* and *Splurge*. Writer Nancy
Naumberg made documentaries. Especially significant was
her film *Taxi* (1932), which presents a strong argument for
trade-unionism. Nancy Ford Cones in 1934 co-directed sev-
eral animated films with her husband, James. They included
Farm Scenes, Goldilocks and the Bears and *Hansel and
Gretel*. Also in 1934, Mina Moise co-directed *Cradle Song*.

Osa Johnson, who made two adventure films with her husband, Martin, in 1923—*Headhunters of the South Seas* and
Trailing African Wild Animals—began making sound films
with him in 1931. These included *Wonders of the Congo*

(1931), *Congorilla* (1932) and *Baboona* (1935). However, the Johnsons used sound primarily for the purpose of conveying their own homey observations, some of which might irritate today's feminists. In *Baboona*, for instance, when Osa arrives at a camp after her husband—because she flies a smaller and slower plane—an impatient Martin asks: "Osa, what time will breakfast be ready?"

Writers and Editors

Still heading the list of women writers in the thirties was Frances Marion, who won an Oscar in 1930 for *The Big House*, and another in 1931 for *The Champ*. In 1932 she was nominated for an Academy Award for *The Prizefighter and the Lady*, but the Oscar that year went to Sarah Y. Mason for her screenplay of *Little Women*. Others who won Academy Award nominations were Sonya Levien for *State Fair* (1933), Adele Comandini for *Three Smart Girls* (1936), Mildred Cram for *Love Affair* (1937), Viña Delmar for *The Awful Truth* (1937) and Lenore Coffee for *Four Daughters* (1938). Other prominent writers of the period were Zöe Akins, Isabel Dawn, Eleanor Gates, Eve Green, Bess Meredyth, Katherine Scola, Bella Spewack, Virginia Van Upp and —yes—Mae West.

A well-established veteran corps of women editors worked on dozens of major pictures in the thirties. Among the credits for Irene Morra were *Connecticut Yankee* (1931), *Bright Eyes* (1934) and *Pigskin Parade* (1936); for Blanche Sewell, *The Big House* (1930), *Grand Hotel* (1932) and *Tugboat Annie* (1933); for Eda Warren, *The Big Broadcast* (1932), *The General Died at Dawn* (1936) and *Anything Goes* (1936); for Viola Lawrence, *The Whole Town's Talking* (1935) and *Craig's Wife* (1936); for Margaret Booth, *Mutiny on the Bounty* (1935), *Camille* (1936), and *Romeo and Juliet* (1936).

In the same decade a new group of editors emerged. Especially prominent among them was Barbara R. McLean, who edited her first feature, *Gallant Lady*, in 1933. Before the decade ended she won Oscar nominations for *Les Miserables* (1935), *Lloyds of London* (1936), *In Old Chicago* (1938), *Alexander's Ragtime Band* (1938), and *The Rains Came* (1939). In 1956 McLean became supervising editor at 20th Century-Fox, and held that post until her retirement in 1969.

Helene Turner edited *Honor Among Lovers* (1931) and a flock of Republic serials. Emma Hill worked on *The Big Pond* and *Young Man of Manhattan* (both 1930). Dorothy Spencer, at United Artists, began a long career with *Trade Winds* and *Blockade* (both 1938) and *Stagecoach* (1939), for which she received an Oscar nomination. The thirties also marked the beginning of Adrienne Fazan's long association with MGM, for whom she edited *The Bride Wore Red* in 1937.

Women producers in the thirties were all but nonexistent. A brief intruder in this male domain was Fanny (Fanchon) Wolfe, who came to Hollywood after a productive career in the theater and produced two films in 1937, *Turn Off the Moon* and *Thrill of a Lifetime*.

The Forties

Except for the last films of Dorothy Arzner and the first of Ida Lupino (who will be discussed later), the 1940s were bereft of features directed by women. Leila Roosevelt directed and also produced a travel film, *The Dangerous Journey* (1944), but that was about it.

Somewhat more numerous were women producers. Virginia Van Upp, the most successful, was the producer of *Together Again* (1944), *The Impatient Years* (1944), *She Wouldn't Say Yes* (1945) and *Gilda* (1946). *Together Again*, directed by Charles Vidor, stars Irene Dunne as the mayor of a small town. Van Upp co-wrote the screenplay with F. Hugh Herbert. *The Impatient Years* depicts the awkward homecoming of a soldier who has been away from his wife for more than a year. Directed by Irving Cummings, this was an original screenplay by Van Upp. *She Wouldn't Say Yes*, directed by Alexander Hall, is about a psychiatrist (Rosalind Russell) who finally recognizes that her advocacy of emotional control has made men see her as a bundle of nervous inhibitions. In *Gilda*, directed by Charles Vidor, Rita Hayworth plays the former wife of the proprietor of a Buenos Aires casino who marries one of his flunkies and makes life miserable for him.

Harriet Parsons, daughter of the columnist Louella and for years a producer of short subjects, produced the features *The Enchanted Cottage* (1945), about a crippled man and a homely woman who have pleasant fantasies of the way they would like life to be, and *Night Song* (1947), about the romance of a blind male pianist. Lillie Hayward produced *Child of Divorce* (1946), which centers on a marital split viewed by a young daughter who is left to fend for herself at a boarding school, and *Banjo* (1947). Constance Bennett's *Paris Underground* (1945) is a story of the French Resistance starring Bennett herself as a woman who smuggles Allied fliers out of France. And Bebe Daniels produced *The Fabulous Joe* (1947) in London.

Women writers in the forties brought a new luminescence to the screen. Their scripts, marked by a sensitivity to female characterization, were a major factor in Hollywood's ascent to a new level of maturity and purpose. Especially noteworthy was the work of playwright Lillian Hellman, who adapted for the screen her plays *The Little Foxes* (1941), *Watch on the Rhine* (1943) and *Another Part of the Forest* (1948). Other distinguished screenplays were Joan Harrison's *Foreign Correspondent* (1940) and *Rebecca* (1940), Gladys Lehman's *Two Girls and a Sailor* (1944), Helen Deutsch's *National Velvet* (1944, co-written with Theodore

Reeves) and *Golden Earrings* (1947), Sally Benson's *Anna and the King of Siam* (1946), Frances Goodrich's *The Virginian* and *It's a Wonderful Life* (both co-written with partner Albert Hackett, 1946), Ruth Gordon's *A Double Life* (co-written with husband Garson Kanin, 1947), and *Adam's Rib* (with Kanin, 1949), Clare Booth Luce's *Come to the Stable* (1949) and Virginia Kellogg's *White Heat* (1949). *White Heat*, not to be confused with Lois Weber's film of the same name, is the violent James Cagney depiction of a psychotic hood ("Made it, Ma! Top o' the world!") which laid to rest for all time the notion that women could write only with a powderpuff.

Editors prominent in the forties were Anne Bauchens, who cut the Oscar-winning *Northwest Mounted Police* (1940), and Barbara McLean, whose *Wilson* (1944) also won an Oscar. McLean also edited the highly successful *The Song of Bernadette* (1943), *A Bell for Adano* (1945) and *Twelve O'Clock High* (1949). Other top editors, again, were Adrienne Fazan (*Anchors Aweigh,* 1944, and *The Secret Heart,* 1946), Viola Lawrence (*Cover Girl,* 1944, and many other Columbia films, including Arzner's *First Comes Courage*), Irene Morra (*The Horn Blows at Midnight,* 1945), Dorothy Spencer (*My Darling Clementine,* 1946), Monica Collingwood (*The Bishop's Wife,* 1947) and Alma Macrorie (*Golden Earrings,* 1947). Helen Van Dongen cut a special niche for herself in documentaries, editing films for Joris Ivens and Robert Flaherty, including Flaherty's *The Land* (1941) and *The Louisiana Story* (1948). Marjorie Fowler, wife of Gene Fowler, and a former contract player, began an editing career in 1944 with *Woman in the Window*.

Lois Weber

Mary Pickford

Frances Marion and Marion Davies

Dorothy Arzner

Anita Loos

Wanda Tuchok

Barbara McLean

Virginia Van Upp

Ida Lupino

Mary Ellen Bute

Shirley Clarke

On a Separate Track, the Avant-Gardists

This recitation until now has concerned itself in a more or less chronological fashion with shorts and feature filmmaking in Hollywood. We will return to this theme after a look at the early contributions of women in the development of the underground film movement—a movement that ran on a separate track.

Underground filmmaking defies precise definition. It is usually anti-establishment, experimental, personal, sometimes a form of protest; it may be a film poem, a film essay, a biography, an imaginative and offbeat view of life. Almost always it is a private kind of work, outside the mainstream of commercial entertainment. Sometimes it is simply a kind of stretching of the instruments of cinematic art to see how flexible they can be. Whatever it is, it is not Hollywood's idea of film entertainment.

An early participant in the avant-garde movement was Mary Ellen Bute, who began her work in the early thirties with her husband, the cinematographer Ted Nemeth, producing, writing and directing abstract animated shorts. In the late thirties she experimented with electronically created and oscilloscope-generated images, sometimes even working in 3-D, to achieve a poetic unity of space, sound, light and color. Her films include *Rhythm in Light* (1936), *Synchrony No. 2* (1936), *Evening Star* (1937), *Anitra's Dance* (1938), *Parabola* (1938), *Toccata and Fugue* (1940), *Escape* (1940), *Tarantella* (1941), *Sports Spools* (1941), *Polka-Graph* (1953), *Abstronics* (1954), *Color Rhapsody* (1954) and *Mood Contrast* (1954). Her films were among the first "art" films to be booked in a first-run theater. In the fifties, Bute turned to directing live-action films, including *The Boy Who Saw Through* (1956-1958) and *Passages from James Joyce's Finnegans Wake* (1965). *Finnegans Wake* isolates passages from the novel, and utilizes stills, stop-motion, montages, and subtitles in an attempt to convey the flavor of Joyce's written words. She is planning a version of Thornton Wilder's *The Skin of Our Teeth*.

Maya Deren, who died in 1961 at the age of thirty-nine, was the major figure of the experimental film movement after World War II. She was among the first filmmakers to distribute her own films, and ardently encouraged other experimentalists to join her. She wrote articles and toured the colleges to lecture on the concept of "personal films." She also pioneered in exhibiting her films commercially by renting the Provincetown Playhouse in Greenwich Village. She was one of the founders and the most vital member of the Creative Film Foundation, which was organized to provide support for other makers of experimental films.

Deren booked her first short film poems—*Meshes of the Afternoon* (1943, 14 minutes), *At Land* (1944, 5 minutes), and *Choreography for Camera* (1945, 4 minutes)—at college campuses, which were to prove an enduring market for art-film rentals.

Meshes of the Afternoon contrasts imaginative and objective reality. At the beginning of the film the division between the two seems clear enough. A woman is sitting in a chair, walking upstairs, listening to a record player. But since ordinary and extraordinary events are intercut dispassionately, imagination has become reality by the end of the film. *At Land* is a poetic story of a search for personal identity. A young woman (Deren) emerges from the sea and climbs a cliff, the top of which becomes a banquet table with people on either side who ignore her. She follows a man whose path first seems to take him toward her ocean home, but when he rejects her she joins other women playing chess and then disappears into the ocean once more. *Choreography for Camera* orchestrates both dancer and camera to make a rhythmic pattern in a constantly shifting space and time.

Later she made *Ritual in Transfigured Time* (1946, 15 minutes), a complex and highly rhythmic dance drama of a widow who becomes a bride; *Meditation on Violence* (1948), which choreographs the movements of two schools of Chinese boxers, and *The Very Eye of Night* (1959, 15 minutes), which emphasizes the use of negative in a singular dance instruction.

Deren's first husband, Alexander Hammid, assisted on *Meshes of the Afternoon*, and her second husband, Teiji Ito, did the score for several of her later films.

Deren was the first recipient of a Guggenheim Fellowship for creative work in motion pictures, and also won a prize at Cannes for her avant-garde work and her activity on behalf of the personal film.

"Cameras do not make films," she once said, "filmmakers make films. Improve your films not by adding more equipment and personnel, but by using what you have to the fullest capacity. The most important part of your equipment is yourself—your mobile body, your imaginative mind, and your freedom to use both."

Another prominent avant-gardist, Marie Menken, who died in 1970 at the age of sixty-one, acquired her first camera when a friend gave her a pawn ticket for it. She used it to photograph husband Willard Maas' *Geography of the Body* (1943). It won her a job as a Signal Corps special-effects expert during World War II. Her career included directing; acting in underground films, including those of her husband, Dov Lederberg's *Eargogh*, and the Warhol-Ronald Tavel *Life of Juanita Castro;* painting; and working as a cable editor at Time and Life. This diversified background led to a variety of films: portraits, diaries, fantasies, and time-lapse studies.

Menken's first personal film was *Visual Variations on Noguchi* (1945, 4 minutes), in which she animated sculptures of Isamu Noguchi through photography and editing. Twelve years later she did *Glimpse of a Garden* (1957, 4½ minutes), an extreme magnification of a flower garden; then *Hurry! Hurry!* (1957, 3 minutes), the adventures of sperm cells in search of an egg, accompanied by sounds of fire and bombardment. Her other films include *Dwightiana* (1957), about painter Dwight Dipley; *Eye Music in Red Major* (1961); *Arabesque for Kenneth Anger* (1961, with sound by Teiji Ito); *Bagatelle for Willard Maas* (1962), set in Versailles; *Mood Mondrian* (1961-1963); *Drips and Strips* (1961-1965); *Notebook* (1962-1963); *Go Go Go* (1963), a look at New York City speeded up; *Wrestling* (1964); and *Andy Warhol* (1965). She left a number of works unfinished at her death in 1970—*Faucet* (a dripping faucet), *Zenscapes* (a rock garden), *Sidewalks* (undercranked footage of pedestrians), *Moonplay* and *Lights*.

In the Fifties: Ida Lupino

In the 1950s there was only one woman director of major films—Ida Lupino.

Lupino was born in London in 1918 to actress Connie Emerald and stage comedian Stanley Lupino; her father belonged to one of England's oldest theatrical families, and she was the first female in it to achieve fame. She got her first film job while still in her early teens when English director Allan Dwan cast her as a flapper in *Her First Affaire* (1933) and publicized her as Britain's Jean Harlow (her hair was bleached blonde). In 1934, after having made several more films in England, she came to the United States, where she worked with regularity, but it wasn't until her portrayal of Bessie in William Wellman's *The Light That Failed* (1939, with Ronald Colman) that she reached stardom.

Many memorable and diversified roles followed. She starred in Raoul Walsh's *They Drive By Night* (1940), Charles Vidor's *Ladies in Retirement* (1941), Michael Curtiz's *The Sea Wolf* (1941), Irving Pichel's *Life Begins at Eight-Thirty* (1942), Vincent Sherman's *The Hard Way* (1942—this one won her the New York Critics Best Actress award), David Butler's *Thank Your Lucky Stars* (1943), Curtis Bernhardt's *Devotion* (1946) and Jean Negulesco's *Road House* (1948)—

and who can forget her torchy "One More for the Road"?

Although the film industry went into a decline in 1949, the next five years were productive ones for Lupino. With Collier Young (her husband for a time), she founded a production company first called Emerald Productions, later Filmakers. The purpose was to make high quality, low-budget independent films on bold themes that would show "how America lives." Between 1949 and 1954, Lupino directed six features and produced two others for Filmakers, wrote a number of them, acted in some of them, starred in three features for other companies, and gave birth to her daughter, Bridget Duff.

Her company's first feature was *Not Wanted*, with Sally Forrest and Keefe Brasselle, in 1949. Direction is credited to Elmer Clifton, but Clifton suffered a heart attack and Lupino took over. *Not Wanted* is the story of a young unwed mother who during her pregnancy commits her baby to adoption, then attempts to kidnap the child and is sent to jail. For all its melodrama, the film deals incisively with the poverty of a woman's fantasy life. It cost a little more than $100,000 and grossed a million.

The second feature Lupino directed, *Never Fear* (1950), again starred Sally Forrest and Keefe Brasselle. Another melodramatic tale, this one deals with a dancing team that is broken up when the young woman is stricken with polio. Although the picture devotes scrupulous attention to medical detail and treats forcefully the anguish of the disease, it is an upbeat film that celebrates a woman's determination to fight back.

The other pictures Lupino directed in the fifties were *Outrage* (1950), with Mala Powers; *Hard, Fast and Beautiful* (1951), with Claire Trevor; *The Bigamist* (1953), with Edmond O'Brien; and *The Hitchhiker* (1953), with O'Brien, Frank Lovejoy, and William Talman.

In *Outrage*, the film again deals with a woman's tragedy —this time rape—and how she attempts to cope with it. We

see the aftermath: how the victim struggles to restore meaning to an existence that has become unreal. *Hard, Fast and
Beautiful* films the fragile relationship between a driving,
ambitious mother and her tennis-player daughter.

The Bigamist is the story of a traveling salesman, sympa-
thetically depicted, who is in love with two women (Lupino
and Joan Fontaine), and wed to both. A tawdry premise this,
but it gives Lupino an opportunity again to manipulate her
favorite cinematic situation—people trying to find their way
out of a bewilderment induced by their own psychogenic
conflicts or the accident of outside events. *The Hitchhiker*
permitted no probing of the personality of women—because
it has an all-male cast—but this gritty thriller set in a Mexican
desert once more draws upon the plight of the victimized,
this time revealing the character of two men brought to the
edge of life by a psychopathic killer. It is Lupino's favorite
film. One reviewer described it as "breathlessly keyed to an
agonizing pitch of terror" from start to end.

The films Lupino produced in the fifties, but did not direct,
were *On the Loose* and *Beware, My Lovely*, both in 1951.
After *The Hitchhiker*, she didn't direct again until 1966,
when she did *The Trouble With Angels*, which stars Hayley
Mills as a wacky student at a convent school who is persuaded by the mother superior, Rosalind Russell, to become
a nun.

One of the most gutsy women in Hollywood, Lupino is
also one of the most talented. In addition to her distinguished
work as an actress, writer, director and all-around filmmaker,
she has directed countless television films. She has also been
a dancer, singer, artist, designer, musician and composer.

In 1950 she told an interviewer, "If Hollywood is to remain
on top of the film world, there must be more experimenta-
tion with out-of-the-way film subjects." Having said that, she
made the plunge herself by forming her Filmakers company.
Lupino was one of the first makers of independent, low-
budget pictures. She eschewed gloss for down-to-earth but

provocative stories that were shot fast in practical locations, with little-known performers. She made it work. Her films, off-beat and innovative, all have an impact on the viewer, and through the grim realities of "how America lives," convey a toughness of the human spirit.

That same toughness of spirit is what enabled her to turn from a successful acting career to new and precarious enterprises. She was dissatisfied as an actress; she wanted a greater freedom to utilize her prodigious energy and to make her comment about life.

Rosalind Russell once observed that she had often worked with directors who were less than confident about themselves and the film they were making. "What I admire about Ida is that she comes to the job each morning thoroughly prepared. She knows what she wants, and knows how to do it. She is clear, concise, and has a sense of humor. Above all, she has vitality and enthusiasm."

Lupino's comment on her choice of unusual stories and her innovative techniques: "That's filmmaking."

Of the other women directors in the fifties, the only one who made any kind of impact on the industry was Ruth Orkin, who worked with her husband, photographer Morris Engel, on three sensitive and pioneering films made in New York. The first of these, which drew international attention, was *The Little Fugitive* (1953), an affectionate story of the wanderings of a small boy. It was followed by *Lovers and Lollipops* (1956), and *Weddings and Babies* (1958). The latter was the first feature to be made using a portable camera with synchronous sound attachment.

Mildred Goldscholl co-directed, with her husband, Morton, the animated *Night Driving* (1956). Their work continued into the sixties, when they did *Shaping the World* (1961), *Intergalactic Zoo* (1965), and *The Great Train Robbery* (1966). Mandy Schefer directed a film called *The Mexican*, and Ingeborg Green, an independent producer-director, made documentaries on wild animals. Virginia Stone, who had been an actress, a band singer, and a swimmer in Billy Rose's Aquacade, teamed up with her husband, Andrew, in directing and producing a number of suspense features. Their pictures in the fifties were *Confidence Girl* (1951), *The Night Holds Terror* (1955) and *Cry Terror* (1957). They continued into the sixties with *Ring of Fire* (1961), *The Password is Courage* (1962) and *The Secret of My Success* (1965). The Stones used their own equipment, employed a small crew of about fifteen, and always shot on location, never in studios. They separated several years ago, but both have continued working in films.

Not every woman in Hollywood in the fifties shared Ida Lupino's conviction that a talented woman could handle any job. One of the doubters was Dorothy Davenport Reid, who held that women could not be producers. Reid based her view on observations over a long career that began in the early silent period when she co-directed a number of films with her husband, the great silent star, Wallace Reid. After her husband's death from drug addiction in 1922, she combined her film work with a crusade against harmful drugs. She collaborated on *Human Wreckage* (1923) with writer C. Gardner Sullivan and went on to direct several other admonitory pictures, including *Quicksands* (1928), *Road to Ruin* (1934, co-director Melville Shirer) and *Woman Condemned* (1934). In 1949 she produced a film called *Impact*, written in collaboration with Arthur Lubin, but this experience failed to fire her confidence as a producer. In fact, when the film was finished she settled for a job as Lubin's Girl Friday. This move seemed to signal the end of her creative career, although in 1952 she confided in an article in the Los Angeles Daily News that "after years of training I feel that I am ready for the post of associate producer in a studio." Not producer, *associate* producer. She explained why she made the distinction between the two jobs: "Women have a lot to give motion pictures, but not in the capacity of producer. Men resent women in top executive positions in films as in any field of endeavor." What's more, she said, "women in executive positions are hard to get along with. They can't retain an impersonal attitude in issuing orders and handling underlings. Also, film production has become a highly technical job, involving a vast knowledge of mechanics, finance, labor problems, and other factors that most women in the industry simply do not bother with."

Editors and Writers

In any case, women in other areas of filmmaking continued to make award-winning contributions to the industry.

Editor Anne Bauchens won an Academy nomination in 1952 for *The Greatest Show on Earth,* and another in 1956 for *The Ten Commandments.* Adrienne Fazan's *An American in Paris* (1951) was nominated for her editing, and her editing of *Gigi* (1958) won an Oscar. Nominations also went to Viola Lawrence for *Pal Joey* (1957), Alma Macrorie for *The Bridges at Toko-Ri* (1954), Barbara McLean for *All About Eve* (1950) and Dorothy Spencer for *Decision Before Dawn* (1951).

Fazan also won an American Cinema Editors' (ACE) award for *Singing in the Rain* (1952) and another for *Gigi.* Alma Macrorie was given an ACE Fifth Critic's Award and an ACE Eddie for *Teacher's Pet* (1958) and an Eddie for *The Bridges at Toko-Ri.* Eddies also went to Barbara McLean for *All About Eve* and Dorothy Spencer for *Decision Before Dawn.* Viola Lawrence received the New York Critics Circle Award in 1956 for her editing of *The Eddie Duchin Story.*

The main addition to the above roster of veterans was Anne V. Coates, whose several credits in this decade included *To Paris With Love* (1955) and *The Horse's Mouth* (1958).

Among the writers, Edna and Edward Anhalt received an

Oscar for their original story of *Panic in the Streets* (1950), and a nomination in the same category for *The Sniper* (1952). They also wrote the screenplays for *Member of the Wedding* (1952), *Not as a Stranger* (1955) and *The Pride and the Passion* (1957). They received associate producer credits on *The Sniper*, *My Six Convicts* (both 1952), *Member of the Wedding* and *Girls, Girls, Girls* (1953).

The *Band Wagon* (1953) and *It's Always Fair Weather* (1955), written by Betty Comden and Adolph Green, received nominations, as did Helen Deutsch's screenplay of *Lili* (1953). Frances Goodrich and Albert Hackett wrote the screenplays for the nominated films *Father of the Bride* (1950) and *Seven Brides for Seven Brothers* (1954), the latter in collaboration with Dorothy Kingsley. Fay and Michael Kanin's original screenplay for *Teacher's Pet* (1958) was nominated, as was Virginia Kellogg's *Caged* (1950, with Bernard C. Schoenfeld) and Isobel Lennart's *Love Me or Leave Me* (1955, with Daniel Fuchs). Sonya Levien won Oscars with *Interrupted Melody* (1955) and *Oklahoma!* (1956), both with William Ludwig. Many of these films also received awards from the Writers Guild, as did Phoebe and Henry Ephron's *There's No Business Like Show Business* (1955), *Daddy Long Legs* (1955) and *Carousel* (1957).

In Recent Years: Shirley Clarke . . .

The big breakthrough for women directors of feature films is yet to come. If indeed it does come, then Shirley Clarke, Elaine May, Barbara Loden, Susan Sontag and Stephanie Rothman constitute a good part of its vanguard.

In this array Shirley Clarke is especially significant because she—along with Mary Ellen Bute, Maya Deren and Marie Menken—was a precursor of the women of today who have made a breakthrough on another level of filmmaking, sometimes known as the underground movement, sometimes as avant-garde. Like Bute, Deren and Menken, Shirley Clarke personifies through her assertiveness, her original subject matter, and her independence of Hollywood, the spirit of the new generation of women filmmakers.

Clarke, who began her artistic career as a dancer, started making films in the fifties. Her avant-garde work, occasionally eerie or romantic, more often forceful and dramatic, is characterized throughout by a strong documentary undertone. At first she did a number of experimental shorts inspired by dance. They included *Dance in the Sun* (1953), *In Paris Parks* (1954), *Bullfight* (1955) and *Moment in Love* (1957, a 10-minute film in which the choreography for boy and girl moves through clouds, under water, and through ruins).

In 1958 she made *Brussels "Loops,"* a series of fifteen shorts providing an imaginative view of the Brussels World's Fair, and *Bridges-Go-Round,* in which bridges are choreographed by the use of superimpositions and a continuously moving camera. In 1959 she was co-director of *Skyscraper,* which documents the construction of a skyscraper. This film won first prize at the Venice Film Festival and was nominated for an Academy Award. The following year she made a film for UNICEF, *A Scary Time,* on the topic of hunger, but it delivered its message in so shocking a way that it was never circulated. It did win a prize at Venice, however.

Clarke's first full-length film, made in 1960, was *The Connection,* based on the Jack Gelber play (performed in New York by the Living Theater) about a group of narcotic addicts waiting for a delivery. The film, translated entirely into cinematic terms, was awarded the Critics' Prize at Cannes. Three years later she made the feature *The Cool World,* filmed in Harlem from the novel by Warren Miller. *The Cool World* is about a fifteen-year-old boy whose dream is to acquire a gun and take over the leadership of a street gang. When the dream comes true and the gun is used in a gang fight, it is suddenly the end of the road for the boy we have come to know and care about.

Clarke followed that film in 1964 with a documentary on the poet Robert Frost—*Robert Frost . . . A Love Letter to the World*—which she made at the request of John Kennedy and Stewart Udall.

In 1967 she made *Portrait of Jason*, a 105-minute condensation of twelve hours of an uninhibited monologue by a black homosexual. That year also she created the continuity and editing concept of *Man in the Polar Region*, an 11-hour carousel film for Expo '67. Since then she has become involved with video to the exclusion of film.

A conversation with Shirley Clarke:

How did you get into film?

SHIRLEY CLARKE: I must be honest; I started at the top and never descended. I knew that if I started at the bottom I would never get any farther than sweeping the floor. Trying to prove myself to the boss was not a trip I could do—teachers never liked me. I knew life was going to be hard. I'd gotten a little money from my grandfather, $1500. And I had a Bolex, which had been given to me as a wedding present. I was going to make three dance films, $500 each, and become the most famous dance filmmaker of all time.

Well, to begin with, I didn't even get one finished for $1500. The film stock alone was more than that.

Then I made a film called *In Paris Parks*. I'd gone to France to do a dance film, so since I was there with my daughter and had to go to the park every day anyhow, I decided to make a film of the park too. It was done as if it were a dance film. That led, in 1958, to getting a job from Willard Van Dyke to make fifteen little 2½-minute films for the Brussels World's Fair. That's how I got to know Willard, Donn Pennebaker, and Richard Leacock—and we all shared this interest in film.

This was all part of the whole *cinéma-vérité* movement. The French called it that. We called it the hand-held-camera-with-sound movement. We all exchanged visits with each other. Godard would come and ask what kind of equipment we used last week.

And from that I got a job making a film for the UN, which I will tell you about later. Then Willard had a job to do, a film about constructing a building [*Skyscraper*]. He asked if I would do it and I said yes, since it was going to let me get into 35mm and he was going to *pay* me. I asked for $3,000, thinking that was an enormous sum. It took me a year to do it, but it was named for an Academy Award and won a prize at Venice. As a result of that I was able to make *The Connection*, because by then I had a successful reputation.

Being an independent filmmaker, not backed by Hollywood, for instance, can be a hard life . . .

SC: You have to realize that I never thought about anything like that. My problem was to learn how to make films. I have never wanted to make a film that wasn't, for me, learning the next thing I wanted to find out about. In each film there's always something that happens that gives me the starting-off place for the next film.

I never thought about the money situation until, one day, I realized there *was* a situation: I had made two successful films and wasn't able to get money to do another. Kubrick had started before me. But the story of Kubrick—who started let's say four or five years before I began—would have been mine, had I been a guy.

Between *The Connection* and *The Cool World*, it wasn't very difficult to get another film, because Kennedy and Udall had asked me to do the Robert Frost film [*Robert Frost . . . A Love Letter to the World*, 1964]. So it was all handed to me, I was in. That was my week of being in. I remember going to see a big agent; I don't know why he asked to see me, but for some reason he did. His whole conversation was, "Now, if you want, I can get you a job right away in Hollywood, but you're doing pretty well the way you are, you know, independent and on your own. I sort of envy you, if you can keep this up." He was selling me a bill of goods not to try Hollywood. It was kind of funny, because a few years later, when I called him and said I *would* like to try Hollywood, he didn't even answer my call.

But there may be with me a problem other than being a woman . . .

Such as—?

SC: Such as, my subjects and my style were a little bit—different.

Non-commercial?

SC: No, more dangerous than that. Dangerous subjects—drug addiction—and not putting it down. Black people, for real, done in Harlem. The last film I made before *The Connection*, a film for the United Nations, was literally banned by them. You can only see it by knowing of its existence and asking for it. It took a prize in Venice and a number of things, but the American committee voted not to put it on the list of films to be shown. They wanted me to change the end.

It was called *A Scary Time*. It was for UNICEF. It's about the fact that there really are skeleton children in the world. It shows a child dressing up as a skeleton on Halloween to go out and get money for UNICEF. It's surrealistically done. At the end, after the kid has been trick-or-treating, he comes running home at night, and it's dark, and he sees all the scary images of starvation that you've seen before in the film. He comes in and his mother and father are watching TV. They say, like, "Go to bed, dear." He goes to bed and suddenly you hear a shriek, and there's this shot of a Moroccan baby in its mother's arms, a great big close-up, and it's covered with flies. Everybody must feel them crawling. It goes on to the point where you want to shriek yourself. And as you do you hear the kid screaming, "Mommy, Daddy, make it stop!" And the whole thing disappears.

It works, which I assume was the purpose for which they hired me to make the film. But the UN wanted just the dance of the children of the world, all happy because the UN had fed them. They wanted to leave out the whole trip about the little boy going home. They thought it was such a horror film it would give people traumatic shock. I hope so!

So they voted it out. And if Rossellini had not said to them, "You cannot do this to a filmmaker's work!" they would have destroyed it. I saw it recently. Unfortunately, it is completely relevant today, the identical film.

Lately you have become interested in video.

SC: Yes, I was given a grant, having already had some success in film. Films presented the very obvious problem of waiting every four years to be allowed to do another. That is, in the beginning, when I was making 16mm films, it was like video, I could do it all the time. But the moment I got into more ambitious projects where hundreds of thousands of dollars were involved, it was bad. So then I found video and now every day I tape. I mean no matter what. Something happens here, it gets taped. Every day I have something to do, which I love. I've got to figure out this wire, I've got to get a set-up done. My life is one long electrical cord.

By the way, I have what must be one of the funniest tapes in the world. Three screens of Alan Watts sitting, waiting for me to say "Begin," and me thinking he's giving some Zen message, by not talking for a half hour! He didn't say a word! Finally I could hear the tape running out, so I turned up the lights and Alan said, "What was that all about?" "We just made a tape." "What do you mean, you just made a tape? Why didn't you tell me to begin?" "Well, I'm sorry, but we don't do 'roll it' and all that any more!"

His son and the third cameraman and I all thought he

was talking to us in Zen fashion by keeping quiet. And how dare I ask the great Alan Watts what he's doing?

You were one of the first important women directors in recent times. What do you think of the fact that more and more women are starting to get into film?

SC: Women have been editors for years, and if you know films you know what editing does. I mean the women have *made* the films the guys have gone out and shot. This has been put into the hands of women, but it's only a tiny line on the credits saying, "edited by —." They've also allowed women to write films, so the original idea is a woman's as well as the finished product. But she gets no equal credit or equal pay.

Now I don't see any way around it still, except to go right in and say, "I'm going to find myself a producer who will produce my film—which I direct, edit, and write."

And I hope that as women make films they will start to say something that is meaningful to women in an entirely different way. And I don't mean just about how women have babies—but with the sensitivity of someone who has looked with double vision, as women have had to, as black people have had to. They will give us a greater understanding, not of men but of humanity, expressed much more broadly than we've been allowed to see.

Elaine May

In Hollywood, meanwhile, directing is still a man's game, a circumstance clearly underscored by the fact that today's leading woman director achieved her singular status on the strength of only two pictures, one of which she sought to disown. Elaine May made her first film, *A New Leaf* (released over her loud objections), in 1971, and her second, *The Heartbreak Kid*, a year later.

Scheduled for release by Paramount in 1975 is her third

film, *Mikey and Nicky,* a comedy she wrote as well as directed. The picture stars John Cassavetes and Peter Falk.

Elaine May was born in Philadelphia in 1932. Her father, Jack Berlin, was a well-known actor in the Jewish theater whose work kept him traveling over much of America, and by the age of ten Elaine had been in fifty schools. At night she was on stage. Her father died when she was eleven, and she moved to Los Angeles with her mother. Bored with school, she cut out at fifteen and a year later married a man named Marvin May. The marriage broke up after the birth of her daughter, Jeannie, and for a few years she worked at odd jobs—including one as a restaurant checker, which required her to sit on a bar stool all night encouraging the bartender to ring up his sales on the cash register.

She wanted to go to college, but no California institution would have her without a high school diploma. Informed that the University of Chicago was somewhat more generous in this regard, she took off one day—with $7—and hitchhiked to Chicago, where without the formality of enrolling she drifted in and out of classes, engaging in sharply worded intellectual debates with instructors along the way. It was at the university that she met Mike Nichols, the leading actor in the student theater group. Out of their initial smart-aleck conversations came one of the greatest comedy acts of show business.

Nichols and May opened as a team in 1954, doing improvisations with Chicago's Compass Players. The act caught on fast. It was a perfect blending of acting talent, wit and keenness of mind—was there ever an act with such a high level of intelligence?

In 1957 Nichols and May moved to New York. Television appearances brought them an immediate national following. There were records, commercials, packed houses wherever they played. But success left May less than satisfied. "There's no way we can top ourselves," she told Nichols, so in 1961 they broke up the act and went their separate ways.

While Nichols went on to become a top theater and movie director, May turned to writing plays. It didn't work out. Neither did her second marriage, to lyricist Sheldon Harnick. She went to Hollywood to write the screenplay of Evelyn Waugh's satirical book, *The Loved One*, but when director Tony Richardson wanted changes she withdrew from the project. Another try at writing for Broadway failed. In 1963 she married a psychiatrist with three daughters and moved into a big brownstone on Manhattan's West Side. She emerged to take the starring role in a play called "The Office," directed by Jerome Robbins, but it closed after a few preview performances.

A few months later May was drawn back to Hollywood by Carl Reiner to play the role of a hard-bitten actress in the movie version of Reiner's semiautobiographical Broadway play, "Enter Laughing." It was her first movie role—she had turned down other offers—and she found working with Reiner a pleasant experience. When *Enter Laughing* was completed she accepted a lead role in the movie of Murray Schisgal's play "Luv," co-starring Jack Lemmon and directed by Clive Donner. There were some difficult moments, but when the film was done Lemmon and Donner were full of praise. "She's the finest actress I ever worked with," said Lemmon. "I think Elaine is touched with genius, like Judy Holliday. She approaches a scene like a director and a writer, not like an actor, and she can go so deep so fast on a scene, and her mind works at such great speed, that it's difficult for her to communicate with other actors."

Having worked in two films (neither of which can be ranked with Hollywood's all-time greats), she was now ready to handle her own film, and the opportunity came from Paramount. She signed on to write, direct and star in *A New Leaf*, a take-off on a 1930-ish comedy of a rich, aristocratic American playboy who loses his money and sets out to snare a rich but klutzy botanist as his bride. May took the role of the pathetic Miss Klutz and Walter Matthau (no Cary Grant—

or was that part of the joke?) was curiously cast as the scheming profligate. If it was to be a black comedy, it didn't turn out that way. When the shooting was over, the film was taken out of her hands by the studio and cut and edited in such a way, according to May, as to make it "a cliché-ridden, banal story." She sued to have it hidden from sight—"it will be a disaster if the film is released"—but she lost her case and in 1971, two years after she had begun working on it, the film was released. One reviewer softened her assessment by saying it wasn't "offensively bad." Others found it a funny and incisive depiction of society's seamier values.

Though not universally embraced as a great work of cinematic art, May's second feature, *The Heartbreak Kid*, brought encomia from many critics. She was described as "one of the most important new American directors" and "a social satirist without peer," and her work was compared favorably with Billy Wilder's.

Based on a story by Bruce Jay Friedman and written for the screen by Neil Simon (without his usual parade of gags), *The Heartbreak Kid* is the story of a sporting-goods salesman who discards his young bride on their Miami honeymoon to pursue a golden-limbed campus queen all the way back to her upper-middle-class, American-ideal home in Minnesota. The young nonhero (Charles Grodin) is an insensitive twerp, his bride (May's daughter, Jeannie Berlin) is an abrasive vulgarian, the campus queen (Cybill Shepherd) is a provocative mantrap, and her father (played superbly by Eddie Albert) is the flinty master of the ideal Wasp household. Out of this melange is fashioned a hard-edged comedy that, depending on the viewer's mood, either knocks the stuffings out of the American dream in the most hilarious manner, or leaves one with a couple of nagging questions that impair appreciation: (a) why did Lenny marry Girl Number One in the first place, and (b) what did Girl Number Two see in *him*? But however one may feel about *The Heartbreak Kid*— or *A New Leaf*, for that matter—it is clear that Elaine May, as a director, brings an original and probing mind to the screen.

May, incidentally, has little patience with people who identify her as a woman director. "There is always some idiot," she told an interviewer, "who will come up to you and say 'You're just great for a girl. You think exactly like a man.' For chrissake, I always thought intelligence was neuter."

Susan Sontag

Essayist, critic, novelist, philosopher, chronicler of avant-garde culture, and now a filmmaker, Susan Sontag commands attention for the sheer power of the intellectuality she brings to her work.

Born in New York in 1933, Sontag grew up in Tucson and Los Angeles, entered Berkeley at fifteen, moved after a year to the University of Chicago (from which she graduated), and married sociologist Philip Rieff. From Chicago she and her husband went to Harvard, where she did graduate work in English and philosophy, and collaborated with her husband on a book dealing with the Freudian influence on modern culture. They were divorced just before its publication (and by mutual consent only his name appears as the author). In 1957 she departed Cambridge for a year of study at the University of Paris under a grant by the American Association of University Women. On her return to New York she was an editor briefly at Commentary, then for six years taught philosophy, first at City College, then Sarah Lawrence, and later Columbia.

At twenty-eight, after years of random writing, Sontag began writing in earnest and produced a novel, "The Benefactor," which got some excellent reviews and a better than average sale for a first novel. About the same time she began publishing criticism in literary journals. In 1964 she wrote an essay for Partisan Review defining "camp," and when Time magazine picked it up she became a pop celebrity overnight. Another novel, "Death Kit," followed, and many more essays, including some that argued that pornography is a valid literary genre and that the non-communicativeness of avantgarde art is a valid quality of art. She kept politics out of her writing until 1968, when she spent two weeks in North Vietnam. The journal of her experiences and observations, "Trip to Hanoi," appeared in Esquire and later as a paperback.

A movie buff since childhood (the cinema, she says, is "the most alive, the most exciting, the most important of all art forms"), Sontag began taking an active interest in films in the late sixties. In '67 she was a member of the jury at the Venice Film Festival, and also helped select films for the New York Film Festival that year. Then she got the opportunity to direct a film in Sweden. "I would have taken any offer," she said, "just to show I could do it. I would have gone to Afghanistan." Her movie, *Duet for Cannibals*, for which she also wrote the screenplay, was shown at the New York Film Festival in 1969 and was distributed in the United States by Grove Press. The story is about two couples, one middle-aged and perverse (the "cannibals"), the other young and vulnerable. The tone of the film is set by the bizarre and erotic games played by the older couple, into which the younger people are drawn. It is an elusive, mystifying film that evokes different reactions in viewers. For Pauline Kael it lacked a sense of drama.

Sontag began shooting her second feature, *Brother Carl*, in 1970 in and around Stockholm. It, too, evolved as an elusive, brooding film. Three of the characters are complex, articulate people—Martin, a handsome man of the theater; Lena, his ex-wife; and Karen, who is involved with both of them. Outside this trio are two figures locked in their own silent worlds. One is an autistic child, Karen's daughter. The other is a famous female dancer, now schizophrenic. One reviewer described the film as "an outsider's commentary, with very personal variations, on those motifs that filmgoers associate with the Scandanavian film tradition." *Brother Carl* premiered at the Cannes Film Festival in 1971 and was shown at the San Francisco, Chicago and London film festivals. It was released in the United States by New Yorker Films in 1972.

Her latest film, an 87-minute documentary distributed by New Yorker Films, is *Promised Lands*, which deals with the tragedy of the Yom Kippur War of 1973 and the conflicts that caused it. Begun just after the war ended, while the agony and destruction still shrouded the landscape, the film was shot in five weeks at the battle sites along the Suez Canal, on the Golan Heights, in the Sinai Desert, and in the villages. Sontag had intended to make this film with all the care and forethought of a feature, all neatly planned and scripted, but she found that "reality was something you didn't invent." "Events were happening first and then written down and constructed into a script later."

The producer of *Promised Lands* was a woman, Nicole Stephane, and women, in fact, dominate the credits. They include: Jeri Sopanen, camera; Annie Chevallay and Florence Bocquet, editing; Monique Montivier, production manager; Nadine Hain, associate producer; and Bonni McCrea, assistant to the producer. (There's a credit also for David Rieff as assistant director. He's Sontag's son.)

Barbara Loden

Barbara Loden, born in the hills of North Carolina, went to Gotham as an eager teenager, and after a fling at modeling and dancing, became an actress. She played the lead in Arthur Miller's "After the Fall" and appeared in several films, two of which—*Splendor in the Grass* and *Wild River*— were directed by Elia Kazan, whom she married.

In 1970 she directed the feature film, *Wanda,* in which she plays the title role. *Wanda* is about a young Appalachian woman, poor and inarticulate, living a dead-end life. Not particularly interested in the traditional wife-and-mother role, Wanda knows no other options—and society offers her none—except to become a honkytonk woman, living off the largesse of contemptuous men. Loden succeeds perfectly in explaining the desolate state of Wanda's mind, which is mirrored by the desolate, strip-mined countryside.

A conversation with Barbara Loden:

Why did you choose such a grim topic for your first film?

BARBARA LODEN: The idea for *Wanda* came from a newspaper article about a woman accomplice in a bank robbery. She received a heavy sentence. By the law of that state, even an accomplice had to get a heavy sentence. She got twenty years with no appeal and said, "Thank you, judge." I wondered why she would be so glad, what kind of terrible life she had had.

I was shooting the film before women's liberation really caught on. It was just during the editing that I became aware of it. So *Wanda* is not specifically about women's liberation, but about *why* women should be liberated. I identified in some way with that girl.

That's something special that women can bring to films. I think they can be very personal. Their films should come from their deep feelings about themselves. Hollywood has made many personal films already, of course, but they're all by men.

So there may be a wave of films by women just like the current wave of films by blacks. Those are *not* really representative of what's happening in the black culture, but it's a start. What'll happen is that they'll give women a chance —and it will be a breakthrough. Unless the women who get the chance are against the women's liberation movement and want to keep things the way they are! What I think is exciting is that we women don't necessarily know what we really think or feel yet. It's unexplored territory, at least in writing and in film, so far.

With your feelings about the woman's point of view, why didn't you use point-of-view shots in Wanda?

BL: I saw her *in* something, surrounded by something. I didn't consciously think about seeing things from her point of view, in terms of camera angles. I didn't think it was necessary to make the film in the standard way—master shots, reaction shots, etc.

If qualified women apply, will you hire women for technical jobs on future films?

BL: Yes, I'll gladly hire women technicians if they can do the job in question. I'll take anyone who will work hard. I think the technology of making a movie is a myth—the idea that you have to be an expert in so many fields. It's simple to learn so many technical film things. It's no harder than learning how to use a washing machine.

How do you and your husband handle the responsibilities of bringing up your children?

BL: There are conflicts in being a woman filmmaker with children. You have a certain responsibility and you can't get away from it. But I figure that's my job. My husband agreed to subsidize me in my films if I agreed to do those domestic things. That's how I make my living. I'd like to be independent, but right now I can't be. My husband is independent, but then he's been making films a long time. I foresee a day I'll eventually be able to make a living for myself, with films or some other way. You see, I don't want to feel I have to create a money-making film, just like I don't take an acting job I feel shouldn't be done by anyone.

I feel a fellowship with other women now becoming directors. I'm glad that women are making films and I'll be making more friends—and contacts—among film women. We all need a lot of encouragement from each other. We're all taking a first step. I was surprised to discover through you how many women are making films. When I made *Wanda*

I didn't know if another woman had ever made a film. I just assumed none ever had.

Now I'm mostly writing, and I'm glad. I'm getting prepared for my next onslaught in filmmaking.

My children are just at the age when I want to be with them as much as I can. Writing is good. You can be there physically, as opposed to being on a location filming.

I have a five-year plan. I'm getting two of the scripts ready. I'm very slow. When the kids are older I'll shoot the films. It's so time-consuming to shoot.

When I was shooting *Wanda* my kids were younger, of course, and I didn't have any domestic help at all. We were out in Pennsylvania most of the time, and I took them with me shooting. Sometimes my husband or one of the townspeople would invite the kids over for a day. When you're in those circumstances you always find a way to get things done. Once you get started you have to go on, even if you have a 104-degree temperature. It's just that one chance and you can't let anything get in your way.

Women should try to do films when they get the urge and the chance. Suddenly things start happening and there's no turning back.

Do you own your own equipment?

BL: No, it's cheaper to buy, then sell when it's over, or rent. Equipment is always changing. I may someday shoot in Super 16, for example, though Super 16 only lends itself to a film with a certain look, a documentary look.

How did you get the money for Wanda?

BL: I financed *Wanda*. I ran into Harry Schuster, after a lot of looking, and he agreed to back me. I set up a nonprofit foundation for the film, the Foundation for Filmmakers. It has a little money yet, but it will eventually be used to finance films of dubious commercial potential.

Men as well as women have trouble getting financing for

their films. People starting to make films should realize that you have to go out and *get* money. It's necessary in large amounts and very hard to get! You have to hunt out rich people, patrons of the arts. Go from one to another. When I was trying to finance *Wanda* that's what I did, and was prepared to keep doing, until my lucky break came along.

I think the big problem is taking the first step. Women are afraid they won't be taken seriously, that people won't feel their work has validity. You have to go about financing in a very tactical way: find out who has the money and get it!

Stephanie Rothman

While Elaine May is the best known woman director of Hollywood features, the distinction of having made the most features belongs to Stephanie Rothman, who has directed six. Her films are produced and distributed by Dimension Pictures, a Los Angeles firm in which she is a vice president and partner.

Graduated from Berkeley, where she majored in sociology, in 1957, Rothman studied in the University of Southern California's Department of Cinema from 1960 to 1963. In her last year she received the Directors Guild of America Fellowship, the first time the fellowship had ever been awarded to a woman.

She directed her first feature in 1966. A beach picture called *It's a Bikini World*, it's about a manufacturer of teenage fad products who sponsors a cross-country race between boy and girl athletes. These films followed:

The Student Nurses (1970), a drama of four young women in their final months of training learning to deal with such problems as malpractice, abortion, drug abuse, and the tragedy of growing attached to terminal patients. *The Velvet Vampire* (1971), a horror tale of a young couple who are the weekend guests of a beautiful woman deep in the Mojave

Desert. The guests have disturbing erotic dreams that foretell their fate at the hands of their vampire hostess. *Group Marriage* (1972), a comedy about a group of friends living and loving communally who decide to legalize a group marriage. *Terminal Island* (1973), an action drama that takes place when California declares the death penalty unconstitutional and permanently exiles all convicted murderers of both sexes to an island off the coast. On the island two groups fight for control, and when the battle is over a new society is born. *The Working Girls* (1974), a comedy about a girl so desperate to find a job that she places an ad that reads "I will do anything for money." She gets some strange offers and finally takes a job as companion and financial adviser to a lonely millionaire who lives in his car.

In the first five films she directed, Rothman also shared writing credits. The last two she wrote herself. She has writing credits also for two Dimension films directed by others: *Sweet Sugar* (1971) and *Beyond Atlantis* (1972).

Conversation with Faith Hubley

Faith Hubley and her husband, John, have been leaders in the field of animated films almost since they began making films together in 1957. Their work includes *Windy Day* (1967, 10 minutes, Academy Award nomination), narrated by their two daughters; *Of Men and Demons* (1969, 10 minutes, Academy Award nomination), in which a man and woman ward off the cackling forces of evil, and *Eggs* (1972, 10 minutes, International Animated Film Festival Award), a complex allegory of the forces of life and death.

Faith Hubley was interviewed in the Hubleys' studio in New York as John wandered in and out.

Your films are credited "John and Faith Hubley." How does your collaboration work?

FAITH HUBLEY: We collaborate on the story. John does

most of the backgrounds and I do some. I do the character rendering. We both work on the sound tracks. As a trained editor it's easier for me. The statement, the content, is made jointly.

JOHN HUBLEY: I direct the film. I time it, direct the set-ups, etc. Faith's credit on *Windy Day*, associate director, applies to almost all the films. The fairest credit is just "a film by John and Faith Hubley," without worrying about the details.

FH: We work this way. Both of us can just about see the whole picture before us before we do the physical work. There's very little improvisation. We do the soundtrack first so we're locked in, in time, to begin with. The visualization is very clear. We work very closely together.

Do you think husband and wife teams are a good idea?

FH: I like it. But the sharing has to be genuine sharing, and it has to exist at home. Any woman who's going to work must be very secure in her mate's convictions—not intellectual, but very real convictions—because it requires a lot of give and take.

Does it help if the husband's a filmmaker too?

FH: The Curies have always been my model. It seems so much simpler that way. Not that I would suggest every woman marry a man in the same line of work. But I think community of interest is very important. It depends, too, on the degree of competition. I don't see myself as an intensely competitive person. I have seen women suffer terribly because of loss of credit and prestige.

In your hallway there are awards on which only John's name appears.

FH: Those are from Europe. Europeans are worse than Americans. We've had three Academy Awards. Two we shared, one no. That was just because we didn't fill out the form properly.

Many of your films deal with little boys and only Windy Day *seems to deal with girls.*

FH: *Windy Day* is interesting from that point of view, because in real life our boys are older and the early films related to them more than to the girls. The girls would say, "You like the boys better!" So we talked about it for a long time. John and I had been wanting to do such a film, precisely because it's very hard for girls to find heroines, characters to identify with. So the girls improvised a soundtrack and a lot of very interesting thoughts emerged, like, "I was really a boy when my father planted the seed, but it came out different and that's why I'm a girl."

The film has been shown very widely, and the effect on young children is just fantastic. One sequence in the film is a dream of Georgia's—she drew the dream also. It's kind of the interior life of two little girls, talking about everything from getting married to death. I think little girls are more forthright about that.

Where are the best opportunities for women in filmmaking?

FH: We were in Teheran for a children's film festival a couple of years ago. Iran is a very backward country in many ways, particularly regarding women. We were invited to go on a television station—and the crew there was fifty-fifty, men and women. I've never seen anything like it in the entire world. There was the best morale I've seen on any set, and the women were charming, they were adorable, they were equally paid! I couldn't figure out how it had come about.

It turned out that the one man at the station who had originally had the technical know-how had gone to film school at UCLA, and he was so impressed by a couple of female students there, he got the message. It was like an oasis.

What sort of work are you doing now?

FH: We've done some work for "Sesame Street," sitting in

on long sessions with them. Suddenly we find ourselves conscious of making characters blue or green, colors that don't identify a specific group, or using surrealism the same way. It's interesting, you've got to keep growing. There's so much educational work that needs to be done.

I've seen more and more films lately which are groping for a new dimension in women's characters. You know, bad as live action has been, animation has been worse. Every female character is either a witch or a sex symbol. But it is changing. I can almost feel it in the air.

The New Producers

Shirley MacLaine, who took her first step in film production in 1973 with a documentary on the People's Republic of China called *The Other Half of the Sky: A China Memoir*, has embarked on an ambitious program for developing her own feature film properties. The objective is to make pictures that depart from the customary depiction of women as either hookers or doormats (roles, incidentally, which have won her three Academy Awards nominations), and show women as independent, strong-minded and vital people.

The first of her projects is *Amelia*, based on the life of Amelia Earhart, the aviation pioneer. Earhart, who was the first woman to make a solo flight around the world, disappeared mysteriously over the South Pacific in 1937, amid speculation that she was on a secret mission for President Roosevelt. MacLaine has raised $5 million for the film, and she looks forward to playing the flyer. She describes Earhart as a relentless advocate of women's rights and a highly vocal foe of fascism. Pete Hamill is writing the script, with MacLaine looking over his shoulder.

The film she made on China grew out of a plan to lead a women's delegation on a six-week tour through the country. Having received permission for the tour, she then asked if she could bring along an all-woman film crew. The Chinese agreed. The group traveled nearly 2,500 miles across China and shot about forty-five hours of film, which later was edited to feature length. Among its highlights are a meeting between MacLaine and Madame Chou En-lai, and a cesarean birth by acupuncture. The film, made with the assistance of Claudia Weill and Aviva Slesin, among others, had its first full-fledged American showing at the Whitney Museum in the spring of '75.

In recent years, MacLaine has been an outspoken feminist, noting that until women's lib started half the human race was virtually left out of the culture. "I'm a middle class girl from Virginia who has done a lot with what she had," she told a reporter for the Christian Science Monitor. "I don't know that I had much more than anybody else, except that I've always wanted to shatter the restrictions and the blinders and the feeling of prejudice I had about my own potential."

A political activist as well, she traveled across the country on behalf of George McGovern, joined peace marches and civil rights demonstrations, and is now working for abortion reform and legalization of pot. She has written two books: the 1970 bestseller "Don't Fall Off the Mountain" and "You Can Get There from Here," published in 1975. Her political work hasn't hurt her career as an actress. One of the few women movie stars in existence, she is still much in demand by the studios. But the roles have to be right.

Francine Parker is one of the few women accorded the distinction of being a director member of the Directors Guild of America. She is a producer and writer as well as a director, and her busy career has encompassed radio, television and theater as well as film. In one way or another, she's been prominently associated with more than a hundred film and videotape documentaries and hundreds of plays and radio shows, but she is best known for the Obie-winning "FTA Show," the satire on army life (and death) which she produced and directed, and the full-length documentary film,

FTA, starring Jane Fonda and Donald Sutherland, which recorded—to much critical acclaim—the "FTA" company's tour through five Asian countries. The film, which she also produced and directed, was released in 1972.

Parker has received a number of grants and fellowships, including a $10,000 American Film Institute Independent Filmmakers Grant (awarded by the National Endowment for the Humanities) and the American Film Institute Directors Internship Grant (awarded by the Academy of Motion Picture Arts and Sciences). Not only is she a filmmaker, she is also a film historian, a writer and lecturer on women's contributions to world history, a collector of rare books on archeology, a producer of rock festivals, and the author of scholarly articles on Greek theater. She is a graduate of Smith, holds a master's in fine arts from Yale, and is currently studying law at Loyola in Los Angeles.

But film remains a major interest. She has completed two screenplays written in collaboration with Delle Coleman and is also engaged in several projects with cinematographer Joan Weidman. The three women have formed a production company known as Pace Three Productions.

Eschewing the appellation of filmmaker, Jane Fonda nevertheless got a very fond reception at the Leipzig Film Festival in December, 1974, for making the new hour-long documentary, *Introduction to the Enemy,* an account of a visit she made to North Vietnam the previous spring with Tom Hayden and their infant child. The film includes interviews with Vietnamese intellectuals, doctors, teachers and peasants, with Fonda doing an on-screen commentary. Acknowledging the participation of a number of people in creating it, she made it clear that she did not regard herself as a filmmaker. "I am a movie actress, and also I am an activist," she told the Leipzig audience. But, she said, she recognizes the importance of documentaries in helping "us raise the consciousness of the American public."

Introduction to the Enemy, she says, "is the first film made by Americans for American audiences that shows the Vietnamese as human beings—not as victims and not as the enemy.

"This is a very modest film, it is not a work of art. It is not meant to be treated aesthetically. It was paid for with money collected in donations around the U.S. This film is for Americans. It's important that Americans see this film." The total cost, she pointed out, was less than the cost of one bomb.

One of the more encouraging signs of the times is that there is an increasing number of women producers. Especially worthy of note is Hannah Weinstein, a veteran of more than two decades who managed to escape attention until 1974, when she turned out the feature *Claudine* for an enterprising New York company called Third World Cinema.

Third World Cinema is a commercial production company which Weinstein formed in 1969 with Brock Peters, James Earl Jones and Diana Sands for the purpose of providing on-the-job technical training for blacks and Puerto Ricans. The training program has worked well. Young men and women who otherwise would never have had an opportunity to get into the film industry have gone on to jobs on features, industrials and commercials, and fifty hold membership in the International Alliance of Theater and Stage Employees. With the company taking firm root, Weinstein looks forward to having a diminishing role in its operation so that minority producers can take over.

As a production company, meanwhile, Third World Cinema has come up with a winner in *Claudine*, which Weinstein produced from a screenplay that had been rejected by Hollywood studios. The film was released by Twentieth Century-Fox in association with Joyce Selznick and Tina Pine. The latter was also co-writer of the screenplay. Hailed by Variety as "an outstanding film—a gritty, hearty, heartful and ruggedly tender story of contemporary urban black family life," *Claudine* stars Diahann Carroll and James Earl Jones. John Berry directed.

Weinstein began her work as a producer in 1953 with an American television series, "Colonel March of Scotland Yard" starring Boris Karloff. Then, in partnership with Brain's ATV she produced the Richard Greene series, "Adventures of Robin Hood," which she made in England (it was shown also on U.S. television), and a number of other series, including "Buccaneers," starring Robert Shaw, and "Four Just Men."

On making feature pictures, Hannah Weinstein makes these observations:

• It's a hard and precarious business, and often discouraging even after you've been at it a while. When you start a new film everything you may have done before is wiped out because every new film is like your first. To cope with the problems of personalities, technical matters and finances you have to have a strong stomach.

• For women it's even more difficult because the major studios constitute one of the last bastions of male domination. Although the upsurge of independent filmmaking broadens the opportunities for women, the major financing still comes largely from the distributors.

• Filmmakers in other countries now have greater opportunities than we do because of government film subsidies, which exist in practically every country in the world but the U.S.

• A motion picture should be entertaining but it also should illuminate and compel the viewer to think and respond.

More cheerily disposed to Hollywood, and sanguine about the future of young filmmakers there, is Julia Miller, who came out of nowhere to share in the producing credits for the Paul Newman-Robert Redford film, *The Sting*, which won seven Academy Awards in 1974, including Best Picture.

Miller didn't exactly come out of nowhere. She came out of Great Neck, N.Y., and Mount Holyoke College, following which she got a job as an East Coast story editor and married a young financial research analyst named Michael Phillips. Over the objections of both their families, Julia and Michael Phillips gave up their jobs for a fling at producing movies. They took an option on a story called "Steelyard Blues" and brought it to the screen in 1971 with some modest success. Then came *The Sting*. Their latest project is *Fear of Flying*, based on Erica Jong's best-selling novel.

Another newcomer who hit the jackpot was Sarah Kernochan, co-producer and co-director with Howard Smith of *Marjoe*, the very successful documentary of an extraordinary revivalist who began his career by performing a wedding ceremony at the age of four and ended it by revealing his cynicism in this film. *Marjoe*, financed and distributed by Rugoff's Cinema V, got great reviews, did a smashing business and won the 1973 Academy Award for documentaries. We couldn't locate Kernochan to find out how she'd gotten involved in the film, so we sought out her co-producer, Howard Smith, a Village Voice editor and columnist. According to Smith, the idea of doing a film on Marjoe was his. He had interviewed the revivalist on a radio show, and he invited Kernochan to join him in making a documentary. Smith says that Kernochan at the time was a twenty-two year old receptionist at the Voice, without film experience, but she flung herself into it with enthusiasm. During the making of the film, relations between the two producers became severely strained, but they finished the job and then parted.

A more durable partnership is the one that links Delores Taylor and her husband, Tom Laughlin. Proprietors of the Taylor-Laughlin Distribution Company, this team operates in a manner that recalls the simpler days when filmmakers wrote, directed and also starred in their films. Taylor and

Laughlin hit the bigtime and big money in 1971 with *Billy Jack*, a warmhearted, if simple-minded, story of the tribulations of an Indian half-breed. Distributed by Warner Brothers, it was one of the big hits of the year. In 1974 they turned out a sequel, *The Trial of Billy Jack*, which runs for almost three hours. It was met by less than universal critical acclaim, but it has the same ingredients—violence, piety, a clear distinction between good guys and bad guys—that attracted crowds to the earlier version. Vincent Canby of the Times, not one of its boosters, described the film as "part pageant, part kung fu action film, part Western, part earnest civics lesson, part Show Boat melodrama, part recollections of the various horrors of the late 1960s and early 1970s." Billy Jack, played by Tom Laughlin, "has a lot of Bruce Lee, Robin Hood, Cochise and Jesus in him." Delores Taylor, as the idealistic Jean Roberts, runs the Freedom School, which engages in exposing abuses by government and big business. (There's some fuzziness about who directed the film. The credits list the Laughlin's nineteen year old son, Frank. Their sixteen year old daughter, Teresa, plays the main ingenue role. The screenplay was written by Frank and Teresa Christina, said to be pseudonyms for Tom Laughlin's parents. Anyway, according to Variety, the movie earned $11,000,000 in its first week of national release.)

Of special interest in '74 was *Alice Doesn't Live Here Anymore*, the Warner Brothers movie which Ellen Burstyn brought to the screen and starred in. The film was directed by Martin Scorsese (Burstyn had considered Barbara Loden, but she opted for Scorsese because she wanted to achieve the "roughness" of Scorsese's *Mean Streets*). Women, however, were involved in other major aspects of its production—Toby Rafelson as production designer, Marcia Lucas as editor, Audrey Maas as co-producer, and Sandy Weintraub as associate producer. (Weintraub, incidentally, also helped produce *Mean Streets*.)

Alice Doesn't Live Here Anymore, some of it improvised by Burstyn from her own experiences, is the story of a woman who buries her aspirations to be a pop singer at the insistence of her crude and insensitive husband. When her husband dies in a road accident, she takes off with her eleven-year-old son on a desperate journey to fulfill her dreams, encountering misadventures and frustration at almost every turn of the road. The film was heralded by Ms. as a "brilliant movie," worthy of an Academy Award for Burstyn. "It is part soap opera, part 1940s romantic comedy—and mostly a damn good documentary-style movie about the conflicts of today's woman," said the Ms. reviewer.

(Burstyn is writing the script for her next movie, *Silence of the North*, which is based on the autobiography of Olive Fredericks, a woman who homesteaded alone with her three children in British Columbia during the Depression years. It should encourage the search for strong-woman roles.)

Women with producing credits in the past few years include (for pictures made in 1969) Helen Silverstein, *Me and My Brother*; Micheline Rozan, *The Immortal Story*; Mary P. Murray, *Kenner*; Betzi Manoogian, *Who's That Knocking at My Door?*; Sylvia Anderson, *Journey to the Far Side of the Sun*; (in 1970) Joyce Selznick, *Children at the Gate* and *Rudi*; Tamara Asseyev, *Paddy*; Evelyn Barron, *Johnny Cash*; Charlotte Zwerin, *Gimme Shelter*; Jo Napoleon, *The Activist*; (in 1971) Paula Stewart, *Dinah East*; Veronica Lake, *Flesh Feast*; Jane Schaffer, *Angels Die Hard* and *The Big Doll House*; Jeanne Abel, *Is There Sex After Death?*; Susan Martin, *Punishment Park*; Zoe Phillips, *Horror of the Blood Monsters*; (in 1972) Jane Schaffer, *The Big Bird Cage*; Rita Murray, *Bury Me an Angel*; Nancy Reals, *Malcolm X*; Linda Gottlieb, *Limbo*; Joanna Milton, *Please Stand By*; (in 1973) Janelle Cohen, with two credits, *Black Caesar* and *Hell Up in Harlem*; June Cash, Reba Hancock and Barbara John, *The Gospel Road*; Joan Shigekawa, *Ganja and Hesse*;

Nancy Romero, *Hungry Wives;* Lois Rosenfield, *Bang the Drum Slowly;* Lynn Pressman, *The Sisters;* Jane Dossick, *The P.O.W.;* Gail Stayden, *I Could Never Have Sex With a Man Who Has So Little Regard for My Husband;* Nina Schulman, *Werewolf of Washington;* (in 1974) Natalie R. Jones, *Two Men of Karamoja.*

Joyce Selznick, a former casting director, has formed a new production company with writer Tina Pine (with whom she was associated in the production of *Claudine*) and is developing several films for Paramount. They are: *The Title,* about a young prizefighter; *Fred,* the story of a Harvard Business School graduate, and *Ask Frankie,* about Frank Lasole, the longest surviving heart transplant patient.

The Screenwriters

Among screenwriters, one of the most gifted—and out-spoken—is Eleanor Perry. A writer of mystery novels and plays before she turned to film writing, Perry scored with *David and Lisa,* a 1962 Academy Award contender produced by her husband, Frank Perry, from whom she is now divorced. Other major pictures she wrote were *Last Summer* (1969) and *Diary of a Mad Housewife* (1970). She was co-producer and co-writer of *The Man Who Loved Cat Dancing* (1973), and also holds credits for *Ladybug, Ladybug, Trilogy, The Swimmer, Lady in the Car With Glasses and a Gun,* and *La Maison sous les arbres.* She has written several tele-vision specials, two of which, "Christmas Memory" and "House Without a Christmas Tree," were awarded Emmies.

An active feminist who has been campaigning for more women power in the film industry, Perry says part of the problem is the attitude of women themselves. "Women have real hang-ups about power," she says. "Power is a dirty word when it's linked to a female." The result is that "the movies we are seeing now offer nothing for women to get involved with or identify with." In a 1974 forum sponsored by the

National Organization for Women and members of the Screen Actors Guild she underscored her argument with the assertion that there were 3,060 men and only eight women in the Producers Guild; 2,343 men and twenty-three women in the Directors Guild; and 2,882 men and 148 women in the Writers Guild.

"The most important thing of all," she says, "is getting the financing for films. I've had three so-called hits, but that doesn't insure at all that I have a bankable script. We've just got to go out and raise the money."

Another leading screenwriter is Jay Presson Allen, whose credits include *The Prime of Miss Jean Brodie* (1969), *Travels With My Aunt* (1972), *Cabaret* (1972) and Barbra Streisand's *Funny Lady*, scheduled for release in 1975. Allen, interviewed by Marjorie Rosen for a Times story on the paucity of good roles for women, said she has never encountered restrictions on depicting women characters. More optimistic than Eleanor Perry, Allen thinks "it's an evolutionary kind of thing" and as soon as two or three dynamic actresses are given strong parts in money-making films, "you'll have women in movies again."

A major writer for some years, Leigh Brackett shared credits for *The Big Sleep* (1946) and *Rio Bravo* (1959). In recent years she has received solo credits for *Hatari!* (1962), *El Dorado* (1967), *Rio Lobo* (1971) and *The Long Goodbye* (1973).

Successful screenwriters also include Harriet Frank, Jr., whose major credits include *Hud* (1964), *Hombre* (1968), *The Reivers* (1969), and *The Spikes Gang* (1974); Isobel Lennart, *The Sundowners* (1960) and *Funny Girl* (1969); Marguerite Roberts, *True Grit* and *Norwood* (both 1970), *Shoot Out* and *Red Sky at Morning* (both 1971); and Tina Pine, *Popi* (1970) and the aforementioned *Claudine* (1974). Maya Angelou, who wrote the screenplay for *Georgia, Georgia* (1972), is planning to direct an adaptation of her autobiographical novel, "I Know Why the Caged Bird Sings," about growing up black in the South. It would be the first feature in Hollywood directed by a black woman. Renee Taylor, one of the world's funniest writers, teamed with her husband, Joseph Bologna, on the script for *Lovers and Other Strangers* (1969). Taylor and Bologna also wrote and starred in *Made For Each Other* (1971).

Other writing credits in recent years: (in 1967) Gladys Hill, *Reflections in a Golden Eye;* Helen Deutsch and Dorothy Kingsley, *Valley of the Dolls;* (in 1968) Ruby Dee, *Uptight;* Joyce Geller, *The Cool Ones;* (in 1969) Bridget Boland, *Anne of the Thousand Days;* Lotte Colin, *Play Dirty;* Jane Klove and Joanna Crawford, *My Side of the Mountain;* Margaret Drabble, *Thank You All Very Much* (adapted from her own book); Jane Gaskell, *All Neat in Black Stockings;* Alida Sherman, *Slaves;* Lois Peyser, *The Trouble With Girls;* Anne Piper, *A Nice Girl Like Me;* Danielle Thompson, *The Brain;* Sylvia Anderson, *Journey to the Far Side of the Sun;* (in 1970) Marjorie Kellogg, *Tell Me That You Love Me Junie Moon;* Jenni Hall, *My Lover My Son;* Gladys Hill, *The Kremlin Letter;* Ann Cawthorne, *Marital Fulfillment;* Betty Botley, *Tropic of Cancer;* Jane Baker, *Captain Nemo and the Underwater City;* Jo Napoleon, *The Activist;* Elinor Kapf, *Adam at 6 A.M.;* (in 1971) Margaret McPherson, *The Pink Angels;* Joan Didion, *The Panic in Needle Park;* Diane Rochlin, *Maidstone;* Jeanne Abel, *Is There Sex After Death?;* Joyce Corrington, *Von Richthoven and Brown* and *The Omega Man;* Sue McNair, *Horror of the Blood Monsters;* (in 1972) Suzanne De Passe, *Lady Sings the Blues;* Joan Torres, *Blacula;* Mary Olson, *It Ain't Easy;* Joanna Milton, *Please Stand By;* Joanna Crawford, *The Little Ark;* Joan Didion, *Play It As It Lays* (adapted from her own novel); Peggy Elliott, *Come Back Charleston Blue;* Joan Silver, *Limbo;* Joyce Corrington, *Boxcar Bertha;* Sandra Scappettone, *Scarecrow in a Garden of Cucumbers;* Sarah Riggs, *Quadroon;* Marlene Weed, *Soul Soldier;* Judith Singer, *Glass*

House; (in 1973) Harriet Rhodes, *Loveland;* Joyce Hooper, *Battle for the Planet of the Apes;* Joan Torres, *Scream Blacula Scream;* Blanche Hanalis, *From the Mixed Up Files of Mrs. Basil E. Frankweiler;* Ann Cawthorne, *The Hitchhikers;* Sue Grafton, *Lolly Madonna XXX;* Lucille Kallen, *Ten from Your Show of Shows;* Joan Huntington, *Manson;* Mona Lott and Joy Box, *The Erotic Adventures of Zorro;* Louisa Rose, *Sisters;* (in 1974) Ruth Wolff, *The Abdication;* Joan Tewkesbury, *Thieves Like Us;* Gayle Gleckler, *Lords of Flatbush;* Jane C. Stanton, *Our Time;* Judith Rascoe, *Road Movie* and *The Life Span.*

Rascoe also has completed a screen adaptation of Isak Dinesen's "Out of Africa." Joan Tewksbury's new credits will include *Nashville,* scheduled for release in '75, and *Maiden,* for which she will also receive directing credit. Another enterprising writer is Joanna Lee, who is directing a film she wrote, *Pocket Filled With Dreams.* Gail Parent, a superb TV comedy writer and author of the novel "Sheila Levine is Dead and Living in New York," has written a screenplay based on her book. Brenda Perla has written an original screenplay about a female car thief in Los Angeles, *The All-American Girl,* to be released by MGM in '75.

Especially promising among the young screenwriters are Gloria Katz and Carole Eastman. Katz works in tandem with her husband, Willard Huyck, and the team has been highly regarded in Hollywood ever since the surprise success of *American Graffiti* (1973), for which they wrote an extremely clever script about growing up in the early sixties. Katz, a product of UCLA, and her husband (USC) originally planned to be directors, and in fact on one occasion they managed to get backing to produce and direct a horror film, but it was so bad that it was never distributed. So they took to writing scripts, and after having amassed twelve of them—none of which were sold—they were hired by George Lucas, the director, to write *American Graffiti.* It was their first break, but success nearly eluded them because the script was rejected by almost every production company until Universal decided to take a chance on it. The movie opened with little promotion, and then, when young America discovered it, it took off. Offers came in abundance after that and the team signed for two films set in the thirties—*Lucky Lady*, starring Liza Minelli and Burt Reynolds, and *Radioland Murders*, a thriller directed by George Lucas—and the saga of a wine-growing dynasty, *The Napa Valley Story*.

Carole Eastman, who won much praise for *Five Easy Pieces* (1970), and also co-wrote *Puzzle of a Downfall Child*, has another big picture scheduled for '75. This one is *The Fortune*, a comedy starring Jack Nicholson and Warren Beatty and directed by Mike Nichols. Eastman also works under the name of Adrian Joyce.

The Editors

Editors singled out for honors in the sixties by the Motion Picture Academy and the American Cinema Editors included some veterans and some newer arrivals. The veterans were Viola Lawrence, an Oscar nominee in 1960 for *Pepe;* Anne Coates, an Oscar winner in 1962 for *Lawrence of Arabia*, also an Oscar nominee and an ACE Eddie nominee in 1964 for *Becket;* Dorothy Spencer, an Oscar nominee in 1963 for *Cleopatra;* and Marjorie Fowler, an Eddie nominee in 1964 for *What a Way to Go* and again in 1965 for *Dear Brigitte*, and an Oscar nominee in 1967 for *Dr. Doolittle*. The newer editors cited were Dede Allen, nominated for an Eddie in 1961 for *The Hustlers* and in 1967 for *Bonnie and Clyde;* Eve Newman, an Oscar nominee in 1968 for *Wild in the Streets;* and Marion Rothman, an Eddie nominee in 1968 for *The Boston Strangler*.

Time, alas, has taken its toll on that remarkable group of women who pioneered in the editing craft and served the industry with distinction for so many years. Viola Lawrence, Anne Bauchens and Alma Macrorie have died. Barbara

McLean, Irene Morra and Eda Warren are retired. But still active are veterans Dorothy Spencer, Marjorie Fowler, Anne Coates, Adrienne Fazan, and, the most durable of them all, Margaret Booth. Spencer's recent credits include *Happy Birthday Wanda June* (1971); Fowler's include *The Strawberry Statement* (1970) and *Conquest of the Planet of the Apes* (1972). The recent credits for Coates include *The Adventurers* (1970), *Friends* (1971), and the British film *11 Harrowhouse* (1974). One of Fazan's recent films was *The Cheyenne Social* (1970). Margaret Booth's credits include *The Owl and the Pussycat* (1970) and *The Way We Were* (1973).

The list of those who have moved to the front ranks of editors in recent years must begin with Dede Allen, who got her start with Robert Wise's *Odds Against Tomorrow* in 1959. Her credits since that time are a roster of moviedom's proudest successes. In addition to *The Hustler* and *Bonnie and Clyde*, they include *America, America* (1964), *Rachel, Rachel* (1968), *Alice's Restaurant* (1969), *Little Big Man* (1970), *Slaughterhouse Five* (1972) and *Serpico* (1973).

As one of the highest-paid, best-known editors in the United States, Allen has the stature to command a contract for each film, whereas most editors are hired on a weekly basis and can be fired at any time. She began her career by working as a messenger at Columbia Pictures in Hollywood in 1943, using "every second on the job to learn moviemaking." Despite being told she wasn't strong enough to carry heavy cans of film, she "pestered" her way into the cutting room and "carried more film and swore more than anyone else, until I felt the men accepted me." She worked in Hollywood until 1950, when she came to New York in search of wider opportunities. After cutting commercials and documentaries for Leon Levy for several years, she left to freelance—only to find that the feature film business in New York was monopolized by a small group of cutters, and she was locked out. Her break came when a friend recommended her as editor for *Odds Against Tomorrow*.

Beginning with *Rachel, Rachel*, Allen has frequently shared in a movie's profits, and her name now appears alone on screen in the credits, like that of the director and producer.

Rita Roland started her editing career in Europe, cutting her first film before she was twenty. After working successfully in Amsterdam, Rome, Paris, London and New York, she went to Hollywood, where she worked at MGM Studios. Her credits here include *A Patch of Blue* and *Girl Happy* (1965); *The Singing Nun, Where Were You When the Lights Went Out?, Penelope* and *Spinout* (1966). For other companies she did *Justine* (1967), *Move* (1970), and *To Find a Man* (1972).

Editor Eve Newman began her career in the film industry as an artist at Disney Studios. Later she specialized in music editing for several years, and then advanced to full editing with *Muscle Beach Party* in 1964 for American International. In the ten years following that assignment she did fifteen films, including the aforementioned Oscar nominee *Wild in the Streets* (1968), *Three in the Attic* (1968), *Bloody Mama* (1970), and *Little Cigars* (1974).

Marion Rothman, who made a strong impression with *The Boston Strangler*, subsequently collected credits for *Beneath the Planet of the Apes* (1970), *Escape from the Planet of the Apes* (1971), *Play It Again, Sam* (1972) and *Tom Sawyer* (1973). Verna Fields, who co-edited *American Graffiti* (1973) with Marcia Lucas, also did *What's Up, Doc?* (1972), *Paper Moon* (1973), and *Sugarland Express* (1974). Joanne Burke did *The Anderson Tapes* (1971), *Child's Play* (1972), and *Lovin' Molly* (1974). Thelma Schoonmaker, before working on *Woodstock*, did *J.R.* (1969). Charlotte Zwerin's credits include *Salesman* (1969) and *The Adventurers* (1970).

Other editors with recent credits: Arline Garson, *House of*

Dark Shadows (1970) and *Rivals* (1972); Virginia Stone, *Song of Norway* (1970); Sylvia Sarner, *Tropic of Cancer* (1970) and *Road Movie* (1974); Karen Edwards, *Brand X* (1970); Thelma Connell, *The Virgin Soldiers* (1970) and *One Day in the Life of Ivan Denisovich* (1971); Millie Paul, *The Big Doll House* (1971); Edna Paul, *Dirtymouth* (1971); Mary Yeomans, *Saturday Morning* (1971); Riva Schlesinger, *Tomorrow* (1972); Anita Kerr, *Limbo* (1972); Pat Somerset, *Black Gunn* (1972); Patricia Lewis Jaffe, *The Friends of Eddie Coyle* (1973); Barbara Connell, *Free* (1973); Lois Fisher, *The Newcomers* (1973); Bea Davis, *Visions of Eight* (1973); L. Deborah Klingman, *The New York Experience* (1973); Barbara Pokras, *I Escaped from Devil's Island, Fly Me* and *The Big Bust-Up* (all 1973); Muffie Meyer, *Lords of Flatbush* (1974); Laura Lesser, *Ladies and Gentlemen, The Rolling Stones* (1974).

A few women have risen through the ranks to become studio executives, among them Judy Feiffer who started at Warner Brothers in 1969 as story editor and became director of East Coast projects for the studio, and Tina Nides, who was also a story editor at Warner Brothers and is now an executive in charge of literary acquisitions. The first woman to become a vice president at United Artists was Marcia Nassiter, who heads motion picture development for the studio. She started her career as an editor at Bantam Books and The Ladies Home Journal, then became story editor for National General Pictures in New York before joining United Artists.

Other women studio executives include Deanne Barkley, vice president for creative affairs at RSO Productions (Robert Stigwood Co.); Andrea Eastman, director of program development for Paramount; Ronda Gomez-Quinones, an executive in the creative affairs department at Twentieth Century-Fox; Rosilyn Heller, vice president for creative affairs at Columbia Pictures; Nessa Hyams, vice president for west coast productions at Columbia Pictures; Monique James, an executive for new talent at Universal; and Helen M. Strauss, head of Reader's Digest Motion Picture Division.

Some Firsts

The woman with potentially one of the largest bankrolls any woman in film has ever had is Pamela Douglas, a producer at Universal Studios, the largest film and television producing company in the world. She also happens to be the first black woman producer at a major studio.

Douglas joined Universal in October 1973, and a year later, when we spoke with her, she was developing several theatrical movies and some television productions as well. Her work, she said, was "involved with moving a gargantuan machine, which survives on making immense motion pictures for the mass audience, to the point of allocating many millions of dollars to me to make the kinds of films I care deeply about, especially in terms of their representation of third-world people and women." How successful has she been? "When the films come out," she said, "we can discuss whether or not I've succeeded. Until that time, it is in the hands of the universal spirit evolving through us all."

Before joining MCA-Universal, Douglas was program director at an experimental television station. Before that she had a fellowship from the University of Chicago to write a book on black television, a project that grew out of her work in organizing people to assert a greater influence by challenging the licenses of TV stations and proposing alternative programming. She wrote critical pieces on the media for a number of publications, including Muhammad Speaks, the Chicago Defender newspaper chain and TV Guide.

A New Yorker, with a background as an artist, she had produced independent films for seven years and directed inner-city filmmaking workshops to "keep the knowledge flowing from me to the young people and from them to me." Even now she drives from Universal to Watts one day a week to teach filmwriting to a group of youngsters.

"This bit about anyone being a 'first,' or being the biggest or best, is not real," she says. "My films will succeed to the extent that they reflect the imagination and cares of millions of people. So if I have any power as a filmmaker or a force in this industry, this is its generator—because none of us is first and nobody is last."

In the spring of '74 Universal reported another breakthrough for women—this one in the area of film music. The news came from Geneva, where director Mark Robson was at work on a feature titled *Chained to Yesterday*, for which all the music was composed, arranged and conducted by a woman—the first time it's ever happened in a major American feature, Universal said.

Chained to Yesterday is a story of the wives of returning Vietnam war prisoners, and it was because of its strong appeal to women that Robson decided to have a woman do the score. The woman he chose was Anita Kerr, a three-time Grammy winner and holder of a gold album for Rod McKuen's "The Sea." Kerr has been living in Switzerland since 1970, when she despaired of ever making it in Hollywood.

There was nothing casual about the decision to engage Kerr. Robson let it be know that he had stuck his neck out for her and that it was something of a test case for women in this area of the film industry. But Kerr did the job in quick order and in a professional manner. Kerr later told a Variety reporter that at the first full recording session the studio was filled with Universal executives who came to watch her fall apart, but as the session went on, and no unusual problems occurred, they drifted away. Kerr made it plain she takes a dim view of producers who feel that their investment is jeopardized when women are given important responsibilities.

Kerr, by the way, is not the only woman prominently associated with *Chained to Yesterday*. The producer is Linda

Gottlieb and the story is by Joan Silver, who also worked on the adaption (with James Bridges). Dorothy Spencer is editor.

As composer, arranger and conductor of a major motion picture score, Kerr may well be unique, but Mark Evans, author of the new book "Soundtrack!" points out that at least two other American women have composed full scores. The first was Elizabeth Firestone, daughter of Harvey S. Firestone, Jr., the tire manufacturer. Elizabeth Firestone, at the age of twenty-five, composed the music for the 1947 romantic comedy *Once More, My Darling*, a Robert Montgomery production for Universal-International starring Montgomery and Ann Blyth.

Firestone—whose grandfather was a close friend of Henry Ford and Thomas Edison—attributed her break to family connections. Montgomery, also a family friend, heard her music on his visits to the Firestone home and one day asked her if she'd like to do a movie score. The young woman said she'd be delighted and Montgomery said, "All right, when I get the right story." "I thought it was just conversation," she recalled, but a few months later Montgomery sent her the script for *Once More, My Darling* and the invitation to do the music.

The second of the two women mentioned by Mark Evans is Ann Ronnel, who did the scores for *Love Happy* in 1949 and *Main Street to Broadway* in 1953. Ronnel actually broke into film music before Firestone, having worked on *The Story of G.I. Joe* (1945), but she shared credits with two others on this film. She also shared credits on *One Touch of Venus* (1948).

Marlene Sanders, who was the first woman to anchor a television network evening newscast, in 1972 became the first woman to be engaged by a network (ABC) as a fulltime documentary producer.

Sanders, a native of Cleveland, got her start in 1955 just

after emerging from Ohio State University when she got a job as reporter and writer for WNEW-TV in New York. The job led to producing assignments, both at WNEW-TV and its parent company, Westinghouse Broadcasting, and then, in 1962 to the position of assistant director of news and public affairs for radio station WNEW, where she also wrote and produced a weekly half-hour documentary. In 1964 she joined ABC News as a radio and television correspondent and that year did the first of a couple of stints anchoring the "ABC Evening News" network newscast. She also anchored her own daytime television news program for ABC News for four years. During her years as a correspondent Sanders also wrote and produced several TV documentaries. These included *Women's Liberation* and *We Have Met the Enemy and He Is Us* (on the population problem), both in 1970, and *Strangers in Their Own Land—The Blacks*, a three-part study aired in 1971. In 1972 she wrote and produced the widely acclaimed *Children in Peril*, a half-hour documentary on child abuse.

As a fulltime producer in '73 she wrote and produced the hour-long *Woman's Place*, an examination of the changing role of women today which won a CINE Golden Eagle certificate. In the same year she wrote and produced the hour-long *Population: Boom or Doom*, a study of U.S. population growth patterns. In '74 she was the writer and producer of *The Right to Die*, dealing with the ethical and legal issues of the hopelessly ill, and *Prime Time TV: The Decision Makers*, an examination of the television industry.

Sanders acknowledges that she "somehow managed to move ahead, on my own, before there was a women's movement," but she sees a need for concerted action to end male domination in television. Keynoting a meeting of the Media Women's Association in December, 1974, she said that although ABC women have excellent relations with management, "we intend to keep the pressure on."

She is concerned, she said, not only with employment opportunities for women, but also the depiction of women on the screen. "The image of women now on the screens of motion pictures and television sets," she said, "is severely limited by the imagination of men. Are we—the women of America—only whores and victims, and only occasionally Mary Tyler Moore? No, we are many things in life, including governors and lieutenant governors. Our possibilities are limitless, but you would never know it from what the screen reveals."

When *Angel Number 9* opened in New York in 1974, ads proclaimed it "the first erotically explicit film ever made by a woman." But actually writer-director Roberta Findlay had already made ten soft-core sex films before this. Findlay, who may be the only woman in the country directing 35mm erotic feature films, is also a professional cinematographer and photographs the films she directs.

Angel Number 9 is the story of a sexually hyperactive young man who gets hit by a truck and goes to heaven, where he meets Angel Number 9. She tells him that he still has a lesson or two to learn on earth, and sends him back down in the form of the creature he has most abused: a woman. He finds out what it is like to be a victim of sexual exploitation, and in the end begs to have his masculine identity restored. So much for the story.

Findlay became involved in making erotic films out of a belief that women's sexual desires are as strong as men's, and that it was time to explore this openly, from a woman's point of view. She puts her own erotic fantasies on film, portraying them, she feels, in a warm, romantic fashion that distinguishes them from most erotic films.

Findlay's childhood goal was to be a concert pianist and in fact she gave several recitals in New York before retiring from the profession at eighteen to begin a film career. With her husband, Michael, Findlay made both horror films and erotic films, including *The Shriek of the Mutilated, Take Me*

Naked, The Touch of Her Flesh and *The Ultimate Degenerate.*

When she felt she was ready to make her own films, she was given the opportunity by Allan Shackleton, a New York distributor. Her first solo venture was *The Altar of Lust*, a low-budget sex film that she wrote, produced, directed, shot and edited. Other films that she has written, produced and directed include *Rosebud, Teenage Milkmaid* and *The Clamdigger's Daughter.*

New York filmmakers Karen Sperling and Doro Bachrach, in the spring of '73, laid claim to a special place in motion picture history by producing the first feature film made with an all-female crew. The film is *The Waiting Room*, written and directed by Sperling, who also stars in it.

First, about the film: *The Waiting Room* (still awaiting a distributor at this writing) is a very personal work that springs from Sperling's own experiences in seeking a relationship with a man, what it seems to have meant to her family and friends, and her realization that there is more to life than birth, marriage and death. Sperling herself describes it as "a psychological drama, based in suspense, which is developed from a series of experiences, dreams and fantasies." It tells of a journey by a young woman through dim hallways and bright institutional corridors into other people's lives; endless doors open and behind each door is a person with a different tale. Bridget Byrne, writing in the Los Angeles Herald-Examiner after a special showing, said "The film is difficult and often infuriating but it is a clever film, often witty and mentally painful. Young men in the audience around me squirmed in a curious mixture of boredom and fascinated discomfort with revelations previously denied them. Women found identity."

About the making of the film: from gaffer to cinematographer, the people who made *The Waiting Room* were women, and assembling them took a bit of doing. Sperling and Bach-

rach found some of the crew in New York, but to round out
the force they sent word out to California, Canada, and even
Europe. The sound stage was to be a vacant hospital on
Ward's Island in New York, and the script called for fifteen
sets that had to be designed and built. Says Bachrach: "We
needed carpenters, scenic artists, assistants, and an art director who could take charge of a large crew. This wasn't a
documentary crew—we needed a feature crew that could
build walls, hang ceilings, paint and light complicated sets.
Some of the chores were heavy, calling for muscle power.
But we stuck to our intention to hire only women.

"We had determined early that the production came first.
If women couldn't hang a ceiling or spackle a wall, we
wouldn't keep them on just because they were women. The
fact is that we found capable, talented women, eager to work,
and men couldn't have done better."

One woman had to get special training as a dolly grip because there were no trained women available. But help came
from New York studio managers and when production began
she was ready to handle the Stindt hydraulic dolly.

In the Village Voice, Molly Haskell told of a trip she made
to Ward's Island while the movie was in production: "I
don't know what I expected to see when I went out—something cute like Santa's elves puttering around the toy shop,
or something scary like clusters of mean-looking militants
eyeing an outsider with suspicion—but what I found were
young women mostly in their twenties scattered here and
there throughout the rooms and corridors of an abandoned
hospital, hammering, drinking coffee, setting up a scene, consulting, scribbling, and in general behaving in the normal,
relaxed way of people who are busy but not frantic."

Union people also came to see what was going on. They
watched with approval and were even cooperative, Sperling
says. "Better yet, when the filming was over they decided to
let some of our crew into their membership."

As a result of their experience, Bachrach and Sperling both

feel that more women should specialize in some particular phase of production work. Does everybody have to be a producer or a director? They point out that men in the film industry can assemble a production team quickly because they know each other by name and specialty. To fill the thirty-two crew positions for *The Waiting Room*, Bachrach and Sperling had to interview 300 women, a procedure that took months of work.

The Waiting Room was shot in 35mm color, using two Arri 11C cameras. Camerawork was by Roberta Findlay. Christine Robinson was art editor and Edna Paul was editor. Other credits: assistant editors, Julia Tanser and Esther Croft; sound recordist, Maryte Kavalauskas; boom operator, Nicola Fisher; gaffers, Celeste Gainey and Nancy Schreiber; assistant camera, Deborah Boldt and Ann Pedersen; dolly grip, Alexis Krasilovsky; carpenters, Judy Van Heyningen and Joann Neuer; props, Laurie Grennan; costumes, Wendy Appel, Amy Kronish and Rita Ogden; make-up, Brooks Riley; production coordinator/casting director, Susan Needles; co-producer, Nancy Littlefield; production assistant, Nancy Oettinger; script, Janet Saunders; unit photographer, Gretchen Berg; location auditor, Mona Shyman.

The Waiting Room is Karen Sperling's second film. In 1971 she produced, co-wrote, directed and edited a 90-minute experimental documentary titled *Make a Face*, which tells of a rich young woman who is terrified by an assortment of people trying to run her life. It was shown at the London, Venice and Cannes film festivals, and produced an income, she says, that helped finance *The Waiting Room*.

Sperling comes from a motion picture family. Her father is the producer-writer Milton Sperling. She is the granddaughter of Harry Warner and grandniece of Jack L. Warner. "Older men in the film business tell me it's great that I do my own films," she says, "but they don't believe it and the next time they see me they ask what school I go to." She recognizes that she can't aspire to the commercial triumphs identified with the Warner brothers because audiences aren't ready for women's films, which are "slower, more sensitive, more aware of the fragments of emotions." Women, she contends, make higher quality pictures—almost out of innocence—and "I hope they don't have to lower their standards to achieve commercial success."

For Doro Bachrach, *The Waiting Room* is the beginning of what she hopes will be a permanent career in making feature-length fiction films, and if sheer determination can do it, she will be heard from again. A graduate of NYU's Institute of Film and Television, Bachrach got her basic training by working for a couple of small production companies, an experience she commends highly because "you do everything," and "everything," she stresses, includes the important work of dealing with finances, logistics, arrangements for locations, and personnel, not to mention unions. She was the producer of a comedy short, *Oven 350* (16 minutes), and Martha Coolidge's long documentary of an addict, *David: Off and On* (42 minutes). She wrote and directed *The Victors* (22 minutes), the story of a breach between a husband and wife, portrayed by John Randolph and Vivian Nathan. It won the Abraham Schneider Award.

Elaine May, directing *A New Leaf*, in which she starred.

Susan Sontag

Stephanie Rothman

Dede Allen

Francine Parker

Marlene Sanders

Shirley MacLaine

Director Karen Sperling briefing some of the members
of the all-women crew of *The Waiting Room*. From the
left: Alexis Krasilovsky, key dolly; Nicola Fisher, boom;
Deborah Boldt, assistant camera; Nancy Littlefield, co-
producer; Roberta Findlay, camera; Ann Pedersen,
assistant camera; Sperling; Janet Saunders, script;
(rear) Judy Van Hook, make-up.

Lina Wertmuller

Beryl Fox, with John Grierson,
documentary film pioneer.

Leni Riefenstahl, with
a Sudanese child.

Around the World

AFRICA

The most prominent woman filmmaker in Africa is Sarah Maldoror, a black feminist whose husband was a leader of the guerrilla struggle against the Portuguese in Angola. Maldoror directed the powerful feature *Sambizanga* (1972). Based on a short story by a white Angolan writer, Luandina Vieira, who spent more than ten years as a Portuguese political prisoner because of his nationalist sympathies, the film was shot on location in the People's Republic of the Congo. It is the story of a tractor driver who is arrested by the Portuguese police and tortured to death for refusing to reveal his underground nationalist contacts. His wife, who was unaware of her husband's clandestine activities, reacts with deep anguish that culminates in her political awakening and commitment to the struggle for Angolan independence. *Sambizanga*, which was awarded several prizes in Europe, was released commercially in the United States in 1973. As a result of this film, Maldoror was commissioned to make a documentary of the guerrilla struggle in Angola for French television.

Maldoror was born in Guadeloupe in the French West Indies, and was educated in Paris and Moscow, where she was a film student. Her films, such as the two shorts *Viva la Muerte* and *The Poor and the Proud*, are concerned mainly with African liberation struggles. She made a documentary on the uprisings against Portuguese colonialism in Guinea and Cape Verde, but this film was never released—it was photographed by an Algerian Army film unit and remains unfinished because of a conflict between Maldoror's feminist views and the traditionalism of the Algerians.

Maldoror, a woman in early middle age with two children, feels strongly about the need for greater involvement of African women in filmmaking. But elsewhere on the continent, south of the Sahara, there is little activity by women. Indeed, because of a distinct preference by black African audiences for Western films, plus a lack of commercial outlets, financing and equipment, the development of the medium here has been slow.

In Egypt, actress Aziza Amir and Turkish writer Wedad Orfyn founded the first Egyptian film production company in 1927; Amir acted and produced. The company's first film, *The Call of God* (1927, also called *Laila)*, is about a pregnant woman who is deserted by her betrothed and driven from her village. Amir also produced *Bint el Nil (Daughter of the Nile,* 1929), and *Kaferi an Khatiatak (Pay For Your Sins,* 1933). The former was co-produced with Rocca and the latter with Mustafa Wali. In the 1930s, another Egyptian actress, Assis, formed her own production company for the films in which she appeared. These included the silent film, *Wakhel Damir,* and the sound films *Endama Tehobel Meraa (When a Woman Loves,* 1933), *Eyoun Sahera (The Enchanting Eyes,* 1934), and *Salaheddin* (1952).

Bahija Hafez founded and headed Fanar Film, producing and acting in *El Dohaya (The Victims,* 1933), *El Etteham (The Accusation),* and *Laila, Bent al Sahra (Laila, Daughter of the Desert,* 1937). Mary Queeny produced films in Egypt in the 1930s, and after World War II Laila Fawzi set up a film production company.

The most recent Egyptian filmmaker to make a name for herself is Hashim el Nahhas, a sensitive young woman who studied film in London. Especially noteworthy is her documentary *On the Nile* (11 minutes), in which her camera depicts, without narration, the ebb and flow of life along the river.

The Tunisian Federation of Amateur Cinéastes has generated so much interest in cinema and television that many of its members have turned professional. Sofia Ferchiou, a producer and director of documentaries, began her work in 1966 with a film on the making of chéchias, a cylindrical coiffure worn by some African women. Her more recent films include *La Zarda*, a report on an annual Moslem pilgrimage, and *Le Marriage de Sabria*, showing the customs of a traditional marriage. Najet Mabaouj directed a different type of film on the same subject, *Marriage* (1967), a fictionalized tale of a young girl who is forced to marry against her wishes. Selma Bakkar, an assistant director for television, has directed film shorts on the theme of women, including *L'Eveil* (*The Awakening*, 1972). Fatma Scandrani, who also works in television, has directed a number of films for children.

In Cameroon, journalist Thérèse Sita-Bella filmed a 16mm documentary, *Tam-tam á Paris*, (1963, 30 minutes), about a Cameroonian national dance troupe that toured France.

In Ghana, poet Efua Sutherland directed *Araba: The Village Story* (1967), a sensitive evocation of village life as seen through the eyes of a little girl. The film was financed by the American Broadcasting Company.

BELGIUM

In Belgium, soon after World War I, Aimée Navarra directed the patriotic *Coeurs belges*. More recent Belgian filmmakers include Claude Misonne, who directed puppet films in the 1940s, including: *Tintin et le crabe aux pinces d'or*

(1946), *Formule X 24, Car je suis l'Empereur, Il était un vieux savant, Dix petits nègres,* and *Concerto.* Misonne also di-directed the documentaries *Ici naît la fantaisie* and *La Huitième Merveille.* Other Belgian film directors are Gene-viève Grand'Ry *(Mardi Gras),* Monique Moinet (shorts, such as *Au bord de l'étang),* nihilist Chantal Ackerman *(Saute ma ville),* Michèle Dimitri *(Tour de chance),* Nicole Gilbert (the experimental film, *Sans parole*), Greta Deses *(Dada),* Françoise Levie *(Le Voyageur),* Lisette de Broyer (films on the Andes), Edith Kiel, and Françoise de Mol.

BULGARIA

Lada Boyadgieva has been directing documentaries in Bulgaria since the 1940s. A few of her recent titles are *How Tales Come to Life* (1965), *Songs and Dances by the River Mesta* (1958), *Story Books* (1963), *Palmira* (1963), *A Trip* (1963), and *Return of the Ikons* (1965). She also directed the features *Return* (1967), *I Dissent* (1969), and *Dignity* (1971).

Radka Bachvarova directs cartoons and popular science films. Her titles: *The Mouse and the Pencil* (1958, co-directed with Zdenka Doicheva), *Long Ears* (1961), *Fable* (1964), *The Star* (1965), *What Shall I Do?* (1966), and *The Balloons* (1967). Nevena Toshevas has directed several documentaries and educational films: *Three Teachers* (1962), *A Sketch* (1963), *International Ballet Competition* (1964), *The Village of Yastrebino* (1965), *Bulgaria: Land, People, Sun* (1966), and *Am I So Bad?* (1967).

Binka Zheljazkova directed the prize-winning feature *We Were Young* (1961), and also *The Captive Balloon* (1967). Ivanka Grubcheva directed *The Mob* (1971), a story of con-flict between citizens and bandits. Irina Aktasheva co-di-rected *Monday Morning* (1965) with Hristo Piskov, and Magda Petkanova co-directed *Shibil* (1967).

CANADA

It took an act of Parliament to get film production going in this country. In 1939 Parliament established the National Film Board of Canada and until the early sixties almost all film production was conducted under its aegis. The picture has changed in recent years, however. The Canadian Broadcasting Corporation (CBC) has been extremely active, and what's more, a wave of independent young filmmakers—many of them women—has begun to rise.

The first woman to make her mark was Evelyn Lambart, who got started with the help of the National Film Board. Lambart was an assistant for a number of years to the ingenious Norman McLaren, who, among other things, devised the technique for painting on film. With McLaren (who had been brought to Canada from England by the National Film Board), Lambart made these colorfully animated shorts: *Begone Dull Care* (1949), *Rythmetic* (1956), *A Chairy Tale* (1957), *Short and Suite* (1957), *Lines—Vertical* (1961) and *Lines—Horizontal* (1965). Her own animated shorts are *Family Tree* (1950), *The Lever* (1966), *Fine Feathers* (1968), *The Hoarder* (1969), and *Paradise Lost* (1970).

Kathleen Shannon has been working for the National Film Board of Canada since 1956. Beginning as sound editor with the NFBC (she had previously edited music for a small independent company), she moved on to writing, editing, directing, and finally producing her own films. Her films include *Goldwood*, a 20-minute short on growing up in the wilds of northern Ontario; *I Don't Think It's Meant for Us*, a half-hour documentary on public housing, and, in 1973, *Films About Women and Work*, a series of thirteen shorts based on interviews with working mothers in all areas of society.

One of the most prolific and versatile of the latter-day filmmakers is Beryl Fox, whose achievements include the memorable *The Mills of the Gods,* an hour-long documentary on combat in Vietnam. *The Mills of the Gods,* which she produced and directed in 1965 (under hazardous conditions), was cited as Film of the Year by the Canadian Film Institute and it numbered among its several other awards the prestigious George Polk Memorial Award.

Beginning with *One More River,* an hour-long documentary on race relations in the U.S. southland which she co-directed for the Canadian Broadcasting Company in 1963, some of her credits are: *Balance of Terror,* about NATO (1963, 1 hour, for NET/CBC, co-director); *The Chief,* about John D. Diefenbaker (1964, 1 hour, for CBC, co-director); *The Single Woman and the Double Standard* (1965, 1 hour, for CBC, producer-director); *Summer in Mississippi,* about black voter registration in the South (1965, 30 minutes, for CBC, producer-director-writer); *Saigon* (1967, 1 hour, for CBS-TV, producer-director-writer); *Last Reflections On a War: Bernard Fall,* about the noted war correspondent who died in Vietnam (1968, 1 hour, for NET/CBC, producer-director); *Memorial to Martin Luther King* (1969, 30 minutes, for NET, producer-director). Her work since 1969, under the auspices of Hobel Leiterman Productions and others, has ranged over many subjects, including nature studies, travel, and an examination of what the seventies have in store.

Fox began her career as a script assistant in the sports department at CBC. "I was so bad at it," she recalls, "they never let me do hockey, only bowling. The only reason I advanced was because of an overriding inferiority complex which drove me to do everybody's donkey work, work nights, work for free, empty wastebaskets, run coffee, and never refuse any kind of work." About her work, finally, as a filmmaker, she says "The greatest difficulty I had as a woman filmmaker was learning to take command." On advising women just starting out as filmmakers, she says "There is one thing I believe in and that is, no matter how scared you are, *never say no.*" Her

most important films, she feels, are *The Mills of the Gods,*
Summer in Mississippi and *Memorial to Martin Luther King.*
"Because they still make me cry."

One of the best known of Canada's experimental filmmakers is Joyce Wieland, who by a variety of techniques (including piercing holes through the film stock) has achieved
effects intended to widen the film viewing experience. Her
films include these shorts: *Larry's Recent Behavior* (1963);
Peggy's Blue Skylight, Patriotism and *Water Sark* (all 1964);
Sailboat, 1933 and *Hand-Tinting* (all 1967); *Catfood* and
Rat Life and Diet in North America (both 1968), and *Dripping Water* (1969). Her major film, made in 1969, is *La
Raison avant la passion* (*Reason Over Passion*), an 80-minute
"whirlwind view of Canada."

Anne-Claire Poirier had planned to go into law, but
switched to writing and interviewing for radio and in 1960
began working in various associate capacities for the National Film Board. Within two years she was directing shorts
for the NFB: *30 Minutes, Mister Plummer* (1962), *La Fin
des étés* (1964), *Les Ludions* (1965), *Impôt et tout . . . et tout*
(1968, five 5-minute films for the Department of National
Revenue), *Le Savoir-faire s'impose* (1971, six 5-minute films
for the same government agency). Her only feature, *De
Mère en fille* (*Mother To Be,* 1968), is based on diaries kept
during her own pregnancy.

A Quebecoise like Poirier, Mireille Dansereau won first
prize at the 1969 National Student Film Festival in London
for a 28-minute movie titled *Compromise.* Her feature-length
film, *Forum* (1969), was originally shot on video, as were *La
Vie Rêvée* (*Dream Life,* 1972) and a series about women
(made in collaboration with Poirier for the NFB).

Other Canadian women directing films are Tanya Ballantyne (MacKay), who did *The Merry-Go-Round,* a short,
and *The Things I Cannot Change* (both 1966); Joan Fiore,
Home Movies (1969); Sylvia Spring, *Madeleine Is . . .*

(1970); Judy Steed, *Clowns and Monsters* (a short) and *It's Gonna Be All Right* (both 1971); and Aimée Danis, *La Croix du Mont-Royal*, *L'Evade*, and *L'Adieu au lys* (all 1971). Danis has also directed a number of shorts.

Still other women directing films in Canada (sometimes exclusively for television) are Susanne Angel, Nancy Archibald, Bianca Barnes, Sara Bezaire (with Burton Rubenstein), Ruth Boughner, Angela Bruce, Myra Changar, Louise Chenier, Barbara Davis, Francine Desbiens, Mary Di Tursi, Alma Duncan (usually in collaboration with Audrey McLaren), Marion Dunn, J. Eglington, Rita Elmer, Viviane Elnecave, Michèle Favreau, Margaret Fielder, Monique Fortier, Elsa Franklin, Suzanne Gervais-L'Heureux, Charlotte Gobeil, Joan Henson, and Mai Hoskin.

Also Elena Jashenko, Isobel Kehoe, Bonny Klein, Judith Klein, Nicole Lavallée, Rhoda Leyer, Peggy Liprott, Jeannine Locke, Sally MacDonald, Shelagh Mackenzie, Monique Pardis (with Lucie Menard), Susan Murgatroyd, Julia Murphy, Carol Myers, Lise Noiseux-Labrèque, Maxine Nunes, Suzanne Olivier, Maryka Omatsu, Yvette Pard, Margaret Perry, Raymonde Pilon (in collaboration with Guy Beaugrande-Champagne), Jean Richards, Nancy Riley, Dodi Robb, Maxine Samuels, Cynthia Scott, Joyce Teff, Doris Toukermine, Roxy Travers, Mary Van Stolk, Patricia Watson, Deanna White, Gloria White, and Donna-Lou Wigmore.

Arla Saare, who came to Canada from Finland in 1924 at the age of nine, is well known as an editor. Since 1963 she has freelanced out of Toronto.

CHINA

Few women have become film directors or cinematographers in China despite the fact that all legal and economic barriers against women were lifted when the People's Republic was founded in 1949. There are many women in lower-echelon jobs—scenarists, artists, photographers, and designers—but by tradition the top creative positions are still monopolized by men.

Among the few women directors are Wang Ping and Shih Mei. Primarily a documentary editor, Shih Mei directed the 1952 film *Harness the Huai River*, and collaborated on others, including *Decisive Struggle Between Two Destinies* (1961). Wang Ping, an actress as well as a director, has had a very productive career, turning out a film every year since 1955. Among the more important are *Story of Liupao Village* (1957), *Constant Beam* (1958), *Battle of Shanghai* (1959), *Meng Lung Sha* (1961), *Locust Tree Village* (1962), and *Sentinels Under the Neon Lights* (1963, with Ko Hsin). Hsia Kuei-ying, a lesser-known director, learned her art in the United States and helped organize China's Documentary Film Studio in the early 1950s.

Chiang Ching, Mao's wife, was once a film actress (under the name Lan P'ing), and has a prominent role in determining the kinds of films to be made in China. In 1950 she was appointed to the Central Steering Committee for the film industry under the Ministry of Culture, and was responsible for closing most of China's film studios in 1966 during the Cultural Revolution.

Hong Kong

Hong Kong has one prominent woman director, Shu Shuen, who made the feature film *The Arch*. Set in a small town in China in the fourteenth century, the story is about Mme. Tung, the widow of a war hero in whose memory the town is building a memorial arch. She falls in love with a handsome captain, but chooses to remain faithful to her illustrious husband's memory. The film is outstanding for its subtle but precise character development and its delicately woven imagery.

CZECHOSLOVAKIA

Women have been involved in filmmaking for many decades in Czechoslovakia. Hedvika Raabeova directed a short, *Ada,* in 1919, and also *Prague in 1549.* Thea Cervenkova directed *Babicka* (1920), *Bludicka* (1921), *The Thief* (1921), and *It Was the First of May* (1922), all adaptations of well-known Czech novels and plays. In 1927 Zet Molas was working as producer, director, writer and actress in the Czech avant-garde. Her films included the experimental *Zavet Podivinova* (1923), *Old House* (1927), *The Miller and His Son* (c. 1930), and *Karel Hynek Macha* (1937), her last film.

Lenka Weissova directed *A Study for Two Hands,* about a young beautician who devotes her spare time to the piano and becomes a virtuoso. Ludmilla Chichkova depicted the hard work involved in ballet in her film *Vera Kirova.* With Karel Zeman, Hermina Tyrlova was one of the pioneers of Czech animation. She began her film career in the 1920s with trick films and animated commercials. After World War II she concentrated on puppet films for children. Her films include *Ferda the Ant* (1944), *Revolt of the Toys* (1947), *Lullaby* (1948), *The Taming of the Dragon* (1953), *Goldilocks* (1956), *The Inquisitive Letter* (1961), *The Woolly Tale* (1964), *The Snowman* (1966), and *The Glass Whistle* (1970). In her more recent films she has used child actors along with the puppets.

Bozena Mozisova invented the character Dorotka for *Dorothy and the Dragon* and *Dorothy and the Ostrich.*

Vera Chytilova, a leading director in the New Wave in Czechoslovakia, studied directing at the Prague Film School (FAMU). There she directed several shorts: *Villa in the Suburbs* (1959), *Mr. K – Green Street* (1960), *Academy Newsreel* (1961), and *The Ceiling* (1961). Her documentary *A Bagful of Fleas* (1962), about young women apprentices in a textile factory, received a bronze medal at Venice. Her next production, *O Necem Jinem (Something Different,*

1963), was a dramatic film in documentary style. The film compares the lives of a gymnast (played by Olympic gold medalist Eva Bosakova) and a housewife (played by Vera Vzelacova). Each conforms to what is expected of her. The gymnast wins a gold medal and the housewife yields to an unhappy marriage. In 1965 Chytilova contributed one episode to the film *Pearls of the Deep* (each of the five episodes was directed by a different New Wave director). In 1966 she directed her second feature, *Sedmikrasky (Daisies)*. This is a satire in which two women decide the world is ugly and evil, and rather than fight it, they join it. A later film was the allegory, *Fruit of Paradise* (1969, also known as *We May Eat of the Fruit of the Trees of the Garden*). Chytilova's husband, Jaroslav Kucera, does the camera work for most of her films, and Ester Krumbachova is co-author of the scripts.

Krumbachova is also a director in her own right. Her films include *The Murder of the Engineer Cert, Valerie,* and *A Week of Wonders* (1971).

DENMARK

In Denmark, comedienne Alice O'Fredericks directed her own films and collaborated on others with Lau Lauritzen, Jr. Their *Vi vil ha et barn (We Want a Baby,* 1949) expressed dismay in a humorous fashion at the falling birthrate. *Calvary of a Child* (1950), which O'Fredericks directed, dealt with Viennese orphans under the care of the Danish Red Cross.

Astrid Henning-Jensen shared credit with her husband, Bjarne, on many documentaries, notably *Dansk Politi Sverige (The Danish Brigade in Sweden,* 1945), about the training of 200 Danish officers who fled the German occupation;

Stemming i April (Impressions of April, 1947), and *Hvor bjergene seljer (In the Country of Icebergs,* 1956). Their feature work includes *Ditte Menneskebarn (Ditte, Child of Man,* 1946). Adapted from Martin Anderson-Nexö's masterpiece about an illegitimate child who becomes an unmarried mother, the film tries to expose the pettiness of false moralists. The Henning-Jensens also directed *Ukjent Mann (The Stranger,* 1952), and *Paw* (1960). Probably every major film library stocks their classic featurette, *Palle, Alone in the World* (1949). Palle dreams he has a streetcar at his disposal in the sleeping city. The Henning-Jensens used Annelise Reenberg as cinematographer on several of their films.

Annelise Hovmand and her husband, Johan Jacobsen, have a studio near Copenhagen, where both direct films. Her *Ingen tid til Koertern (No Time for Tenderness,* 1957) tells of the lurid sexual adventures of the daughter of an actress. But there was no sensationalism in her *Krudt og Klunker (Powder and Shot,* 1959) or *Fridehens pris (The Price of Liberty,* 1960), about the anti-Hitler resistance. *Gøngehøvdingen (Goinge, the Akvavit Champion,* 1961) dealt with the war in 1657 between Denmark and Sweden. In *Sekstet (Sextet,* 1964) Hovmand turned to a daring treatment of homosexuality.

Other Danish filmmakers include Marguerite Viby (*Bolettes Brudfaerd* and *Sorensen and Rasmussen,* co-credited with Emmanuel Gregers); Annelise Meineche *(Soya's Seventeen,* 1965); Else Gress Wright *(Boxiganga,* 1968); Lisbeth Movin, who works with her husband, Lau Lauritzen, Jr., and Annelise Reenberg, who did the camerawork for the Henning-Jensens and directed *Hurray for the Blue Hussars,* (1970). Trine Hedmann does films for children. Mette Knudsen co-scripted and starred in the feature film *Dear Drene,* directed by Christian Braad-Thomsen. Other Danish women filmmakers include Lisa Roos; Astrid Pade; Charlotte Strandgaard (*The Case of Lone,* 1970); and Kirsten Stenbaek (*Miss Julie, The Mad Dane, Lenin, You Rascal,* and *The Dreamers*).

EAST GERMANY

East Germans Annelie and Andrew Thorndike made films after the war which exposed corruption in the West German government and the presence of war criminals in influential positions. *Du und Mancher Kamerad (You and Other Comrades/The German Story*, 1956) is about fifty years of German history, seen as the struggle of the Communists against the Kaiser, the Junkers, the industrialists, and finally, Hitler. The Thorndikes' many films include *Weg nach Oben (The Way Up*, 1950), *Freundschaft Siegt (Friendship Wins*, 1952), *Sieben vom Rhein (Seven From the Rhine*, 1954), *Urlaub auf Sylt (Holiday on Sylt*, 1957), *Unternehmen Teutonenschwert (Operation Teutonic Sword*, 1958), *Das Russische Wunder (The Russian Wonder*, 1963, in two parts), *Tito in Deutschland* (1965), and *Du Bist Mein, Ein Deutches Tagebuch (You are Mine, A German Diary*, 1969).

Also in East Germany, Katja Georgi has directed animated films such as *The Princess and the Pea* (1959) and *The Thorn* (1967). Winifred Junge specializes in educational documentaries. They include *Until Man Came* (1960), *The Ape Terror* (1961), *Girl Students: Impressions of a Technical College* (1965), *The Brave Truants* (1967), and *With Both Legs in the Sky* (1968).

One of the most active documentary filmmakers in East Germany today is Gitta Nickel, whose film on Vietnam—*Tay Ho, The Village in the Fourth Zone*—won a first prize at the 1973 Leipzig International Film Festival. To find out how women filmmakers fare in the DDR, Prof. Norman R. Seidei, a filmmaker and Director of Cinema Studies at the C. W. Post Center of Long Island University, interviewed Nickel in Leipzig. Part of the interview follows.

How did you get into film?

GITTA NICKEL: I studied at Humbolt University in Berlin to be a teacher of German and German literature, but then

I went to the Studio for Popular Science Films to become an apprentice. I didn't really fit in there so I changed to the Studio for Feature Films. I became an assistant director and worked with Konrad Wolfe, who is one of the very best directors in our country. I also worked with several other directors, including Ralph Kirsten. It was a period of great learning. Then I met Karl Gass, who is one of the best known documentary filmmakers in the DDR. I worked with him for several years, keeping one foot in documentary films and the other in feature films. I finally found that I was really drawn to documentary films because they are so direct, so much closer to the thing I really want to do.

When did you begin making your own films?

GN: I directed my own first film in 1965. My earliest films dealt with German-Soviet relations. To be specific, the first film was about a kindergarten in a section of Berlin where most of the Soviet soldiers were stationed. The situation in this school was sort of experimental in the sense that both German and Soviet children were together. It was very interesting. The next film was about a group of Soviet singers and dancers—all soldiers who were stationed here—and about their travels around the DDR and their relationships with German people.

In 1970 you made a film called She. *Tell me about it.*

GN: *She* deals with the practical problems of women trying to achieve equal rights and emancipation. We present a garment factory in Berlin where women work at sewing on an assembly line. We meet and get to know four different women from different groups and backgrounds. One woman works on the line, another is a trade union functionary. The third woman is a production director and the fourth is a gynecologist and an intellectual. We found, with regard to the question of equal rights, that we've trained huge numbers of women who have received their college diplomas but usually end up as deputies. It is almost always the men who are the bosses. Since this film deals exactly with this problem, it is both a critical and important film.

You are saying that there are problems of equal rights for women in the DDR?

GN: Of course there are problems. We have all of the laws which guarantee equal rights here. They are on the books, but how the women themselves achieve these rights, how they put them into practice, remains to be seen. There are all kinds of problems. For example, not every woman who works is able to bring her child to a kindergarten or nursery. A great many do, but there is never enough room for all of them. This remains, for the present, an unsolved problem. There are many nursery schools and kindergartens, but never enough to fill the demand. You must realize that eighty-five percent of our women work. Of course we have equal rights here, but not every man has understood this.

Are there many women working in film?

GN: No, there are relatively few. Fewer than in New York.

How many women film directors are there in the DDR?

GN: There are only two that I know of.

How many camerawomen are there?

GN: There are none in film, but there are a number in television. Television is very different. There is a greater percentage of women working in that industry as directors and camerawomen. I do not know why that is so. Perhaps it is because television needs more people. There are more television programs than films, so it is easier to break into television.

How many women work on your production crew?

GN: Two—a production director and an assistant director. However, when we go abroad, the crew is male.

Why?

GN: We can't find a sound woman or an assistant camerawoman. Besides, I have a regular team that I work with all the time. My cameraman is very important to me. He sees as I do. His eye is my eye. If I found a good woman, I would take her.

Do you personally edit your films or do you use an editor whom you supervise?

GN: I edit myself. It is most important for me to do so and I would not let anyone else do it. I must do it alone. I must have the film in my own hands. I like to experiment and try one thing or another. With someone else, there is always the possibility of back and forth discussion, little disagreements, possible resistance to ideas. I don't want to worry about what the other person is thinking. I want to do it all myself. In this regard, I direct, I edit, and I write as well. However, sometimes another person writes the scenario with me. I have never done a film written by someone else. I couldn't do that. I will also work without a script. I will work from a general conception as I did in my recent film, *Tay Ho*, which we made on location in Vietnam. I knew exactly what I wanted and actually the story tells itself. Often, I will write a scenario because it must be submitted in order to get the commission and the money for production. But I don't stick to the exact script. For a documentary filmmaker that would be impossible, so many things happen when you are shooting.

Do you personally select the subjects of your films?

GN: Usually, yes. Occasionally, I get a commission to do a film for television. There have been three such films, each a portrait of a famous person. One of them was Walter Felsenstein, the head of the Comic Opera in Berlin. I also did a portrait of Palucca, a famous teacher of modern dance, and of Paul Dessau, who is one of our most famous composers. I think well of these films, but I don't want to do too many since they tend to become routine.

How did you get started on your Vietnam film?

GN: It was my idea to do this film. I wanted to be in

Vietnam when the war ended. The peace came earlier than expected and I got there a little late because my proposal got snagged in a bit of red tape.

To whom do you make proposals for films?

GN: To the Dramaturgical Committee of the Studio For Documentary Film. This group works out a yearly plan of work for the studio.

How are you paid? Do you receive a fixed salary?

GN: I get a fixed sum each month as a director and I receive a special fee for scripts I write myself. For several years the studio has also worked out "predicates" which are listed as good, valuable, and especially valuable. If a film is awarded one of these "predicates," the filmmaker receives a bonus.

Would you say this is an incentive program?

GN: Yes, it does create incentive. It is a pity that we don't have this in all areas. Many people do a great deal of work on their own and are not rewarded. Of course, people don't always need material incentives, but you can't expect them to labor all the time on purely a moral basis.

Gitta, do you feel creatively fulfilled at the Studio For Documentary Film?

GN: Absolutely one hundred percent!

ENGLAND

The first woman to direct films in England probably was Dinah Shurey, but little is known of her work besides two titles: *Carry On* (1927) and *Last Port* (1929). Alma Reville wrote scripts for her husband, Alfred Hitchcock, and assisted him on many of his British films. These include *The Ring* (1927), *Rich and Strange* (1932), *The 39 Steps*

(1935), *Secret Agent* (1936), *Sabotage* (1937), *Young and Innocent* (1937), and *The Lady Vanishes* (1938). Later in the United States she wrote, sometimes in collaboration with other writers, Hitchcock's *Suspicion* (1941), *Shadow of a Doubt* (1943), *The Paradine Case* (1947), and *Stage Fright* (1951).

Mary Field, a specialist in children's films, joined British Instructional Films in 1926, then in 1934 transferred to Gaumont-British Instructional Films. Her major work consists of the two series, *Secrets of Nature* (begun in 1928) and *Secrets of Life* (begun in 1934). Her documentaries include *The King's English* (1932), *The Changing Year* (1932), *They Made the Land* (1938), and *The Medieval Village* (1940). From 1944 to 1950 she was executive producer of children's entertainment for J. Arthur Rank, and from 1951 to 1959 executive officer of the Children's Film Foundation. From 1959 to 1963 she was children's program consultant for British television and wrote several books in the field.

Elinor Glyn, a best-selling author of the 1920s and the writer of original screenplays for a dozen or more films in America and England, produced and directed *Knowing Men* (1929). To preserve her creative independence she financed the film herself. One example of the kind of prejudice faced by women directors is shown in a contemporary review that appeared in the London Daily Mail: "Many a hardened filmgoer might well be sickened by the underlying implications of sly cynicism and the general tone of the talking film, *Knowing Men.* One is forced to regret that it is an English film. Mrs. Glyn's picture depicts man as possessing one characteristic alone, which compels him to ogle, then maul, every woman he meets." Another film directed by Glyn, also released in 1929, was *The Price of Things.*

Joy Batchelor entered film in 1935, and five years later formed a team with her husband, John Halas (Halas-Batchelor Productions). She worked as producer, scenarist, and technician on their animated films. They co-produced, co-directed, and co-authored the first British feature-length cartoon, *Animal Farm* (1954), adapted from the George Orwell novel.

Their other productions include *The Pocket Cartoon* (1941), *Dustbin Parade* (1942), the *Abu* series (1943, four films), *Old Wives' Tales* (1946), the *Charley* series (1947, seven films), *First Line of Defense* (1949), *As Old as the Hills* (1950), *Magic Canvas* (1951), *The Figurehead* (1952, with puppets), *The Owl and the Pussycat* (1953, not to be confused with the later Broadway play and film of the same title), *Power to Fly* (1954), *Speed the Plough* (1955), *The History of the Cinema* (1956), *All Lit Up* (1957), *The Christmas Visitor* (1958), *The Cultured Ape* (1959), the "Foo Foo" television series (1960, 39 programs), *The Columbo Plan* (1961), *Hamilton, the Musical Elephant* (1962), *Automania 2000* (1963), the "Hoffnung" television series (1965, four programs), *Ruddigore* (1967), and *Children and Cars* (1970). They currently make only educational films, primarily cassettes. Theirs is the first English film company to use computer animation for math and science films.

Muriel Box began her career as a script girl for Anthony Asquith. By 1946 she and her husband, Sydney, had founded London Independent Producers, and she had written the original story for *The Seventh Veil* (which she produced with Sydney), as well as directed her first film, *The Happy Family*. She then produced *Smugglers* and *Dear Murderer* (both 1948), and *Girl in a Million* (1950).

In 1952 she directed *Mr. Lord Says No!*, about a London shopkeeper who refuses to vacate his premises in time for the Festival of Britain. Then followed *Both Sides of the Law* (1954), the adventures of a woman on the police force, and *The Beachcomber* (1954), adapted by Sydney Box from Maugham's *Vessel of Wrath*, about a missionary woman and a wayward male beachcomber in the tropics. *Simon and Laura* (1955) concerns a married television actor and actress who are chosen to play a loving couple while they are on the verge of separation. In *Cash on Delivery* (1956) a divorced and re-married couple vie to fulfill the requirements of a $2-million inheritance. In *A Novel Affair* (1957) a writer's manuscript is discovered by her chauffeur, who imagines it is a secret plea for his love and sets out to make the fantasy come true. *The Truth About Women* (1958) depicts a male diplomat's ad-ventures with women. After fifty years he concludes, "It's tough with them, but tougher without them." *Rattle of a Simple Man* (1964) chronicles the relationship between a childish bachelor and a prostitute.

Box has also written the screenplays for at least twenty films, as well as a novel, "The Big Switch," a futuristic account of a world dominated by women. A contemporary review in *Variety* reflects the usual complacency that even in a world dominated by women the sexual status quo would continue. "Mrs. Box makes some shrewd observations about the re-spective worlds of men and women [but] it's reassuring to know that she does not visualize any new substitute for love and propagation."

Jill Craigie wrote and directed various documentaries: *Out of Chaos* (1944) for the Boxes, *The Way We Live* (1946-1947) for Two Cities, *Blue Scar* (1950), and *To Be a Woman* (1951). In the late 1930s and early forties Yvonne Fletcher directed documentaries for Paul Rotha Productions. Budge Cooper, who had entered film in 1934 as a shorthand typist and then did continuity for British International Pictures, began work for Rotha in 1942, di-recting *Rat Destruction, China, C of C,* and *Birthday*. In 1944 she joined Data Films as director. In that year she directed *Children of the City,* a documentary on juvenile delinquency. Mary Marsh wrote and directed educational films for G. B. Instructional Films beginning in 1946. In 1949 Marjorie Deans formed her own company, Touchstone Films, directing *The Girl is Mine*.

In the 1950s, Margaret Thompson directed *Child's Play* (1952) and Wendy Toye directed *In the Picture* (1955)—part of the *Three Cases of Murder* series—as well as *The Mechman Mystery* (1955) and *Raising a Riot* (1957). Michaela Denis, actress, explorer, and writer, made films in over forty countries. *Among the Headhunters* (1958) is a record of her trip through New Guinea with her husband, Armand Denis.

In 1963 Joan Littlewood, a well-known director of plays, directed the all-Cockney film *Sparrows Can't Sing*.

Several women have produced theatrical films in England. Among them is Betty Box, sister of Sydney, who produced several dozen films for the Box company, including *The Blind Goddess* (1949).

Joan Harrison, longtime assistant to Alfred Hitchcock, is a noted British screenwriter who has been working in the United States for many years. She wrote *Jamaica Inn* (1939), *Rebecca* (1940), *Foreign Correspondent* (1940), *Suspicion* (1941), *Saboteur* (1942), *Dark Waters* (1945), and many others. She has produced several features, including *Phantom Lady* (1944) and *Ride the Pink Horse* (1948). Beginning in 1958 she produced the "Alfred Hitchcock Presents" series.

Joy Harrington produced several films including *Our Hearts Were Young and Gay* and *National Velvet* (both 1944). Jean Carmen Dillow, president of Carmen Productions, has produced films for John Croydon and Frank Solento. Penelope Gilliatt wrote the widely-acclaimed *Sunday, Bloody Sunday* (1971).

The late Canadian-American actress, Helen Winston, produced *Hand in Hand* in London in the 1960s. Diana Morgan's moving script is about a friendship between two children, a Jewish girl and a Catholic boy.

Among prominent film editors is Thelma Connell, who worked on *Alfie*, one of the top hits of 1966. Other films she edited include *Stranger on the Prowl* (1952) and *The Hill* (1965).

FINLAND

Occasionally in Finland's dim past, some actress married to a producer might have gotten a chance to direct a film, but women didn't really break into the industry until 1966 when the government set up a grant system for young film-makers. Many women benefitted from this program including Eila Kaarresalo-Kasari, who used her grant to produce and direct *Ampumarata* (*Finnish Frustrations*, 1970, 7 minutes)—a film that won a special prize at the Jury Tampere International Film Festival and the Jussi Award of the Finnish Film Critics in 1970. One American critic said, "In seven minutes Ms. Kaarresalo-Kasari isolates an aspect of sexual inequality with a narrative starkness that recalls the paintings of George Grosz." She was also director-producer of *Kotimaani ompi Suomi* (*Finland, My Sweet Home,* 15 minutes) and *Salliiko Aiti* (*Would Momma Allow?,* 2 minutes), and production coordinator for two feature films, *The Kremlin Letter* and *Vodka, Please, Mr. Palmu*. Kaarresalo-Kasari is now working in the United States.

Other women active in Finnish filmmaking are Ritva Arvele, who directed *The Golden Calf* (1961); Eija-Elina Bergholm, director and scriptwriter of *Poor Maria* (1972); and Elina Katainen, animator of *Jalmari and Hulda* (1972).

FRANCE

Germaine Dulac

Alice Guy Blaché's successor in French filmmaking was Germaine Dulac, well known in the early 1900s as a feminist and socialist. After an active involvement in theater, music and journalism (she was a writer for the feminist publication La Française), she founded a film production company, Delia Film, with her husband, Albert Dulac, and writer Irene

Hillel-Erlanger. Her first film was *Sœurs ennemies* (*Enemy Sisters*, 1915).

Other early films included *La Vraie Richesse ou Georges le mystérieux* (*True Wealth or Mysterious George*, 1916) and *Vénus Victrix* (*Venus Victorious*, 1917). The films were artistic yet remained commercial enough to warrant distribution by Pathé. During the shooting of *Ames de fous* (*Souls of the Mad*, 1918), she met Louis Delluc and began a long collaboration with him. One of her better known films of this period was *La Souriante Madame Beudet* (*The Smiling Madame Beudet*, 1923). It was one of the few films of that era in which a woman was the main character. It portrays a repressed and unfulfilled Madame Beudet, who silently dreams of revenge against her domineering husband.

Dulac subsequently directed *Le Diable dans la ville* (*The Devil in the City*, 1924), a tale of fanaticism in the Middle Ages. She harmonized music with images in *La Folie des vaillants* (*The Madness of the Valiant*, 1925). This was followed by the surreal *La Coquille et le clergyman* (*The Seashell and the Clergyman*, 1927), with a scenario by Antonin Artaud. In this film, which exposes male sexual fantasies, a frustrated man of the cloth pursues a white-robed woman in weirdly shifting surroundings suggestive of Freudian symbolism. The film created a great deal of controversy, and Artaud denounced Dulac for having "feminized" his script. Immersed in the relationship of film images and music, Dulac directed *Disque 927* (1928), inspired by the music of Chopin, and *Thème et variations* (1928), inspired by classical melodies. She was attempting to achieve what she called "cinéma pur," similar to the "pure poetry" of the period. *La Princesse Mandane* (1929) was her last major work. By then, enthusiasm for sound had temporarily deflected public interest away from subtle visual imagery.

The intent of Dulac's work was to explore the uniqueness of film and articulate the difference between it and the other arts. Like Alice Guy Blaché, she felt films could do more than tell stories. Her theories and experiments formed the basis of the avant garde. She was one of several filmmakers reviving the art after World War I. With her friends, Louis Delluc, Abel Gance, Marcel L'Herbier, Jean Epstein and his sister Marie, she formed a group of radical filmmakers who called themselves Impressionists.

Other films directed by Dulac include *La Fête espagnole* (1919), *La Cigarette* (1919), *Malencontre* (1920), *Gosette* (1920, six episodes), *Antoinette Sabrier* (1927), and Baudelaire's *L'Invitation au voyage*. From 1930 to 1940 Dulac returned once more to commercial work, as head of newsreel operations, first for Pathé, then for Gaumont. Her career came to an end early in World War II, and in 1942 she died.

In 1918 Suzanne Devoyod directed her only film, *L'Ami Fritz*, with René Hervil. In 1921 Gabrielle Sorère and American-born dancer Loie Fuller collaborated on the fairy tale, *Le Lys de la vie (The Lily of Life)*, which is one of the first recorded uses of a negative print, employed here to set the real apart from the imaginary. In 1922 actress Renée Carl directed her only film, *Un Cri dans l'abîme (A Shout from the Abyss)*, which evoked some of the less pleasant aspects of country life. Rose Pansini and Georges Monca directed *Le Sang des Finoëls (The Blood of the Finoëls)*.

The well-known actress Musidora (Jeanne Roques), to whom the poet Louis Aragon in 1919 gave the title "The Tenth Muse," directed and starred in *Vicenta* (1918), her original script. Between 1920 and 1923 she collaborated with Jacques Lasseyre to direct *La Flamme cachée (The Hidden Flame)*, *Pour Don Carlos*, and *Soleil et ombre (Sun and Shadow)*. In 1924 she traveled to Spain to shoot *La Terre des taureaux (Land of the Bulls)*. During the filming she tested her courage in the bullring to demonstrate that women were brave enough to "deserve" the vote. Her last film was *La Magique Image (Magic Image*, 1951). She died in 1957.

In 1927 Jane Bruno-Ruby, a novelist, filmed *La Cabane*

d'amour (Cabin of Love) and Lucy Derain directed *Harmonies de Paris* and the short film *Désordre*. Actress Marie-Louise Iribe founded a production company in 1927 and directed *Hara-Kiri* (1928), the story of a woman's suicide, and *Roi des aulnes*. When sound came, Elyana Tayer, a silent-film actress, turned to directing documentaries (among them, *Versailles*). Marguerite Viel co-directed *Jungle d'une grande ville (Big City Jungle,* 1929) with Léo Marten, a film about a young woman abandoned by her family. She later directed *La Banque Némo* and, with René Weissbach, an adaptation of Feydeau's *Occupe-toi d'Amélie! (Take Care of Amelia!)*. In 1930 Claude Revol co-directed *Retour de bonheur (Return of Happiness)* with René Jayet, later working with the Egyptian singer Réda Caire on *L'Enfant de minuit (The Midnight Child)*.

Marie Colson-Malleville was a friend and collaborator of Germaine Dulac until the latter's death. On her own, she directed these documentaries: *Escale à Oran (Port-of-Call at Oran), El Oued, la ville aux mille coupoles (El Oued, City of a Thousand Domes),* and *Baba Ali,* all in Algeria. She also made *Du Manual au robot (From Manual Labor to the Machine),* about the industrialization of Algeria; *Solidarité; Les Doigts de lumière (Fingers of Light); La Route éternelle (The Eternal Road); Des Rails sous les palmiers (Rails Beneath the Palm Trees); Les Tapisseries de l'Apocalypse (Tapestries of the Apocalypse); Pierre de Lune (Moonstone); Delacroix, peintre de l'Islam (Delacroix, Painter of Islam); Croyances (Beliefs);* and *Simple Histoire d'amour (A Simple Love Story)*.

Titayna, a journalist, filmed *Indiens, mes frères (Indians, My Brothers)* in Mexico, then *Tu m'enverras des cartes postales (Be Sure and Send Me Postcards),* about a Marseilles-to-Saigon steamer cruise, and a documentary, *Promenade en Chine (Walking Through China)*. These films were made in the 1930s.

Marie Epstein collaborated on scripts with her brother,

Jean, and Jean Benoît-Lévy, and co-directed several films with the latter, including the classic *La Maternelle* (1933) and the shorts *Hélène* and *Altitude 3200* (both 1934-1937). In 1953 she co-directed with Léonide Azar *La Grande Espérance (The Great Hope)*, a documentary on atomic energy.

Solange Bussi (Solange Térac) was encouraged to direct by her friends G. W. Pabst, Béla Balázs, and Bertolt Brecht. She adapted Colette's *La Vagabonde* (1931) and *Mon Amant l'assassin (My Lover, the Murderer*, 1932), then returned to writing. In 1952 she directed an adaptation of *Koenigsmark.*

American-born Claire Parker co-directed the animated film, *Une Nuit sur le Mont Chauve (A Night on Bald Mountain*, 1933), with her husband Alexandre Alexéïeff, using the "screen of pins" technique he invented. They moved to Canada and made shorts and commercials for the National Film Board and later returned to France to devote themselves to commercials. Marion Vandal directed the comedy *Monsieur le vagabond* (1933).

Lucette Gaudard directed her first film, *Paris-Berlin*, in 1935. She had worked for 18 years as a secretary for a production company, then became a script girl, later an assistant, and finally a director. She specialized in documentaries such as *L'Industrie du verre (The Glass Industry)* and *Les Hôtes de nos terres (Guests on Our Land)*, a report on wild animals in France. She joined Claudine Lenoir (Charlette Terrus) to direct *Souvenirs de Paris (Memories of Paris)* and *C'est un vrai paradis (It's a Real Paradise)*. Lenoir headed firms that produced short films, several of which she directed herself, including *La Belle au bois dormant (Sleeping Beauty)*, *La Prisonnière (The Captive)*, and *Le Rendez-vous sauvage (The Wild Rendezvous)*. In 1956 she directed a feature, *L'Aventurière des Champs-Élysées (The Adventuress of the Champs-Élysées)*.

Among husband-wife teams in France were Monique Muntcho and J. J. Raymond-Millet. On her own, Muntcho directed several films made in Madagascar: *Réalités mal-*

gaches, Tamatave la marine, and *Il etait une montagne.*
Madelaine and Jacques Guillon worked on *Monsieur Rameau*
and *Images sur les musiques françaises.* She directed and he
did the camera work. She also directed the series *Souvenirs
de cinématographie.* Yvonne and Roger Leenhardt also
worked as a team. On her own, Yvonne directed *Jacques
Copeau,* about the pioneer French theatrical producer in
the early 1900s. Irene and Ladislas Starevich were a daughter-
father team who worked on the puppet films for which the
father became famous. These included *Zanzabelle à Paris,
Fleur de fougère (Fern Flower), Gazouly, petite oiseau (Little
Bird, Gazouly),* and *Nez au vent (Nose to the Wind).* Most
critics felt that his preoccupation with technique prevented
his films from achieving their full potential. Ladislas died
in 1965, and Irene went blind and had to abandon film work.

Nicole Vedrès came to filmmaking quite by chance. In
1946 she realized that segments of the film she had been
given for her picture book, *Images du cinema français
(Scenes from the French Cinema),* could be made into an interesting film. With the well-known editor, Myriam, and her
young, then-unknown assistant, Alain Resnais, she created
her first compilation film, *Paris 1900* (1947), a panorama of
life at the turn of the century. The success of this film enabled her to direct *La Vie commence demain (Life Begins
Tomorrow,* 1950), a series of interviews with leading French
personalities, including Jean-Paul Sartre, Jean Rostand, and
Pablo Picasso. Although this type of feature was to become a
familiar genre a decade later, on both the screen and TV,
Vedrès' early film was a commercial failure and a major set-
back. She was able to make only two more short films:
Amazon, a segment of *L'Encyclopédie filmée (Filmed Encyclopedia,* 1951), and *Aux Frontières de l'homme (The
Limits of Man,* 1953), with biologist Jean Rostand.

The most important editor of the 1930s was Marguerite
Renoir, who worked on thirteen films over the course of the
decade, including many major ones. Among her films are:

Madame Bovary (1934); *Le Crime de Monsieur Lange* (1936); *Les Bas Fonds (The Lower Depths*, 1936); *La Grande Illusion* (1937); and *La Regle du jeu (The Rules of the Game*, 1939).

Yannick Bellon, after an editing apprenticeship with Myriam on several animated films and documentaries, worked with Nicole Vedrès on *Paris 1900*, as well as with Denise Tual. But she was determined to become a director herself. Her short, *Goemons* (1948), a realistic film about seaweed-gatherers on three small islands, won the Grand Prix International du Documentaire at the Venice Biennale of 1948. However, as no opportunity arose to make longer films, she returned to editing and directed only the short subjects, *Varsovie quand même (Still Warsaw*, 1954) and *Les Hommes oubliés (Forgotten Men*, 1957).

Jacqueline Audry first entered a studio in 1933 at the age of 25, intending to become an actress. But when the time came for her to join the rows of silk-stockinged legs for an advertising film, she realized that she would much prefer to be in charge, to be the director. She became an assistant to Pabst, Delannoy, and Ophuls, among others, then director of a Resistance documentary in 1943, *Les Chevaux du Vercors (The Horses of the Vercors)*. This was followed by two features, *Les Malheurs de Sophie* (1945) and *Gigi* (1949). Her lasting affinity for stories by Colette began with the latter film. *Gigi* is about a young woman, groomed by her mother and grandmother to become a courtesan, who rebels and insists upon marriage.

Audry's next film, Colette's *L'Ingénue libertine* (1950, also known as *Minne*), traces the amorous affairs of a young Parisian wife in the Gay Nineties. Despite her eventual discovery that her husband is the best lover of them all, the earlier scenes of sexual exploration were heavily cut by the censors. *Olivia* (1951), retitled in English *The Pit of Loneliness*, develops innuendos of Lesbian love as young women in a fashionable French boarding school compete for the affection of the headmistress. *La Garçonne (The Bachelor Girl,* 1957) is an adaptation of a controversial story of the 1920s about a young woman who wishes to live as a man. In *Mitsou* (1958)—Colette again—a cabaret girl persuades her sugar daddy to teach her the manners necessary to capture the heart of a young lieutenant. Audry's other films include *Un sombre dimanche (Gloomy Sunday,* 1948); *Huis Clos* (Sartre's *No Exit,* 1954); *L'École des cocottes (School for Strumpets,* 1957); *C'est la faute d'Adam (It's All Adam's Fault,* 1958); *Le Secret du Chevalier d'Éon (The Secret of the Chevalier d'Éon,* 1960), about a famous transvestite; *Cadavres en vacances (Corpses on Holiday,* 1961); *Les petits matins (Early Mornings,* 1961); *Soledad* (1966); *Fruits amers (Bitter Fruits,* 1967); and *Le Lis de mer (The Sea Lily,* 1970).

Two other French directors to be noted in passing are Denise Charvein, who worked entirely on animated films during the 1960s, and Nina Companeez, whose one film thus far, *Faustine,* appeared in 1972.

Denise Tual (née Denise Piazza) began an editing career in 1928 under the name of Denise Batcheff, her first husband having been Pierre Batcheff, the leading man of the famous film by Salvador Dali and Luis Buñuel, *Le Chien andalou.* Later she collaborated with her second husband, Roland Tual, on all of his productions. On her own, she directed *Ce Siècle a 50 ans (The Century Is Fifty),* using the compilation methods of *Paris 1900.*

Renée Cosima, an actress, produced short films and directed the documentary *Sur la Route de Key West.* Other directors of short films include Francine Premysler, Sylvia Hulin, Vergez-Tricom, Lucile Costa, Colette Harel-Lisztman, Anne Dastrée, Paule Delsol, Simone Crozet, and Yolande du Luart.

Actress Nicole Stéphane was in the front lines during the war between Israel and Egypt in 1949. On her return to

France she founded the Ancinex production company and directed *Les Hydrocéphales (Hydrocephalics,* 1965), *La Génération du desert (The Desert Generation,* 1957), and *Le Tapis volant (The Flying Carpet).* This last is a Zionist fairy tale in which a tractor changes into a flying carpet to take Jewish wanderers to Israel. Stéphane has continued actively as a producer of documentaries, such as *To Die In Madrid* (1963), and other features, including Racine's *Phèdre.* She was the producer of Susan Sontag's *Promised Lands* (1974).

Two major women directors in France today are Nelly Kaplan and Agnès Varda. Kaplan was born in Buenos Aires, but has lived in France since the 1950s. She began film work as assistant to Abel Gance on *La Tour de Nesle,* the triple-screen production comprised of *Magirama, Austerlitz,* and *Cyrano et D'Artagnan.* She then directed shorts on art including *Gustave Moreau; Rudolph Bresdin* (the engraver); *Dessins et merveilles (Drawings and Wonders,* drawings by Victor Hugo); *Abel Gance: hier et demain (Abel Gance: Yesterday and Tomorrow);* and *A la source de la femme aimée (At the Fountain of the Beloved,* the erotic drawings of André Masson). Her 60-minute film, *Le Regard Picasso (The Picasso Look,* 1967), won the Golden Lion at the Venice Film Festival.

Kaplan's first feature, *La Fiancée du pirate* (English title: *A Very Curious Girl),* appeared in 1970. It tells of Marie, a young gypsy suspected of witchcraft, who gives or sells her sexual favors to many local men (and one woman) in order to publicly expose the town's pettiness and hypocrisy. Picasso described the film as "insolence raised to a fine art." Marie is a stronger character than Cookie, the heroine of Kaplan's next film, *Papa, les petits bateaux* (1971). Cookie is a rich blonde being held for ransom by kidnappers, who discover she is not as empty-headed as she appears. Although by the end of the film she has killed all seven of her ab-

ductors and won the two-million-franc ransom for herself,
the emphasis on her dizzy-blonde Betty Boop characterization somewhat spoils the film, especially after the initial surprise at her resourcefulness fades away.

Agnès Varda was originally a still photographer. In 1954
she founded a filmmaking cooperative with Alain Resnais
as producer and Carlos Vilardebo as technical advisor. The
first feature film she directed was *La Pointe courte* (1955),
in which a young couple's struggle to save their marriage
is presented against the background of a fishing village's
fight against the big combines. This very personal film is
considered one of the forerunners of the *nouvelle vague*,
though it received limited distribution at the time. The
success of the three short films she made next—*O saisons,
ô châteaux* (1957), *L'Opéra-Mouffe* (1958), and *Du côté de
la côte* (1958)—encouraged her to make a second feature.

This was *Cléo de cinq à sept* (*Cleo From 5 to 7*, 1961), for
which she also wrote the script. In each sequence Varda
uses a slightly different style, adapted to the people Cleo en-
counters on the day she discovers she may be dying of cancer.
Cleo feels deserted by her friends as she realizes they can
appreciate her only in certain stereotyped roles: singer, pal,
docile mistress. She finally confides her fears to a gentle
stranger, but soon he too is forced to leave her and she
realizes she must confront life—and death—entirely alone.

Le Bonheur (1965), won a top prize at Cannes. Its theme
is that happiness is a "given" of life and can never really be
lost. *Les Créatures* (1966), starring Catherine Deneuve, draws
a parallel between two stories, one real and the other developing in the mind of a novelist. *Lions Love* (1970) is
115 minutes of Viva, Jerome Ragni, James Rado, Shirley
Clarke, and Eddie Constantine in a rented house in Hollywood. The absence of a recognizable plot might not be a
weakness in this free-flowing film if the people were more
interesting.

Varda's other films include the documentary, *Salut les*

Cubains (1963), *Elsa* (1966), and the short, *Oncle Janco* (1967). Her recent film, *Mon Corps est à moi (My Body Belongs to Me)*, deals with abortion.

Nadine Marquand Trintignant worked her way up from script girl to editor before directing the short film, *Fragilité, ton nom est femme (Fragility, Thy Name is Woman*, 1956), and several television shows. In 1967, her husband, Jean-Louis Trintignant, starred in her *Mon amour, mon amour.* Her next films were *Le Voleur de crimes (The Crime Thief,* 1969), and *Ca n'arrive qu'aux autres (It Only Happens to Others,* 1971), starring Catherine Deneuve and Marcello Mastroianni. The latter film, based on the tragedy of her own child's death, depicts the parents' shock and pain in an extremely personal and moving manner. Most recently she completed a thriller, *Défense de savoir*, starring Jean-Louis Trintignant.

Marguerite Duras is a major screenwriter and novelist who wrote *Hiroshima mon amour* (1959) for Alain Resnais. She collaborated with Paul Seban on the first film she directed, *La Musica* (1966), and directed *Détruire, dit-elle (Destroy, She Said,* 1969), adapted from her novel. In 1971 she directed *Jaune le soleil;* in 1972, *Nathalie Granger;* and in 1973, *La Femme du Ganges (Woman of the Ganges).*

Jackie Raynal began her film career as an editor; her credits include *Paris vu par . . . (Paris Seen By . . . ,* 1964) and Rohmer's *La Collectioneuse (The Collector,* 1966). In 1971 she directed her first feature, *Deux Fois (Twice).*

Especially active among the editors during the 1960s was Agnes Guillemot, who worked on fifteen films in that decade, including *Les Carabiniers (The Soldiers,* 1963); *Les Mepris (Contempt,* 1963); *Alphaville* (1965); *La Chinoise* (1967); and *Weekend* (1968).

Annie Tresgot, whose *El Ghorba* (English title: *The Passengers,* 1971)—about the plight of Algerian emigrants to France—was shown in the Critics Week of the 1971 Cannes

Festival, is another French director. Sylvia Jallaud has directed several shorts, beginning with *Des Maisons des hommes* (1953) and including *47, rue Vieille-du-Temple* (1960) and *Comme un reflet d'oiseau* (1961). Nine Mayo's films include *L'Arbre* (1961) and *Les Six Jours de la Création* (1962). Monique Lepeuve has done the animated films *La Chanson du jardinier fou* (1960) and *Concerto pour violincelle* (1962). Another animator, Yona Friedman, made *Les Aventures de Samba Gana* and *L'Origine des Kabouloukou* (1962).

Several women producers are currently active in France. Mag Bodard did *Les parapluies de Cherbourg (The Umbrellas of Cherbourg*, 1964), *Je t'aime, je t'aime (I Love You, I Love You*, 1968), and *Peau d'âne (Fairy Tales*, 1970). Others include Christine Gouse-Rénal, who produced *Les amitiés particulières (Special Friendships)*; Nicole Stéphane, previously mentioned; Lucy Ulrych; Jenny Gérard; and Vera Belmont.

A final note of interest: Françoise Giroud, who in 1974 was named to the newly created Cabinet post of Secretary of State for the Condition of Women in France, was once a script girl and then a scriptwriter for Jean Renoir. That was in the thirties, before she rose in prominence as a magazine publisher and journalist.

HUNGARY

Hungary's Judit Elek directed her first feature, *The Lady from Constantinople*, in 1969. In it a nostalgic old woman tries to connect with modern life by moving to a new apartment and subletting her old one. She spends her remaining money on a party for her prospective subtenants, and then moves. But her new apartment is even more isolated than the old one, and she is still not able to achieve a sense of belonging. Elek's short films include *Meeting* (1963), *Occupants of Manor House* (1966), and *How Long Does Man Matter?* (1967).

Márta Mészáros, also Hungarian, graduated from the Moscow Film Academy, where she directed documentaries. Her first feature, *The Girl* (1967), is about a young woman born out of wedlock and raised in a Budapest orphanage. As the film begins, she is making her first visit to her mother, a frightened, repressed peasant. The young woman slowly realizes that despite her family background she is a city person and must create her own happiness rather than search for it in the past. Mészáros also has directed several shorts, including *They Smile Again* (1964), *Care and Affection* (1963), and *The City of Bells* (1966). In 1973 she completed her second feature, *Good Riddance*.

Marianne Szemes is a screenwriter and documentary director, specializing in social problems handled in *cinéma-vérité* style. She wrote the screenplays for *The Sledge* (1955) and the feature *Dam* (1957), directed by her husband, Mihály Szemes. The documentaries she directed include *Divorce in Budapest* (1964), *Women Will Do Everything* (1964), *I'm Sorry for Your Sake* (1967), *It's So Simple* (1968), and *I Do What I Like* (1969).

Judit Vas directed the educational films entitled *Polarized Light* (1960), *Who Can Carry on Longer?* (1962), *Circadian Rhythms* (1965), *Who Is Your Friend?* (1967), and *Trio* (1967). Livia Gyrmathy directed the short *58 Seconds* (1966), the documentary *Message* (1967), and *Do You Know Sunday-Monday?*

INDIA

In India, two Bengali women—both former actresses—made commercially successful feature films in 1967. Manju Dey made *Abhisapta Chambal (Accursed Chambal Valley)*, the saga of a dancing girl who becomes a highway robber but is ultimately transformed into a virtuous woman. Arundhati Debi made *Chhutti (Vacation)*, a delicate film of youthful love and innocence. One reviewer said the film "projects the woman's mind and achieves a quality which would be hard to find in a man's work."

Other Indian filmmakers include Vijaya Mulay, an official in the Education Ministry who began making films after she became a grandmother, and has now completed several documentaries and educational films; Sai Paranjpe, who does documentaries for Delhi-TV, including *The Little Teashop;* and Shyama Habeebullah, who returned to India in the late 1960s to make documentaries, after having studied in England. Habeebullah's most important film is a documentary, *No Tree Grows*, about university students.

ISRAEL

The most prominent person in the Israeli film industry is a woman. She is Margot Klausner, head of the country's oldest and largest film company, the Israel Motion Picture Studios at Herzliya. Klausner was born in Berlin and came to Israel in 1926. A writer and patron of the arts, she first was active in promoting theatrical organizations (Habimah and later Ohel) and as far back as 1935 helped produce Israel's first film, an hour-long documentary which won first prize at Venice. She founded the Israel Motion Picture Studios in 1949, and since that time her firm has produced or provided services for more than 1,000 documentaries, ninety features and countless TV productions, commercials and newsreels.

American-born Ellida Geyra, a former dancer and choreographer who has been living in Israel since 1963, was the first (and still the only) woman to direct a feature film, *Before Tomorrow*, made in 1968. Since her feature, Geyra has been writing and directing shorts and documentaries.

Another American whose reputation is growing is Ruth

Broyde, a Chicago filmmaker who came to Israel in 1971 to make a documentary for the Encyclopaedia Britannica and decided to be part of what she believes is Israel's great film-making future. A graduate of Northwestern's Medill School of Journalism, Broyde had worked for several Chicago film companies (as assistant director, editor and camerawoman), then produced and directed a couple of short films of her own which resulted in the assignment from Britannica for a film about life on a kibbutz (*Israeli Boy*, 13 minutes). She now has her own company, Ariella Films.

Israel's leading camerawoman is Nurith Aviv, a Sabra who studied filmmaking in Paris. She shot the feature film *Shablul*, and recently was head camera for a full-length French-Swiss production. She is also active in documentary work.

Abigail Yoresh, a painter from Transylvania, joined her husband in organizing Yoresh Ltd., a company that special-izes in animation, illustration, titling and graphic design. Since 1968, they have turned out about forty shorts.

Among the screenwriters is Alima Dai, whose credits in-clude the feature *Adam,* a suspense thriller produced and di-rected by her husband, Yona. Editors of feature films include Nelly Gil'ad, Anna Gurit, Tova Biran and Anat Lobarsky.

ITALY

Lina Wertmuller, Liliana Cavani

The two most widely known women filmmakers in Italy are Lina Wertmuller and Liliana Cavani, both of whom have had extensive international exposure.

Wertmuller, who is of Swiss ancestry, was born in Rome in 1930. For ten years her life was the theater, where she worked as an assistant director and writer, but in 1963 she got a job as an assistant to Fellini in the making of the film 8½, and the association with Fellini, as one might expect, set off sparks of cinematic creativity. That same year she wrote and directed her first film, *I Basilischi (The Lizards)*, the story of a young man in a small town in southern Italy who tries to buck the social structure and fails. It was, for Wertmuller, an expression of her anger with the middle class. The film won a Silver Ribbon at the 1963 Locarno Festival, and she was on her way. In 1966 she made a tragi-comedy with the Anglicized title of *This Time Let's Talk About Men*, an episodic film depicting the victimization of women. In 1972, after some work as a radio and television writer, she wrote and directed *Mimi mettalurgico ferito nell'onore*, a well-received bedroom farce which came to the United States as *The Seduction of Mimi*. It is a wild tale, set in Italy and Sicily, of a round of sexual jousts in which even the Mafia gets involved. Her greatest acclaim came with *Love and Anarchy*, which she wrote and directed in 1973, and which has been a rousing box-office success, particularly in the U.S. The story, which takes place in the 1930s, is of an idealistic but naïve young man from the country who is given a political assignment—to assassinate Mussolini. He goes to the city, takes up board in a brothel, falls in love with a prostitute, and is consumed by the conflict of completing his mission and pursuing his love.

Wertmuller's more recent *Everything Is Ready, But Nothing Works* (1974), was described in Variety as "a disappointing third film on the subject of over-exploited southern subproletarians looking for roots and a life mission up north." (The film has not yet been released in the United States.) Another recent Wertmuller film is *Swept Away by an Unusual Destiny in the Blue Sea of August*.

Wertmuller says she prefers making "popular cinema" rather than films for the cultural elite because she wants to reach the neglected masses. The way she does this is by relying heavily on comedy, which not only attracts a bigger audience but permits her to advance serious ideas at the same time she's making them laugh. Even in dealing with feminism, a cause she espouses, she is inclined to make it funny because that is the way she works.

She has encountered prejudice on the part of producers, she says, and it has made her career a difficult one, "but when you really get down to work the sex thing is overcome."

Liliana Cavani, a graduate of Rome's Centro Sperimentale, began her career in 1960 making films for television. They included documentaries (*History of the Third Reich, The Woman of the Resistance, The House in Italy*) and dramatic films (*Francis of Assisi* and *The Guest*, about a female inmate of a mental hospital). In 1970 she made the feature film *The Year of the Cannibals*, which tells of two idealistic young people fighting for decency amid Fascist repression. In 1974 she directed *The Night Porter*, which was heavily promoted in the U.S. and drew large audiences despite the fact that many critics rapped it. The film deals with the sado-masochistic relationship between an ex-Nazi officer and a young woman he had raped years earlier when she was an adolescent in a concentration camp. One critic, who called the movie "romantic pornography," wrote that "if you don't love pain, you won't find it erotic." After *The Night Porter*, Cavani began work on a film called *The Eternal Return*, about the German philosopher Nietzsche.

Cavani says she has not run into any obstacles as a woman filmmaker; her main problem is persuading film producers and TV executives to let her make films that deal boldly with political and social problems. She doesn't feel that a woman brings any special qualities to filmmaking if she has grown up in a free environment; if she has not, then she expresses in her films the distortions of her condition.

Cavani is not impressed by the feminist movement in the United States, labeling it elitist. It has not touched the workingwoman, she contends. What's more, she says, the feminist struggle cannot go forward apart from a general political struggle.

Lorenza Mazzetti had such a difficult time as a filmmaker in Italy that she went to England to direct *Together* (1956). The film, which won a prize at Cannes, is about two male deaf-mutes in London's East End and the difficulty they have in maintaining their friendship while the world of sound revolves around them.

When Mazzetti first became interested in films, she was given a choice by her husband: films or marriage. As she put it, "I chose love and started washing my husband's socks. But he left me anyway. He said he could not love such a silly woman, who wanted to direct films." Despite the success of *Together*, it remained impossible for her to make films in Italy. She joined a French film collective to do a sequence of *Les femmes accusent (Women Accuse,* 1961), then deferred her film aspirations and returned to Italy where she works as a sociologist.

Other women directing films in Italy include Anna Gobbi, who directed the short avant-garde film *Tre e due (Three Plus Two)* in the 1940s. She became a script writer and costume designer, then returned to directing in 1967 with *The Scandal.* Maria Basaglia directed *Sua Altezza ha detto, No!* (1954) and *Sangue di Zingara* (1956). Cecilia Mangini co-directed *All'armi siam fascisti* (1961), *Processo a Stalin* (1963), and the short *Essere donne (To Be Women,* 1964). In 1969 Sandra Franchina directed *Morire gratis (To Die for Nothing),* and in 1972 Dacia Mariani, a novelist, directed *Conjugal Love,* after the novel by Alberto Moravia.

Women producers are very scarce in Italy, but one in particular has been succesful since the early 1960s, Countess Marina Cicogna, of Euro International Films. Suso (Giovanna) Cecchi d'Amico is one of the most influential screenwriters. Her work includes *To Live in Peace* (1946), *The Bicycle Thief* (1948), *Miracle in Milan* (1951), *Bellissima* (1952), *I Vinti (The Defeated,* 1952), *Le Notti bianche (White Nights), I Soliti Ignoti (Big Deal on Madonna Street,* 1958), *Salvatore Giuliano* (1961), and *Rocco and His Brothers* (1961).

JAPAN

Although women filmmakers were virtually nonexistent in Japan prior to World War II, a few have emerged since then. Among them is Kinuyo Tanaka, who became Japan's first woman film director in 1953 and has since directed a film every two years. Tanaka began her career as an apprentice in a musical troupe before joining the Shochiku film production company as an actress in 1924. By the 1930s she had become one of the top stars in Japan, and has continued to act as well as direct. Western audiences know her primarily as the actress who played the potter's wife in *Ugetsu*.

The director Toshie Tokieda is best known outside Japan for her documentary, *Report from China*. In 1966-67 she took her crew into the People's Republic of China to shoot a full-length color film on the social and economic transformation of the country and the everyday lives of its people. Tokieda and her team dressed like the Chinese, mingled with them, and were able to film freely without calling attention to themselves. They shot rare scenes of China's largest steel mill, heavy machinery factories and motor vehicle plants, and visited farm communes, day nurseries, schools, and individual homes. *Report from China* was released in 1970 and has received excellent notices in both Japan and the United States. One reviewer said "The camera tells it all, capturing what amounts to a gigantic anthill of human dedication and productivity. . . . The days of 'The Good Earth' are gone forever."

LATIN AMERICA

In Colombia, Gabriela Samper was virtually a one-woman film industry until her death in 1974 at the age of 56. Working under near-primitive conditions, she produced six films portraying the rapidly vanishing native culture of her country. Although she often had to transport her equipment and crew to location by means of public buses, and had very limited facilities for processing and developing films, she managed to turn out award-winning documentaries. Her aim, she said, was "to use the film medium to arouse in my fellow Colombians an awareness of our identity, to project on the screen for them an image of our culture and its authentic roots."

In 1970, Samper produced *The Salt Man*, which won the Maltese Cross at the Cordoba Film Festival in Argentina. Her other films are *A Story of Long, Long Ago* (1965), *The Paramo of Cumanday* (1966), *Cities in Crisis* (1968), and *A Mask For Me, A Mask For You* (1968), all of which she produced with Ray Whitlin; and *The Holy Brotherhood* (1970), produced with Rebecca Puchi and Ernesto Sabogal.

Samper was a visiting scholar at Cornell in 1963-64.

Argentinian Renée Oro did a long documentary, *Argentina*, at the end of the silent era. In Venezuela, Margot Benaceraf directed the short, *Reveron* (1952), about the man who was to become the country's most famous artist. Her feature *Araya* (1960), won a prize at Cannes. *Araya* is about the inhabitants of Venezuela's salt desert, where living conditions have not changed in more than 400 years.

Carmen Toscano, in Mexico, compiled the film *Memories of a Mexican.* Her father, Salvador, had introduced the motion-picture camera to Mexico in 1897, and before his death had accumulated about 165,000 feet of film on many major news events. This film footage was the source of his daughter's documentary.

POLAND

Poland's Wanda Jakubowska directed the important film, *The Last Stop* (1949). In the 1920s, Jakubowska and the filmmakers Eugeniusz Cekalski, Tadeusz Konalski, Stanislaw Wohl, Jerzy Zerzyski, and Jerzy Toeplitz co-founded the Society of Devotees of the Artistic Film (START), which later became the Cooperative of Film Authors. By 1930 Jakubowska was in the vanguard of the pre-war documentary movement, with *Report I* and *Report II*, followed by *Impressions* and *The Sea* (1932). She then collaborated with Cekalski on *We Build* (1934), and with K. Szolowski on *The Banks of the Nieman* (1939). During the German occupation of Poland she was deported to Auschwitz and Ravensbruck, and upon her return she drew on her experiences for *We Are the Builders of the Country* (1946) and her best film, *The Last Stop*.

The Last Stop is one of the most straightforward films on Nazi concentration camps ever made. It is also the only one directed by a woman, with a cast and crew composed mainly of women who had been in the camps. The film shows how the Nazis pitted woman against woman by giving special privileges to a few. The women become so dehumanized that finally a woman in childbirth is tortured by a female guard and her baby is murdered. The two heroines of the film are a doctor, Eugenia, and an interpreter, Anna. When they learn that the Germans intend to destroy everyone in the camp before the impending arrival of Soviet forces, each tries in her own way to break through the prisoners' terror and hunger-induced apathy to organize a resistance.

With *The Last Stop* and her subsequent films, Jakubowska established herself as one of the leading filmmakers in Poland. Later films directed by her include *The Puppet of Warsaw* (1953), also called *Soldier of Victory*, a biography of General Swierczewski; *Confidences* (1955), about conflicts between East and West Germany; *Goodbye to the Devil* (1957), a drama of peasant life and the assassination of a Communist; *King Matthew I* (1958), a philosophical story; *Encounter in the Shadows* (1960), in which a pianist finds she must give a concert in the village to which she was once deported; *It Happened Yesterday* (1960); *The End of Our World*

(1964), a return to Auschwitz 20 years later; *The Hot Line* (1965); and *The Big Wood* (1966).

Eva Petelska was co-director for the features *Shipwrecks* (1957), *The Sky is Our Roof* (1959), *Mountains on Fire* (1961), *Black Wings* (1962), *The Beater* (1963), *The Wooden Rosary* (1965), *Don Gabriel* (1966), *A Matter of Conscience* (1967), and *Empty Eyes* (1969).

Other women filmmakers in Poland include Marta Flanz, who in 1935 co-directed the comedy *Love Only Me* with Mécislas Krawicz; Marta Marczakowi, who co-directed *Grzyby* (1949); and Natalia Brzozowska, who directed *Music* (1949). Walentyna Uszycka co-directed *End of Night* (1957). Helina Bielinska directed *Hanging the Guard* (1958), *Wlodzimierz Haupe* (1958), *Zmiana Warty* (1958), *The Circus Under the Stars* (1960), *Lucky Tony* (1961, co-directed), and *Godzina Pasomes Rozy* (1963). Maria Kaniewska directed *Not Far From Warsaw* (1954), *Much Ado About Little Basia* (1959), *On the Threshold of Art* (1962), *Panienka z Okienka* (1964), and others. Anna Sokolowska directed *Beata* (1965).

SWEDEN

The first woman to direct films in Sweden (and the second anywhere after Alice Guy Blaché) was Anna Hoffman-Uddgren. She directed *Blott en Drorn* (1911), *Stockholms-damernas* (1911), *Systrarna* (1912), and Strindberg's *Miss Julie* (1912).

Today, one of the leading Swedish filmmakers is former actress Mai Zetterling. First seen in the United States in Ingmar Bergman's *Torment* (1944), she starred in many films until early in the 1960s, when she decided to direct. Her acting films include several by Bergman, and Muriel Box's *The Truth About Women* (1958).

Zetterling and her husband, the writer David Hughes, collaborated on documentaries for English television. She then turned to features with *Alskande par (Loving Couples)*, which was shown at Cannes in 1965. In this film all three main characters are pregnant and in the same hospital. The film investigates the childhood, love affairs and childbirth of each character by means of a complex construction of flashbacks and a constantly moving camera. The latter is used also in Zetterling's film, *The Girls. Langtan (Night Games,* 1966), again through the use of flashbacks, examines both the present and thirty years ago, as a woman helps her husband escape the mansion which represents his *dolce vita* past and adjust to the rapidly changing present-day world.

Zetterling's *Doctor Glas* (1967) was similarly concerned with the decay of a civilization, but *Flickorna (The Girls,* 1967) is a humorous positive look at three women coming to terms with themselves. In this film the actresses on tour with *Lysistrata* become immersed in their roles off stage and on, and see the Greek women's oppression as mirroring their own. Zetterling also directed a segment of *Visions of 8* (1973), a documentary on the 1972 Olympics. She covered the wrestling matches, while seven other international directors filmed different events.

As a woman director, Zetterling has had to fight her share of oppression and prejudice. In an interview in the New York Times in 1972 she said "You come up against all sorts of silly little prejudices. People think you don't know what you're doing, or that you'll go away and cry in a corner if you can't get what you want. It's so stupid." As for her themes, which are mainly about women, she said "There are many things I feel haven't been aired on the screen, haven't been looked at from a woman's viewpoint. So naturally I make films about women."

Between the time of Hoffman-Uddgren and Zetterling there were no more than a handful of female directors in Sweden. Pauline Brunius directed short comedies and farces including *Stenaldermannen* (1919), *Trollslandan* (1920), *De*

Lackra Skaldjuren (1920), *Ombytta Roller* (1921), *Ryggskott,* and *Lev Livet Leende* (1936). Alice Eklund co-directed *Flickorna pa Uppakara* in 1936. Other Swedish women directors are Margareta Rosencrantz (*Kuckelikaka,* 1949), Mimi Pollack (*Rattan Att Alska,* 1956), Elsa Colfach (*Suzanne,* 1960), and Karin Falck (*Drompojke*n, 1964). Actress Ingrid Thulin directed *Devotion* (1964) and co-produced *La guerre est finie* (1965) with Alain Resnais, a film in which she also starred.

U.S.S.R.

Russia's first woman director was Olga Preobrazhenskaya, who began her career in 1913 as assistant to director W. R. Gardin. Her early films include *Miss Peasant* (1916) and *Locksmith and Chancellor* (1923, co-credited with Gardin). In 1927 she directed *Women of Ryazan,* an important contribution to the Soviet Union's golden age of cinema. In this film a young woman whose husband is at war is seduced by her father-in-law. She is thrown out of the house when her husband returns, and kills herself before her husband realizes who the father of her child is. The story is told from the woman's point of view, though the emphasis is on the change that takes place in the husband. Among Preobrazhenskaya's later works were *The Last Attraction* (1929); *Paths of Enemies* and *Grain,* both made in the 1930s; and *The Quiet Don* and *Children of the Taiga* (1941), both done with Ivan Pravov. Her work was cut short by the Stalin purges.

Olga Chekhova, a niece of Anton Chekhov, founded a production company in England in 1927, producing several films and directing *The Victorious* and *Poliche* (both 1928).

Esther Shub was director of editing for the Soviet Cinema Archive, and it is said that she gave Eisenstein his first film job. She was one of the first Russians, along with Dziga Vertov, to create feature films entirely from newsreel and archival footage, turning the accumulated material into valuable documentaries of daily life. With tremendous patience she reconstructed significant moments of Russian history: *The Fall of the Romanovs* (1927), *The Great Road* (1927), *The Russia of Nicholas II and Tolstoy* (1928), *Today* (1930), *Komsomol* (1932), *The Subway* (1934), *Spain* (1938), and *The Country of the Soviets* (1937). Her last films were *Twenty Years of Cinema* (1940), in collaboration with Pudovkin; *The Face of the Enemy*, a short (1941); and *By the Arax* (1947). As she explained her philosophy: "We believe that in our epoch we can film newsreels and thus preserve our epoch for future generations. This means that we want to film the present day, today's people, today's events. What is the difference when you watch a wonderful fiction film made three years ago? You cannot stand to look at it—it becomes simply indigestible. But when you see a nonfiction film, you watch it, and it comes across and it is interesting because it is a piece of genuine life which is now in the past."

Vera Stroyeva began in film as a writer of scripts with her husband, director Gregori Roshal. In 1931 she directed *The Rights of Fathers*. Her other films include Dostoyevsky's *Petersburg Nights* (1934, co-credit with Roshal), *Generation of Conquerors* (1936), *Marite* (1947), *The Grand Concert* (1951), *Boris Godunov* (1955), and *La Khovanschina* (1959). She and Roshal also collaborated on *Search for Happiness* (1940).

Yulia Solntseva, an actress, collaborated with her husband, Alexander Dovzhenko, on films such as *Shors* (1939), *Liberation* (1940), *The Fight for Our Soviet Ukraine* (1943, co-directed with Yakov Avdeyenko), *Victory in the Ukraine* (1945), and *Life in Bloom* (1947). In 1952 she made her first film on her own, *Igor Bulichov*, and in 1955 directed *The Unwilling Inspectors*. After Dovzhenko's death she completed his *Poem of the Sea* (1958) and went on to direct *The Years of Fire* (1961), *The Desna* (1963), and *The Unforgettable* (1969), again about the war in the Ukraine.

Margarita Barskaya wrote and directed *Torn Shoes* (1933), a popular children's film.

Valentina and Zenajeda Brumberg, veteran cartoon directors, are still active at the Soyuzmultfilm Studio. Their postwar films include *Great Troubles* (1961), *Three Fat Men* (1963), *The Brave Little Tailor* (1964), *An Hour Until the Meeting* (1965), *The Golden Stepmother* (1966), and *The Little Time Machine* (1967).

Other Russian women filmmakers include Z. Touloubieva *(Swan Lake* and the documentary *Along the River Kama)*, Lana Gogoberidze *(Under the Same Sky)*, Nadezhda Kocheverova (films for children), I. Troyanova *(The Little Horse)*, N. Bebderskaya *(The Wolf and the Crane)*, O. Khodatayeva *(The Little Room, Tom Thumb,* and many others), Natalya Rashevskaya *(Fathers and Sons)*, and Irina Poplavskaya *(Revenge, Jamilya)*. Olga Ulitskaya co-directed *Ataman Kodr*, Marija Andjaparidze wrote and directed *Aniuta* (1960), Aida Mansarova co-directed *The Trial* (1962), Larissa Shepitka directed *Heat* (1963), *Wings* (1966), and *You and I* (1972). Vera Plivova-Simkova directed *Mice, Foxes, and Gallowshill* (1970). Margarita Pilikhina is an important Russian cinematographer with many films to her credit, including *Man from Planet Earth, Forna Gordeyev, Ginger, I Am Twenty, Day Stars,* and *Tchaikovsky.*

WEST GERMANY

Leni Riefenstahl

Leni Riefenstahl may well be the most gifted of all women filmmakers. She is also, because she made propaganda films for the Nazis, the most controversial.

Riefenstahl began her career as a dancer and actress, and starred in nine films in the late twenties and early thirties. The first, a silent picture made in 1926, was *Der Heilige Berg (The Holy Mountain)*, in which she plays a young dancer who becomes enthralled with mountain climbing. In 1932 she directed her first feature film, a movie called *Das Blaue Licht (The Blue Light)*, in which she also starred. It is an allegorical story of a mountan peak (mountains were very big in German filmmaking) which emits a strange blue light that lures the heroine to her death. Hitler, it is said, became enamored of her work, both as an actress and a director, and their friendship led Riefenstahl into a new phase of her career, making "documentaries."

The two documentaries for which she is known are *Triumf des Willens (Triumph of the Will)*, made in 1934, and *Olympiad*, a film of the 1936 Olympics in Germany.

A depiction of the massive Nuremberg Rally, *Triumph of the Will* in its original, full-length version seeks to convey the glory and mystique of Germany recovering from the effects of a devastating war, proud of the military regime which had produced endless rows of clean, healthy young men, while covertly stressing the power of disciplined multitudes. It is one of the most effective propaganda films ever made; in the view of many, the most successful.

For many years and in many places Riefenstahl has defended herself vigorously against charges that the film revealed her as an ardent supporter of the Nazis. Typical of her arguments is this one, which appeared in Femmes Cinéastes: "You must remember that I made *Triumph of the Will* in 1934, when Hitler had just been brought to power not by a coup d'état but by a parliamentary majority freely elected . . . Why should I have been the only person to foresee the future and to know that Hitler would lead Germany and the world to catastrophe? Many filmmakers made films and followed orders then. None has been accused as I have. Why? Because I am a woman or because the film was too successful? My film is nothing but a documentary, a newsreel, different from normal newsreels only because I made it *artistically*. I did not make it as propaganda. I was apolitical during the Nazi era."

Was *Triumph of the Will* purely a documentary, a genuine record of an historical event, as Riefenstahl has claimed? Not so, says Susan Sontag, who takes the filmmaker apart in a powerful article in the February 6, 1975, issue of the New York Review of Books. Citing Riefenstahl's own book, "Hinter den Kulissen des Reichsparteitag Films," published in 1935, Sontag says the rally was actually staged for the purpose of making a propaganda film. It was conceived as "the set of a film spectacle" and Riefenstahl was involved in the planning of it. In her book, long forgotten, Riefenstahl herself says "The ceremonies and precise plans of the parades, marches, processions, the architecture of the halls and stadium were designed for the convenience of the cameras."

According to Hans Barkhausen in the fall 1974 issue of Film Quarterly, Riefenstahl also has spread some myths about *Olympiad*—which really is two films, *Fest der Völker (Festival of the People)* and *Fest der Schönheit (Festival of Beauty)*. While Riefenstahl has maintained that both films were commissioned by the International Olympics Committee and produced by her own company, Barkhausen holds that they were actually commissioned and financed by the Nazi government, engineered through a dummy company set up in Riefenstahl's name, and filmed with the close cooperation of Goebbels. Riefenstahl spent two years editing *Olympiad* and arranged its world premiere in 1938 in Berlin as part of the celebration of Hitler's forty-ninth birthday. It was the main German entry at the 1938 Venice Film Festival, where it won the Gold Medal. (Riefenstahl had also won the Gold Medal in 1932 for *The Blue Light*.)

Sontag says Riefenstahl's involvement with the Nazis goes beyond the making of *Triumph of the Will* and *Olympiad*. She points out that Rienfenstahl made other films for the Nazis which somehow have dropped out of sight. The first, in 1933, was *Sieg des Glaubens (Victory of Faith)*, a joyful depiction of the first National Socialist Party Congress after Hitler came to power. The second, released in 1935, was

Tag der Freiheit: Unsere Wehrmacht (Day of Freedom: Our Army). Made for the army, this film tells of the glory of bearing arms for the Führer. In 1938 (after *Triumph of the Will* and *Olympiad*) Riefenstahl rhapsodized Hitler in a 50-minute portrait called *Berchtesgaden über Salzburg*, which employs as a backdrop the rugged mountains of his aerie. In 1939 she was on hand with a camera crew when the Wehrmacht invaded Poland, but there is no record of any film she may have made there.

The Allies briefly arrested Riefenstahl in 1945 and seized her homes in Berlin and Munich. Intermittent examinations of her past began in 1948 and continued for four years, when she was finally declared "de-Nazified." The court found "no political activity in support of the Nazi regime which would warrant punishment."

Riefenstahl's last film, finished in 1944, was a feature called *Tiefland*, in which she was the star again. It was released in 1954 and quickly sank into oblivion. In 1965 she began but did not complete a documentary called *Schwarze Fracht (Black Cargo)*, a film on the East African slave trade.

Riefenstahl's most recent work is a book of photographs, "The Last of the Nuba," published here by Harper and Row. The book deals with an obscure people in the desert of southern Sudan who subscribe to a culture in which success in fighting "is the main aspiration of a man's life."

Sontag says the "purification of Leni Riefenstahl's reputation of its Nazi dross has been gathering momentum for some time," and she attributes it in part to the fact that Riefenstahl is a woman. In the fall of '74 Riefenstahl was guest of honor at a film festival in Colorado. The event drew criticism but it created something less than a furor.

The first woman director, preceding Riefenstahl by just a year, was Leontine Sagan. In 1931 she filmed *Mädchen in Uniform*, an adaptation of a play by Christa Winsloe. Set in a German school for girls, and without any male characters, the film contrasts the innocence and need for individuality of the students with the senseless uniformity exacted by the stern school head. A young student's repressed love for her teacher leads to suicide (or, in another ending, attempted suicide). This film was widely interpreted as a plea for humanism at the time the Nazi regime was coming to power. Sagan emigrated to England in 1932 to escape persecution by the Nazis. Her second film, *Men of Tomorrow* (1932), produced by Alexander Korda and set at Oxford, was based on Anthony Gibbs' "Young Apollo." She was on unfamiliar ground, and the film was a failure. Her career as a director ended, and she moved to South Africa, where she helped found the National Theatre in Johannesburg.

In the early 1920s writer Thea von Harbou had begun working closely with her husband, Fritz Lang. Through him she exerted a strong influence on the German cinema of the day, which to that time had been more of a screenwriter's medium than a director's. She wrote all of Lang's scripts from *Der Müde Tod (Between Two Worlds,* 1921) to *Das Testament des Doctor Mabuse (The Last Will of Dr. Mabuse,* 1933), including *The Gambler* (1922), *The Nibelungen Saga* (1924), *Metropolis* (1926), *Spies* (1928), *Woman on the Moon* (1928), and the sound film *M* (1931). She also wrote scripts for F. W. Murnau and Carl Dreyer. With the rise of National Socialism, Lang left Germany, but von Harbou, a Nazi, remained. She directed two films, *Elizabeth und der Narr* (1934) and Gerhardt Hauptmann's *Hanneles Himmelfarht* (1934), and wrote scripts for Richard Eichberg, Lamprecht, Viet Harlan, Von Baky, and others. She died in 1954.

Other women filmmakers of this period were Bauer-Adamara, who directed a film report of a German expedition to the Amazon, *Die Grüne Hölle (Green Hell,* 1931) and Lore Bierling, who worked on animated films (and conformed to Nazi standards of art). Else Wegener accompanied her husband, Alfred, on his 1936 expedition to Greenland and, in collaboration with Dr. Paul Kunhenn and Svend Noldan, made the documentary *Das Grosse Eis.*

Lotte Reiniger began by making "silhouette films," having started her experiments with this special animation technique in 1919 with her husband, Carl Koch. In 1926 they made *The Adventures of Prince Achmed,* the first full-length feature cartoon. They made over twenty films before fleeing to England in 1936, but most of the negatives were destroyed in the bombing of London. In London, Reiniger founded the film-production group, Fantasia Productions, Ltd., and continued for many years to make silhouette films. Her best-known surviving films include *The Gallant Little Tailor* (1954), which won first prize in the television category of the 1955 Venice Film Festival; *Jack and the Beanstalk* (1955) and *The Star of Bethlehem* (1956), the first color silhouette films; and the *Doctor Doolittle* series, as well as many fairy tales. Since 1951 she has been working on children's programs for British television.

Current West German filmmakers include Dore Nekes, who, with her husband, Werner, has been active in underground films since 1960. Daniele Hullet and her husband, Jean-Marie Straub, developed a spare style in their *Machorka-Muff* (1963), a short; *Nacht Bersohnt* (1965); *Chronik der Anna Magdelena Bach* (1967), a feature; and *Der Brautigam, die Komödiantin und der Zuhalter* (1968), a short. Birgit and Wilhelm Hein directed *Rohfilm* (1968), *625* (1969), and *Work in Progress, Part I, Part II* (1969-1970). Helke Sanders directed *Gewalt* and *Eine Prämie für Irene,* a feminist film about a woman factory worker. Claudia Alemann's *Tu Luc Van Doan* concerns women in the Vietnam war. Charlotte Kerr-Sokal did a 1969 documentary on the Antarctic, while Rosa von Prauheim specializes in avantgarde shorts. Karen Thome directed and stars in *Over Night* (1973), a portrait of hippie life in Bavaria. Other German women directing films include Mai Spils and Isa Hesse (*About a Tapestry*).

OTHER COUNTRIES

AUSTRALIA

Women in Australia have played a very small part in films. The McDonagh sisters made two films, *The Cheaters* (1926, silent; re-released in 1930 with sound), and *Two Minutes Silence* (1934). Dymphna Cusack wrote the screenplay for *Red Sky at Morning*, released in 1951 as *Escape at Dawn*.

AUSTRIA

Luise and Jacob Flack formed the Weida production company in 1910, and by 1914 they had directed about 100 short films. Some of their longer silent films later included *The Czarevich*, *The Poor Student* and *Yoshiwara*. Most notable of their sound films was *The Citadel of Warsaw*. The company closed when Austria succumbed to Hitler.

NORWAY

In Norway, Anja Brien has made two short films, *Visages* (on the paintings of Eduard Munch) and *May 17* (a satirical treatment of a national festival); and a feature called *Rape*.

ROMANIA

Romanian filmmaker Elizabeth Bostan has directed three features: *The Kid* (1962), *Recollections from Childhood* (1964), and *Youth Without Old Age* (1968), and three shorts: *The Brood Hen and Her Golden Chicks*, *Three Romanian Dances*, and *The Hora-Dance*. She has also done a series about a little boy, *Naica*. Malvina Ursianu, another Romanian director, is known for her film *The Smile*.

SPAIN AND PORTUGAL

In Spain, Rosario Pi directed *The Wild Cat* (1936). In Portugal, Barbara Virginia directed *Three Days Without*

God (1946). This film is about a priest who leaves his small mountain village in charge of a schoolteacher. In his absence the community accuses the teacher of complicity with the devil. The film met with some success.

TURKEY

The best known actress in Turkey is Türkan Soray, who in 1973 began to produce movies as well as act in them. Her first film, *Dőnűs (Going Back)* is about a woman from a small village who migrates to Istanbul, endures the hardships of city life for several years, and then returns to her village with her baby. The film probes the difficulties of rural-urban migration, and has been highly acclaimed as one of the few Turkish movies that has social relevance. Soray financed the film, wrote the script, starred in it, and helped direct. Two more films are scheduled to complete a trilogy.

PART TWO

THE NEW FILMMAKERS

WOMEN WHO ARE MAKING MOVIES
OUTSIDE OF HOLLYWOOD

In New York, California and many places between, a different breed of women filmmakers has emerged. Some are militant feminists, some are indifferent to feminism, some are hostile to it. Some specialize in one aspect of movie-making—producing, directing, writing, editing, sound, or camerawork—and others range over two or three of these areas, or seek to encompass all of them. Some are motivated by a desire for creative expression, others by commercial interest. Many have been trained in colleges and studios, others are self-taught. A great number are pursuing their craft with professional earnestness and are turning out good films, or will, in time; others, less dedicated, less talented, will no doubt find other avenues for their energies after a while. But good or bad, professional or otherwise, a lot of women are now

145

making films, and more are entering the field with every passing day.

In the pages that follow is a description of women filmmakers outside the Hollywood establishment who have achieved at least some recognition. There are no dilettantes here, but neither is this a complete listing of all the capable and productive women engaged in the work of making films. What follows is only a sampling, chosen pretty much at random, and presented here for the purpose of providing a general picture of who these filmmakers are, the kind of problems they have faced, and, in some instances, what they have to say about their work.

◦   ◦   ◦

PERRY MILLER ADATO, New York, is an award-winning producer and director of documentary films for television. Her film, *Dylan Thomas: The World I Breathe*, won an Emmy in 1967. Before moving to NET in 1968, she was a film consultant for the Columbia Broadcasting System for ten years. Her feature, *Gertrude Stein: When This You See, Remember Me* (1970), is a lively biography of Stein, combining photographs, paintings, music, rare bits of Stein-Toklas home movies, and live reminiscences by some of the people who knew her. The use of both compilation-film and new footage achieves a most effective result.

Adato's other films include *The Great Radio Comedians* (1972), *Norman Corwin's 'Untitled'* (1972), and *The Film Generation and Dance* (1969), all produced for NET.

YVONNE ANDERSEN, Lexington, Massachusetts, is the director of the Yellow Ball Workshop, where filmmaking is taught to children. She is an accomplished director of films for children, including *One Hot Dog with Mustard* (1962), *Spaghetti Trouble* (1963), and *Let's Make a Film* (1970). She notes that "boy students—especially those up to the age of thirteen—make films with a lot of physical violence," while girls seldom portray violence. But "girls are very good technicians at an earlier age than boys, and take a lot of responsibility." Andersen has been a film consultant to educational institutions in the United States and abroad, and her work has included coordinating an animation project for the Center for Understanding Media, involving elementary school children in Alaska, Nebraska, New York, and Kansas.

MADELINE ANDERSON, Brooklyn, New York, was the second black woman to be admitted to the editors' union. In the 1960s she was the producer of Richard Leacock's *Integration Report I*, later she assisted Shirley Clarke on *The Cool World*, then edited and occasionally produced films for NET's "Black Journal." In 1970 she produced, directed, and edited *I Am Somebody*, a film dealing with the 1969 Mother's Day March in Charleston, South Carolina, where 400 medical workers, nearly all of them black women, decided to form a union. As one woman in the film explains, "We were sick and tired of being sick and tired!" In a powerful scene, the women engage in a battle with white police. The narrator, Claire Brown, declares: "More than a thousand of us went to jail. . . . My kids were in jail, too." Later, their fervor aroused by a speech by Coretta King, they organize a black boycott of local business. The weeks drag by, but finally the hospital recognizes the new union. Anderson is currently making films for "Sesame Street" and the Children's Television Workshop, and teaching at Columbia University.

EVE ARNOLD is an American still photographer now living in London. Her *Beyond the Veil* (1971, 50 minutes) is a delicately photographed documentary of harem life in eastern Arabia. A popular proverb is quoted in the film: "An Arab loves first his son, next his camel, then his wife." We see the women spending most of their time indoors, only venturing out with veils covering their faces. But times are changing. Noura, the narrator, drives a jeep. Young women studying to be doctors assert that they will not consider marrying a man who does not believe in equality for women. And a young woman of the aristocracy, the most confined class of all, sits smiling among her costly perfumes, cutting her veil away to a bare minimum.

In the course of putting together a crew for her film, Arnold spent many months searching for women technicians until she finally found two camerawomen and a soundwoman. She plans a series of films dealing with the Middle East.

ANNETTE BACHNER, New York, began in the forties as a director and stage manager for NBC-TV. Since then she has become a director and producer, recently starting her own production company for commercials, industrials, and documentary films. Her commercial films have won many prizes, including the Gold Lion at Cannes for *Sinclair Gas* (1969). She has also directed films for Sunshine Bakers, Kinney Shoes, Woolworth, General Mills, and the federal government.

MIRRA BANK, New York, an artist and still photographer, was a producer of radio shows in Boston before apprenticing in film at the London School of Film Technique. She was first assistant editor on the feature *Gimme Shelter* (1971), and edited *The Conspiracy* (dealing with the Chicago conspiracy trials), *Dybbuk*, and *Crazy Years* (a special on Warner Brothers in the 1930s).

CONI BEESON, Belvedere, California, is best known for her films for the National Sex and Drug Forum, such as *Unfolding* (1970, 17 minutes), which she wrote and directed, and on which she did the camerawork. A film about human desire and lovemaking, it has been through the courts on pornography charges, but has been cleared each time and judged to be a work of art. "It is not so much a woman's viewpoint," Beeson has stated, "as it is an artist's statement through theater-piece collages in which the subject matter is man's universal need to touch and be touched. . . . The film differs from pornographic films, as it is about feelings, emotions, relationships." Beeson's other films include *Thenow* (1971, 14 minutes), in which a black woman dreams of being black and being white, and has both black and white lovers; *Ann, A Portrait* (1971, 21 minutes), an American Film Institute-sponsored film about dancer Ann Halprin; *Holding* (1971, 13 minutes), about two women falling in love with each other. Other Beeson films: *Watercress* (13 minutes), *Stamen* (6 minutes), *Women* (12 minutes), *Firefly* (6 minutes).

Beeson prefers to work alone or with just a sound-person. She explains: "I like to keep people and equipment at a minimum when I shoot. If I bring along a tripod I rarely end up using it. I like to work with the person or people in the scene with no one else around. There is an intimacy, an understanding, and an excitement that belongs to the scene, and there are many times when I could not have gotten a scene if there had been the slightest outside disturbance. The kind of films I make are delicate; they could not be made with an audience. I want to shoot life and real feelings being felt at the instant I am shooting. I was a still photographer for so long that there is an instinctive compositional feel on my part to capture the fleeting glance, the quick nuance. What I always seek is to make a special reality of that moment when bare feet touch hot sand."

How does a married woman with children manage a career in film? It's not too difficult, says Beeson, if you have money coming in, if you can organize your time, if you can keep your sense of humor, and if you can maintain a flow of ideas despite the inevitable distractions. It's also important to have a cooperative family, which she has. "I like to cook," she says, "so most of the time I do the cooking, but I don't think it's necessarily a woman's job to cook or even get the food—though I admit I'd feel guilty not doing it. I don't think the kids are necessarily the woman's sole job either, but most of the time I make it my first concern. I find this rather easy to do. And I compulsively do the housework first thing on getting up. I like combining my home and my studio."

HORTENSE BEVERIDGE, New York, was part of a group of young black artists, writers and filmmakers who came together in the early 1950s to inspire and help each other under the auspices of the Committee for the Negro in the Arts in Harlem. "Today it might be called a consciousness-raising group," says Beveridge, "but at that time we had no label for it. We were just a group of people looking for ways to expand and express ourselves." When they discovered that there were almost no black technicians in the film industry, the Committee set up an informal school where rudimentary filmmaking skills were taught. Beveridge learned the basics of editing, and went on to become the first black woman admitted into the film editors union.

"Even though our school operated on practically no money and was a very casual, free-spirited operation, some of the top people in the field came to teach us, such as Joe Kohn, the director; Leo Hurwitz, the director and editor; and cameraman Richard Leacock. We learned by doing—we went out into the community and shot newsreels of neighborhood activities and events. It was an excellent way to learn, and almost all of us who were in the school then are working in the film industry today."

Despite its success, the film school was short-lived because the Committee for the Negro in the Arts ran afoul of Senator Joseph McCarthy and his investigating committee. "We were agitating for change in the creative arts, and that alone made us suspect," Beveridge says. The Committee landed on the Attorney-General's list of "subversive" groups, and used up its meager financial resources in a futile legal battle to clear its name. The group fell apart, but many of its members subsequently rose to prominence, including authors John Killens, Rosa Guy and Alice Childress.

In breaking into the film industry, Beveridge encountered hostility primarily because she was a woman, she feels. "At that time, New York was a center for newsreel productions, and the field was totally dominated by men." Opportunities for women began to open as New York also became a center for the production of commercials. Beveridge's first job was as an apprentice in a commercial editing firm; then she became an assistant and eventually an editor.

"I supported myself with commercials, but by the 1960s my main interest was in doing films on the civil rights movement. I got together with others to film various demonstrations and marches on Washington. We didn't do this for money—we gave these films to organizations like the NAACP. Also, we trained people in the Student Non-Violent Coordinating Committee to make their own films. Our concern was mainly in the area of social documentaries, whereas many of today's young filmmakers are more involved in self-expression. I don't mean this as a put-down, it's just that our orientation was different."

Beveridge was Director of Photography and Films for Bedford Stuyvesant Youth in Action in 1964. She was associate producer and editor of *Morris, Time to Make It*, an abstract film about the ghetto, that was made in 1972 for the New York City Youth Board. More recently, she edited *Honey Baby—Honey Baby*, a feature-length thriller starring the late Diana Sands, which is due to be released in 1975. For the past eight years, Beveridge has been an editor at Professional Films, Inc., which produces promotional featurettes.

SUE BOOKER, Los Angeles, is the only black woman director on the West Coast who is currently a member of the Directors Guild of America. From 1970 to 1973 she was a director, producer and writer for KCET-TV, the public television station in Los Angeles, where she worked on documentaries, videotape series and special features. After leaving KCET-TV to freelance, she produced a program for KNBC-TV, *As*

Adam Early in the Morning, which won an emmy as the best entertainment special in the Los Angeles area in 1973.

Recognition did not come easily. She points out that often she was not given director's credit for her television films. She was finally able to join the Directors Guild with the support of KNBC.

Booker got started in film in 1968, after receiving a master's degree in journalism from Columbia University. She worked as a girl-Friday on a film that was being shot on location in New York, and then became a production assistant for the Children's Television Workshop. She stayed on this job for nine months before heading west—to Lincoln, Nebraska—to be associate producer for a national PBS film series on the history of blacks in the American West, a project funded by the Ford Foundation. Booker produced and wrote one of the four films in this series, *The Exodusters,* and was associate producer of the others.

Later, while working in Los Angeles on KCET-TV, she founded "The Storefront," a community news bureau serving the black population of south central Los Angeles. "The Storefront"—located, literally, in a storefront in the heart of the community—also served as a studio for a weekly public affairs program on black news and cultural events.

Among the television films and documentaries Booker has worked on are: *Compton: A Restless Dream* (1974, KNBC); *And Now the Children* (1973, KCET); *Just Another Day* (1973, KCET); *Walk On, Vinnegar* (1972, KCET, later broadcast nationally by PBS); and *Soledad* (1971, KCET).

SHEILA BOOTH, Half Moon Bay, California, works on sound in independent productions with her husband, Larry. They have opened a film school in Half Moon Bay (near San Francisco). Larry Booth's films are often abstract, and the sound that Sheila provides accounts for a good measure of their success. *The Rose,* a film about childbirth—in which she was the subject and did the sound as well—made them eligible for a $10,000 grant from the American Film Institute in 1969. On her very sophisticated sound equipment, Sheila Booth also creates "sound paintings—an audio film you can watch in your head" for radio and recordings.

"In my particular working situation," says Booth, "I've had no problem with discrimination, but then I've been working with tape recorders for fifteen years. My hassles have been with the unions, not with men. Now I work non-union, with non-union crews on location. The crew is always male, and I've had no static at all. A lot of gallantry and no static. If you know what you're doing and are not uptight about sexual discrimination, there appears to be no problem. I've climbed through cattle pens to record sync sound for auctions, done interviews under the best conditions, and sync sound for an anti-war film under really nasty conditions. The thing I've found important is not being 'one of the boys,' but being one of the crew and really knowing your tools."

LIANE BRANDON, Brighton, Massachusetts, teaches film production and media studies at the University of Massachusetts at Amherst. She became a filmmaker when she began helping her students make films as an alternative to traditional classroom teaching methods.

Many of Brandon's films have feminist themes. In *Anything You Want to Be* (1971, 8 minutes), she humorously portrays the conflicts and absurdities that beset a high school girl who tries to break out of her traditional sex role. The girl wants to be class president but is coerced into running for class secretary; she goes to the guidance counselor determined to become a doctor, but comes away wearing a nurse's cap and clutching a bedpan; her chemistry texts mysteriously turn into "The Joy of Cooking."

Brandon's other films include *Not So Young Now As Then* (1974, 18 minutes), about a high school class's reunion; *Betty Tells Her Story* (1972, 20 minutes), a study of a woman's anxiety about beauty and status; and *Sometimes I Won-*

der Who I Am (1970, 5 minutes), a sympathetic look at a young mother's dilemma.

"The roughest part of filmmaking is getting the money," Brandon says. "If you work as an independent you have to hunt for grants, borrow money from friends and borrow equipment. Even if you've gotten some recognition and won awards, there's still a constant hassle for money."

Distribution of independent films is another problem. New Day Films, a distribution cooperative that Brandon helped found several years ago, deals specifically with feminist films. "At first our films went only to metropolitan areas," Brandon says, "but now they are going to towns I never even heard of. In the last four years our films have reached over 800 groups, as diverse as the Girl Scouts, a women's prison in Kansas, a consciousness-raising group in Texas, and Mademoiselle magazine.

But Brandon does not want to be stereotyped as a feminist filmmaker. "Now that people are accepting women's films about women, they want us to make only films about women. I don't want to be forced into this position. I don't want to deal only with women's issues. Women should have the freedom to deal with any subject that concerns us as human beings."

CHRIS BURRILL, Beverly Hills, is a cinematographer, director and editor. In the graduate program at the University of Southern California she directed *King Arthur* (15 minutes), the secret world of a young boy in the country. She also did camera for *Prizefight* (20 minutes), the choreography of a fight. More recently she co-edited *Brazil—A Report on Torture* (Haskell Wexler—Saul Landau), directed *Victim* (12 minutes), and was assistant cinematographer for Francine Parker's *Free the Army Show* (as it is known in polite circles).

WENDY WOOD CHAPPLE, Storrs, Connecticut, became interested in directing while at Stanford. Her many educational and industrial films include *New Design for Education* (28 minutes); *More Different Than Alike* (27 minutes), about innovations in education across the country; *Teaching the One and the Many* (28 minutes); the award winning *Promises to Keep* (28 minutes), about inner-city poverty projects; and *Yankee Craftsman* (20 minutes), which compares work done by an old cabinet-maker with modern factory methods. This last film won a Cine Award. Her more recent films are *Alcoholism: Industry's Hangover* (28 minutes), and *America at Sea* (20 minutes).

Says Chapple: "The most difficult thing for me to accomplish as a filmmaker was to find a job. I'm sure women do have an advantage in getting some film jobs because of their attractiveness to men—secretarial jobs, 'assistant' this or that, make-believe jobs of all kinds. Most women will work harder and accept less pay for these jobs, as they will in any profession. But if, as a woman, you apply for a traditional man's job—forget it! My first job offer after I received my MA in Communications from Stanford was from a man who had advertised in the San Francisco Chronicle for a camera girl. I replied to the ad and was asked for my measurements. Naively, I thought it must have something to do with the size or shape of the camera I was going to be carrying around. He asked me what kind of film I was particularly interested in and was delighted when I responded, 'Documentary.' He, too, was interested in documentary-type films—mainly involving 'interracial sexual events.' Apparently I was going to be the event.

"The second most difficult thing about being a woman in film is a lack of technical knowledge. Everything I have learned I learned the hard way. Things men are brought up knowing from childhood (building ham radios, etc., while I was playing with dolls) I have had to teach myself. What is a watt, a circuit, an ohm—how do you fix a motor, wire a lamp? All of these things you *have* to know to be a competent independent filmmaker.

"I do wish I had been taught at film school how to light a set, how many lights a certain circuit can take, etc. I think this lack of training in technical details of film affects women more than men, because most men do have the basics.

"Third problem: Most sync cameras, fully loaded, are too heavy for me to carry around a day at a time. I would probably hire a male cameraman myself for any project I did involving long, hand-held moving-camera scenes. I did carry around a blimped Arri in England for two weeks and almost broke my back (I was in bed for two weeks). However, I think this problem will be overcome as cameras become lighter—and they are becoming lighter every day. At present, though, when I go out to shoot my own films I am pretty much limited to non-sync cameras unless I use a tripod, and this is a handicap."

Being a woman, Chapple has found, sometimes has its advantages. "Very often on locations I get help from men that I suspect would not be offered to men filmmakers. I am very often given company electricians and extra help to carry my equipment from place to place. On the other hand, I find I often have to pay for this sort of help by getting into sticky situations with the opposite sex."

Chapple's advice to women considering a career in film: "Get a good grounding in all those boring, maddening details of electricity and basic mechanics. And marry a good man."

ABIGAIL CHILD, New York, a graduate of Radcliffe and Yale's School of Art and Architecture, was a still photographer before going into filmmaking. She produced, shot, and edited several documentaries before directing her first film, *Game* (1972, 90 minutes), a documentary about a hooker and her pimp. The film combines *cinéma-vérité* and psychodrama to explore their lifestyles and motivations. Above all, it is a vision of how Tina and Slim see themselves. Her other films include *Except the People* (20 minutes), *Mother Marries a Man of Mellow Mien* (7 minutes), *Will You Still Be a*

Mother? (23 minutes), and *Savage Streets* (24 minutes). Her most recent film, *Angel Baby*—about a woman on the verge of insanity—is being produced with the help of a grant from the American Film Institute.

What problems has she faced as a woman? "What's most difficult," she says, "is to convince people that I am responsible and able, and to sustain that conviction myself. I suppose it is a problem for both men and women, but I feel additional pressure to be 'responsible and able' in everything: as a filmmaker, businesswoman, cook, and womanly woman. Though I have decided to forego everything for film and am happiest when working on my own project, I still find I want to eat, love, and live well. I think a large part of the incompatability of these things stems from the basic unreality between an education and an upbringing promising 'everything will be yours if you work at it' and a film world in which women are second-class and money rules.

"As for specifics, it is difficult for me to deal with a 400-foot-load sync camera for a long time because I am small. I have never met with direct discrimination, though Bill Jersey suggested once that my husband should make the presentation of our ideas because he had found that in conferences with producers they do not listen to a wife.

"The advantage of being a woman is that I appear unthreatening and so, in some cases, achieve easier success. While filming pimps, for example, I found they would talk to me, viewing me as some sort of 'crazy woman' who could probably be persuaded to join their stable. I didn't, but their attempt is on film."

Phyllis Chinlund, New York, who studied at Smith and Stanford, has been working mainly in the production of training films for personnel in health and social welfare. An early film was *If You Want to Be a Camper* (28 minutes), dealing with a summer camp for diabetic children. *Robin, Peter and Darryl: Three to the Hospital* (53 minutes) is an excellent study of three hospitalized children frightened at being separated from their parents. ("I'll be back in a few minutes," says one mother—and leaves for the day.) *Two Worlds to Remember* looks at the problems of the aged in a nursing home without attempting to provide any answers to the problems. Like life itself, the film just ends. *Family Planning: More Than a Method* (27 minutes), for volunteer workers in family-planning centers, shows a cross-section of women being interviewed by a counselor.

(All the films mentioned above were made under Chinlund's married name, Phyllis Johnson.)

JOYCE CHOPRA, Cambridge, Massachusetts, entered film as an apprentice to Richard Leacock and D. A. Pennebaker in 1960, and has made films on a variety of topics. She codirected and edited a film on quintuplets, *A Happy Mother's Day* (28 minutes), with Richard Leacock (and although she received equal screen credit, it is invariably referred to as Leacock's film). She has made films on a rock group's bid for fame, *The Wild Ones* (54 minutes), and on the role of environment in pre-school learning, *Room to Learn* (22 minutes). She co-directed the widely-acclaimed *Joyce at 34* (1972, 29 minutes) with Claudia Weill. This film is especially relevant for women filmmakers who are considering having children. It is about Chopra's first pregnancy, at age 34, and the baby's first year. Emphasis is on the equal sharing by husband and wife in the raising of children, and there is a wonderful scene in which her husband, writer Tom Cole, feeds the baby while discussing a plot outline with a fellow writer. The film was a winner at the Venice Film Festival.

JULEEN COMPTON, Bel Air, California, began her career as an actress in New York at sixteen, and studied film at New York University and later in Paris. She first won attention as an independent filmmaker at Cannes with an out-of-competition showing of her first film, *Stranded*, an avant-garde comedy about three hippies on a summer cruise through the Aegean. The film was enough of a success in Europe to pay off the investors. After returning to the United States, Compton raised $125,000 for *The Plastic Dome of Norma Jean*, which she wrote and directed in the high-art manner of the French *nouvelle vague*. A fantasy set within a realistic context, *Norma Jean* is the story of a naïve clairvoyant who is cruelly exploited by a showbusiness promoter. Completed in 1966, the film received the Special Award at the San Francisco Film Festival and the Jury's Grand Prize at the Cannes Festival, and was widely distributed in Europe. Compton's more recent work is a documentary, *Women in Action*, a history of women directors in Hollywood.

MARTHA COOLIDGE, New York, a producer and director, became involved in filmmaking while studying at the Rhode Island School of Design in 1965. Her first films were self-financed, and were used to obtain sponsor backing. In 1972 she made *David: Off and On* (42 minutes), a portrait of her addict brother, which has been shown twice on NET. With this film she won the first John Grierson Award for the best young documentary filmmaker at the American Film Festival in 1973. Her other films are *More Than a School* (1973, 55 minutes) and *Old-Fashioned Woman* (1974, 45 minutes). The latter film, a portrait of her grandmother, was partially financed by a grant from the National Endowment for the Arts. Coolidge has taken an option on the novel, *The Desert*, for her first full-length feature. She organized the Association of Independent Video and Filmmakers with Ed Emshwiller and Ed Lynch.

SHARON COUZIN, Goleta, California, teaches film aesthetics in the College of Creative Studies of the University of California at Santa Barbara, and heads her own production firm, Augenlust Films. Her 1974 experimental art film *Roseblood* (7 minutes), won the Silver Medal at the Atlanta International Film Festival, and Second Prize at the Ann Arbor 8mm Film Festival.

She functions as producer, director, camerawoman, sound recorder, writer and editor on all her films. Among her other works are *True Flick* (1973, 4 minutes), *Nimbusodilongradiva* (1973, 7 minutes), *Dance for Well-Spaced Teeth* (1972, 5 minutes) and *Some* (1972, 5 minutes).

NELL COX, New York, is an independent producer-director and head of Nell Cox Films. Now a highly-regarded veteran, her work spans a wide range of film activities. She wrote, produced, directed, and edited *French Lunch* (15 minutes), shot in the kitchen of the renowned La Caravelle restaurant; *Operator* (15 minutes), a recruiting film for AT&T; and *A to B* (36 minutes), a sensitive film about a sixteen-year-old girl in a conservative Kentucky town who learns to identify with progressive new friends. The film won a 1974 Cine Golden Eagle Award. The same year, Cox completed *Trial* (54 minutes), a documentary of a murder trial.

"There are so many more women working in films now than when I started," Cox observes. "And it's so pleasant. It's not just me up there. And men don't apologize when they swear. They're getting used to us. Someone actually turned me down for a job one time when I was on the verge of starvation because he said the men around me wouldn't be able to be free with their language!"

On her background: "I started out as an apprentice editor with the whole *cinéma-vérité* movement—Ricky Leacock and Pennebaker, the Maysles brothers, and Bob Drew, when they were just beginning. Quite a few women got their start there. Ricky would fight for me, so I got to go out and take sound, which is really important. If you are ultimately going to produce and direct, you really have to get out of the editing room and into the field.

"Eventually I got associate producer credits, too, which meant I helped decide where to film, and went out on locations. That was a great opportunity to learn. But in the very beginning, though, I was an apprentice editor and logged quarter-inch tapes on a typewriter."

Her advice to newcomers: "I was working with a woman once, editing a short film with her. She was so competent, so sharp. We spent three days, really intense, editing. Then the producers came in. And she became a person I couldn't believe. They teased her, practically pinching her cheeks, it was that kind of thing. And she played their game!

"A lot of guys will come in and tease you and say, 'Aren't you cute!' It's easy to fall into that. Never let them do it, unless they're really good friends and you know where you stand."

STORM DE HIRSCH, New York, a published poet, is one of the few women filmmakers honored with a mention in Lewis Jacobs' "The Emergence of Film Art" (possibly because the increase in women making films has become truly conspicuous only since that book was published in 1969).

Her many abstract and experimental films include *Journey Around a Zero* (1963, 3 minutes); *Goodbye in the Mirror* (1964), a dramatic feature about three women living in Rome; and the impressive color trilogy titled: *The Color of Ritual, The Color of Thought*, which consists of *Divinations* (1964, 26 minutes), *Peyote Queen* (1965, 8 minutes), and *Shaman* (1966, 12 minutes). She uses many innovative technical devices in her films, including the frame-by-frame etching of the oxide layer of 16mm sound film to produce visual effects, black-and-white negative and paint-on-film. She also performed the fast, twangy music that sets the mood for the visuals—a Maori chant and a Sicilian tarantella.

Her *Sing Lotus* (1966, 18 minutes) is an exotic landscape of Indian miniatures, and *Cayuga Run* (1966, 12 minutes) is a contemplative film about a train named Cayuga. *Third Eye Butterfly* (1968, 10 minutes), an adventure in dual-screen projection, won the Maryland Film Festival Award. De

Hirsch won the American Film Institute's first independent film grant for *The Tattooed Man* (1969, 35 minutes). The live images in *The Tattooed Man* (naked man, ginkgo tree, water reflections) create patterns similar to the calligraphic style of her trilogy. A more recent film, *An Experiment in Meditation* (1971, 18 minutes), is an investigation of memory and change.

JOHANNA DEMETRAKAS, Tujunga, California, broadened her work in 1974 by directing *Womanhouse*, an imaginative 47-minute documentary based on a project of the Feminist Art Program at the California Institute of the Arts headed by Judy Chicago and Miriam Shapiro. The project involved acquiring an old mansion in Hollywood and altering its interior "to search out the female experience . . . the dreams and fantasies of women as they have sewed, cooked, washed and ironed their lives away." Demetrakas' film, which combines a tour of the house with interviews and glimpses of the sponsoring group's consciousness-raising sessions, was described by one reviewer as "warmly comical, chilling, and finally almost devastating in its impact."

Demetrakas, a 1959 graduate of the Rhode Island School of Design, got into film as an art editor, then began editing. (Her editing credits include the features *Naked Angel, Once There Was a Flower* and *Caged Heat.*) With her husband, Baird Bryant, she co-directed *Celebration at Big Sur*, a feature-length documentary of a rock festival, and the success of this film pointed her toward a directing career. In the summer of '74 she taught filmmaking at a new Buddhist school, the Naropa Institute, in Boulder, Colorado. She has begun work on a documentary about the institute.

KAYE FINCH, Madison, Wisconsin, received a degree in filmmaking from Bob Jones University in 1961 and subsequently went to work as a film editor for the National Aeronautics and Space Administration, making films about the seven original astronauts and their space adventures. Later she made industrial films in Iowa and Tennessee, and for a time she headed the Motion Picture Unit of the University of Iowa.

Her films there were *Elusive Shadow* (15 minutes) and *Blindness Is* (28 minutes), both of which she directed and edited, and *Quartet* (57 minutes), which she wrote, produced, and edited. *Elusive Shadow*, about still photography, conveys a veneration for subject matter while at the same time suggesting techniques for obtaining good pictures. *Blindness Is*, narrated by Danny Kaye, is the story of young people in a school for the blind. *Quartet* is a documentary about a professional string quartet, including a performance of music by Haydn. Finch hopes to make theatrical films in the future, and is working on an idea for a television series. She is now at the University of Wisconsin, where she has written, directed, and edited *The Plan, Quarry, Kitchen,* and *Buzz* (all 1972), a series of shorts for teenagers on the subjects of drinking and driving.

CINDA FIRESTONE, New York, produced and directed her first film in 1973, and it was a blockbuster. The film was *Attica*, a documentary of the 1971 prison uprising in which forty-three died and more than 200 were wounded.

The idea of doing a film on Attica first took hold when Firestone was writing a piece for the Liberation News Service based on taped interviews with some of the prisoners. At first she thought of doing a 5- to 10-minute film combining the tapes with some still photographs, but as she got deeper into it her ardor grew. With a great deal of persistence she got footage from NET and then bought additional footage from UPI and an ABC subsidiary. One further step remained —a visit to Attica to shoot the grim confines of the place in order to provide a better understanding of what happened there. This part of the project started badly. On the way up her cameraman confided he couldn't see how a mere slip of a girl could handle the job and he predicted a lousy film. Aware of her lack of experience, it had a shattering effect, but the worst was still to come—the prison itself. No amount of research could have prepared her for the terrifying impact of the brutalizing environment she found there. For all the battering, Firestone's sense of mission was never shaken, and when the work of editing began, her confidence in what she was doing was restored. And fortunately so. For what she produced was a searing indictment of the conditions that led to this tragedy: ineptness and cowardice in high places and a penal system that corrupts the instincts of humanity and reduces them to unspeakable malevolence.

Distributed by Newsreel, Tri-Continental and the Attica Defense Committee, the film has evoked outrage throughout the United States and incredulity in Europe, where it has been widely shown in theaters and on television. Vincent Canby of the Times called it "a superior example of committed filmmaking . . . an exceptionally moving outraged recollection of that terrible event." The New Yorker's Penelope Gilliatt described it as "an aching, precise study." She said "If Attica disturbed our slumber for a month or two, one of the qualities of this trumpet-call of a film is that it makes the disturbance enduring."

Attica was first released in October, 1973, and had its premiere at the Mannheim (German) Film Festival, where it received the only unanimous choice for a Golden Ducat. Additional awards at other international festivals followed. In 1974 it won the John Grierson Award.

Although Firestone's experience in filmmaking was limited to a brief association as assistant editor for the documentary filmmaker Emile de Antonio (her job mainly was putting away film trimmings), she had some positive things going for her. Not the least of these was the financial support she got from her family, the Firestones of rubber fame. It was her family that put up the $40,000 needed to make the film. Incidentally, first year profits from U.S. distribution went to the

Attica Defense Committee to help cover the legal costs of prisoners still facing charges.

Her next film: a documentary examining the abuses of another beleaguered segment of our society, the aged.

LYNN CONNOR FISCHER, Virginia Beach, Virginia, entered film production after acting in fifty films and working as an account executive in an advertising agency. She produces and directs television commercials and industrial films, and has often written and edited films as well. She comments:

"Films, like other pursuits in the business world, cost money, and are financed by people who expect a profit. Books must be kept, releases signed, exotic equipment rented, talent hired, and large groups of diversified people handled.

"It's a big order, and usually women just haven't had the opportunity to get the necessary experience. If a film backer sees two filmmakers with equal experience, he'll pick the man to make the film every time. He feels that even if the woman is an expert in all the facets of filmmaking, she might not be able to handle male subordinates. But that is not true at all. Ask any man who has worked for a woman. If he respects her and her work, he is just as loyal and hard-working as he would be if his boss were male. I know, I've been there. But it's difficult to convince men of that, unless *they've* been there.

"I'll never forget the first production conference I had with a group of men from a production company. I was the client, hence the over-all producer. They had never seen me, and because my name is Lynn I suppose they thought I was a man. Anyhow, as I went into the conference room to sit at one of the eight chairs I was greeted with 'Hi, honey.' Someone asked, 'Are you going to serve coffee?' It took a while before they could get adjusted to the idea that the client was not *Mr.* Connor but Miss Connor."

She got her start as a filmmaker in an indirect way. She was working as an actress in an industrial film and one day told the man in charge she thought the film could be improved. "He stopped production," she recalls, "and I rewrote the script. Incidentally, I wrote myself out of it because I was too old for the kind of film they needed. He accepted it piece by piece and I finally filmed and edited it."

What advice does she have for the aspiring filmmaker? "Go into editing," she says. "That way you're hidden from the client. Forget about joining a directors' or cameramans' or sound union. Production is damn hard too. Be an assistant something or other. There's always an assistant producer who's a woman. Be a secretary to a producer. Learn who his clients are, what costs are, and all the details of filmmaking, then compete directly against him."

She sums up her experience as a woman filmmaker this way: "Being a woman has meant that I've had to work harder and make damn sure I didn't make any mistakes."

BONNIE FRIEDMAN, New York, a camerawoman, editor and director, has been concentrating on films that deal with alternative life styles for women. In *Chris and Bernie* (1974, 30 minutes), she studies two single mothers from different class backgrounds, and the alternatives they have chosen for themselves and their children. Among her other films are *How About You?* (24 minutes), about birth control and sexuality; and *Childcare: People's Liberation* (20 minutes), a documentary showing how a group of people formed their own day care center. Friedman is a member of Pandora Films, a women's film collective.

CHARLOTTE GAFFORD, Birmingham, Alabama, is a writer and head of the story department of the Interlock Film Studio. She works with industrial and documentary films, but hopes eventually to work in the experimental and/ or theatrical fields. The films she has written include *Fiesta '65* (28 minutes), *Cut Through the City* (17 minutes), *A New Look at the Old Address* (28 minutes), *On With the*

Flow (20 minutes), and *Born to Build*.

Says Gafford: "Men in commerce and industry never say anything to *me* about doubting my ability to write a technical script because I am a woman. My male colleagues tell me that the clients sometimes mention this doubt to them. They come on strong in my behalf because I happen to have done some extensive engineering, construction, industrial, and technological freelance writing in a variety of media."

JILL GODMILOW, New York, and folksinger Judy Collins turned out the most successful full-length documentary of 1974, *Antonia: A Portrait of the Woman*. The film, which describes the life of Antonia Brico, the indomitable seventy-three-year-old conductor, opened the New American Filmmakers Series at the Whitney Museum and got raves. "It is a feminist documentary about the still overwhelmingly male chauvinist world of classical music, made by women working in the male chauvinist world of film," Grace Lichtenstein observed in the Times. "Yet it delivers its message with a kiss, not a punch in the nose." Nora Sayre, also writing in the Times, commented: "*Antonia* is biographical cinema at its best, and it will also encourage many women in fields other than music, thanks to Dr. Brico's determination, her refusal to be defeated. The film ends, as it should, with bravos and applause."

It was Judy Collins who came up with the idea of making this film. She had been one of Dr. Brico's students in the fifties (when Collins was an aspiring concert pianist) and had stayed in touch with her teacher through the years. Collins brought Godmilow into the project, and for the next six months the two women, with a small camera crew, followed Dr. Brico through her daily activities—including her music classes and performances with her symphony orchestra in Denver. The cost of the film eventually stretched to $75,000, which was borne by Collins' company, Rocky Mountain Productions, but the end product was worth it, and the collaboration, despite occasional shouting matches, was a satisfying one.

Jill Godmilow, the team's professional filmmaker, got her start in films in the most casual way. Here's how she tells it:

"I had a Puerto Rican boyfriend who was a painter (and wasn't middle class and over-educated like me), and one day he said to me 'Let's make a film,' and I said 'We can't. It's a very tricky thing to do and we don't know anything.' He said, 'That's okay. We'll make it in Spanish for the Puerto Rican market. P.R. films are terrible—full of beautiful blondes and handsome dark men in nightclubs—so we can make every mistake in the book and still come out with a good film. We'll show how it really is in Spanish Harlem—no nightclubs, no blondes.'

"So, in 1967 we made a black-and-white feature film for $2,000, *La Nueva Vida*. But we ran out of money in the editing stage, and one of us had to get a job where there was editing equipment. I volunteered, and after going around to about eighty companies, one of them finally hired me to sync up 10,000 feet of around-the-world Quaker Oats dailies—something with nuts and raisins in it. And that was it, I was hooked. I came down with a chronic case of editing fever, and after that I learned all about commercials (which is an excellent way to develop technique and skills because companies spend so much money on sixty seconds of film).

"*La Nueva Vida* still sits in a closet somewhere, unmixed and unloved. Nevertheless, my career was launched and I spent three years in the commercial game until I noticed I was getting fat and lazy on my weekly staff salary. I cut the cord and entered the world of freelance, where I have been ever since."

As a freelancer, Godmilow cut documentaries for KQED in San Francisco, and then in 1969 made a film with Cassandra Gerstein, *Tales* (70 minutes), a documentary about people's attitudes towards their own sexuality. "Now that I've had a taste of directing," she says, "I find I'm loath to sit down and work on editorial solutions to other people's film problems—unless, of course, its really interesting and they give you some space, some credit, and some money."

After finishing *Antonia*, Godmilow directed a 60-minute documentary for WNBC-TV, *Where Do All the Mentally Ill Go?*, which probes into the New York State Department of Mental Health, and explores the problems of mental patients after they are released from hospitals.

Godmilow says: "I worry a lot about what's happening with film schools these days. It takes too much time and costs too much money to learn techniques that could be learned out in the real world. Also, it is unrealistic, perhaps unfair, for film schools to turn out thousands of graduates a year into an industry with so many unemployed. Why not pay people to learn in beginners' jobs instead of in film schools? This is how the industry really works anyway."

DIANA GOULD, Los Angeles, graduated from UCLA in 1967 with a major in filmmaking. Her original screenplay, *Jenny*, a feature, was bought by a major film company and, in her words, "rewritten beyond recognition." Essentially, the story is about a pregnant young woman who marries a young man in need of a wife and child to avoid the draft. At the outset the wife thinks this is the solution to her problems, but she grows more independent and in the end leaves him. As rewritten in Hollywood, Jenny remains the same through the film and the man leaves *her* at the end. Having a screenplay rewritten is a common experience for writers in Hollywood, particularly new writers. What is significant about the doctoring of the script of *Jenny* is that the female character was made weaker (not stronger as the author intended) so that the focus could then shift to the male character.

AMY GREENFIELD, Cambridge, Massachusetts, a choreographer and filmmaker, makes dance films. She directs and edits, leaving the camerawork to someone else so that she can participate in the dances herself.

Greenfield has been making dance films since 1965. These include *Image to Remind Me* (13 minutes), a duet for woman and child; *Transport* (6 minutes), a duet for man and woman; *Dirt* (3 minutes), a solo dance by a woman; two educational films on dance, made for junior and senior high school audiences; and *Film in Progress* (12 minutes), another solo by a woman.

Greenfield describes the special situation of a woman filmmaker who is also involved in dance:

"Being a dancer/choreographer in a field where women are prevalent, and sometimes predominate, lessens my contact with prejudice against women. I was able to show my work and to be instructed by excellent filmmakers because they (male) dug my being a woman. They didn't feel the same kind of ego-competition hassles they might have felt with a male who asked the same kind of attention of them as teachers and helpers as I did."

MOLLIE GREGORY, Reno, Nevada, is co-owner and operator of Thunderbird Film Enterprises, Inc. She is the producer, editor, and writer for Thunderbird films, including *Cities Are for People* (25 minutes), a documentary on pollution, city planning, and prejudice in Las Vegas; *The Transportment of Ken Shores* (14 minutes), a documentary of a sculptor working in clay and feathers; *ERA and the American Way* (1974, 20 minutes), a study of the issues involved in the inception and passage of the Equal Rights Amendment; and *Welfare: Exploding the Myths* (an 18-minute documentary which she directed as well). Mollie Gregory discussed some of the benefits which accrue to women in filmmaking:

"If she is starving, I imagine a woman can always get a foot in the door as a secretary or research assistant. In terms of my own film business, I've discovered that other business people (the competition) are more likely to tell you about their projects with candor, because a woman in the business still doesn't seem like much of a threat. Then, too, if a woman says she 'doesn't understand' something, a man is likely to go into greater detail to 'teach' her—by giving her even more information about the competition."

Says Gregory: "The jobs I got were never what I wanted, so I formed my own business to create exactly my kind of films, edited in my kind of way.

"The problem for women, of course, is outright discrimination. Most of all it consists of (a) not being taken seriously when she applies for a film job, and (b) if she manages to get one, not being treated in a professional manner by male co-workers."

DEEDEE HALLECK, Stony Point, New York, began working in movies at the age of sixteen as an inker and opaquer in a small animation studio in Chattanooga. "I worked with an old-time animator who claimed to have originated Felix the Cat. I went after school and during vacations for fifty cents an hour." After attending Antioch College she moved to New York to study at Pratt Institute. She got a job as an art teacher at the Lillian Wald Community Center, and it was here that her interest in filmmaking came alive. The kids, she found, were fascinated with film, so she helped them make one. "The film we made, *Children Make Movies*, was one of the first to involve kids in the medium," she says.

Halleck also worked at New York's Henry Street Settlement, and here, too, her program of activities concentrated on film. At this center she produced *The Mural on Our Street*, a documentary on a mural project; it was nominated for an Academy Award in 1964 and won a Cine Golden Eagle.

Halleck later introduced a successful film program at the Otisville School for Boys, a state correctional institution. The program drew wide interest among education officials, and films made at the school were shown throughout the state at professional meetings.

Halleck's own films include the documentary *Jaraslawa*, a 10-minute study of an old woman, with background music by a women's folk singing group, the Penny-Whistlers. She received a grant of $10,000 from the National Endowment for the Arts for a 40-minute experimental documentary, *Halleluia: Domestic Resurrection Circus*, about the Bread and Puppet Theatre. Other films are *Mr. Story* (1973, 30 minutes), which she made with Anita Thacher; *Morag* (30 minutes), a lyrical portrait of batik artist Morag Benepe; *Peter Pie* (8 minutes), about Halleck's son; and *Drawing Series # One*, a collaborative work with the French artist Jean Du Puy.

MARIA HARRITON, New York, was a dancer, choreographer and teacher before becoming a filmmaker and editor. Four 10-minute educational films she edited—*Cylinders, Boxes, Clay*, and *Sugar*—won a Golden Eagle Cine Award. *Nine Variations on a Dance Theme* (1966, 13 minutes), which she edited for Hilary Harris Films, won short-film awards at five international festivals.

Harriton was writer and editor of *Work* (1971, 15 minutes), a study of alienation among auto assembly workers, and has written, produced and directed *The Island* (1972, 7 minutes), a film about childhood. Among her other films are *The Draftcard Burners* (1966, 7 minutes), about anti-war protests in New York; and *Seafall* (10 minutes), a dance film featuring Michael Utoff and Lisa Bradley.

She comments, "It has been difficult for men to accept the idea that I could be as good with film machines as they, could handle 'masculine' subject matter in film, in fact was as intelligent or talented as they, or more so. Let's face it, a strong, creative woman is a threat to all but the best of men. I think the sensibilities I have developed in my experience of being a woman have helped me be more aware of the humane potentials of film, and to express myself in my work with freedom and security."

Amy Greenfield

Wendy Chapple

Barbara Kopple, with Hart Perry, after filming in a "low coal" mine which required crawling through a tunnel two feet high.

Louva Irvine, filming a reception at the Guggenheim Museum for *Portrait of Thomas Messer*, president of the museum.

Storm De Hirsch

Juleen Compton

Jean Hoelscher

ELDA HARTLEY, Cos Cob, Connecticut, began her film career in front of the camera, appearing in many silent and talking pictures, including the first color film ever made, *The Vagabond King*. Although she was on top of the world as an actress, she was still searching for the meaning of life until she discovered Buddhism. It brought her a spiritual revelation. "I knew then," she says, "that I wanted to do something for the good of mankind."

She gave up her acting career and studied for a master's degree in fine arts at Columbia University, then became North Carolina State Supervisor of Visual Education. It was in this job that she met her husband, Irving, a filmmaker. In 1964 the Hartleys took a trip to Japan guided by Alan Watts, the scholar of Eastern philosophies. One day, while meditating with the monks, she got an inspiration to do a film on Zen. Her husband didn't think it would work because they didn't have the right equipment, but gripped by a sudden fervor she insisted. "I shot in the rain," she recalls, "and broke every rule there was." The film, *The Mood of Zen* (14 minutes), narrated by Watts, won an award at the American Film Festival. It was the first of many awards to come. Since then she has become a prolific filmmaker and her husband has given up his own film career to concentrate on handling and distribution. Their company, Hartley Productions, specializes in philosophical and religious subjects, including studies of Zen, Yoga, and Buddhism, as well as psychic and scientific phenomena. Their films on ancient cultures include: *Requiem For a Faith* (28 minutes), a study of Tibetan Buddhist customs and traditions, narrated by Prof. Huston Smith of M.I.T.; *Psychics, Saints and Scientists* (35 minutes), a film on spiritual healing, biofeedback, ESP and brain-wave conditioning, which is narrated by Prof. Thelma Moss of U.C.L.A.; and *Islamic Mysticism—The Sufi Way* (27 minutes), a study of Islam and its mystic core, Sufism, which brought Hartley and her camera into mosques in India, Iran, Turkey, Morocco, and Tunisia. Recent films include two with

Capt. Edgar D. Mitchell, Apollo 14 astronaut. They are *Inner Spaces* (28 minutes), which explores "intuitive and religious ways of knowing," and *The Ultimate Mystery* (40 minutes), which presents scientific data supporting claims of mystics through the ages that there is a oneness to all living things.

ROBERTA HODES, New York, a feature-film script supervisor, produced, directed, edited, and did some of the photography on her excellent film, *The Game* (20 minutes), in which black children play abstract, dance-like games on city streets. As the film progresses the games become vicious and create problems the children are unable to cope with, symbolizing the frustrations and violence of the adult world. The film, in black and white, is directed and shot in a sharp abstract manner that is both visually and emotionally striking.

Hodes teaches film at New York University's Graduate Institute of Film and Television. She was script supervisor for *On the Waterfront, Rachel, Rachel,* and *Where's Poppa?*

JEAN HOELSCHER, Austin, Texas, was the first woman to graduate from the radio-television-film department of the University of Texas, where she received her MA in 1969. She and her husband, Clifford, run Film Enterprises, working together on all projects. They occasionally work on an independent basis for special film productions, but generally they initiate their own projects, seek out funding, and do most of the work themselves, from script work to negative cutting. Their company got its start with the assistance of several private investors. It was Jean's first job.

Their films include *Central Texas College* (15 minutes), a promotional film; *Join Hands* (14 minutes), for the Texas Conference of Churches; *Careers in Law Enforcement* (16 minutes); *War in the Crimea* (28 minutes); *Dust to Dust* (14 minutes), a prediction of a world without water; *Next Time No Brains* (14 minutes), about water pollution; *Before*

Gutenberg (16 minutes); *The Great Depression: A Human Diary* (52 minutes); and *For Such as We* (80 minutes). *For Such as We* combines still photographs and live action as a young man travels around the country trying to find a place the Great Depression has not touched.

"I don't expect any conflict between marriage and a career," says Jean Hoelscher, "because the two are so closely related in my case. Of course, I do worry that if and when we do have children, I may be out of the picture—no pun intended—as far as a career is concerned. But since we work at home and plan to continue to do so, no matter how successful we may be, I think we can work out our child-rearing responsibilities between us."

JOAN HORVATH, New York, was an off-Broadway producer and director before shooting her first film, *Nobody Goes There* (1965, 10 minutes), a documentary about Ellis Island. Her next effort, *Jenny Is a Good Thing* (1969, 18 minutes), a film about nutrition for Operation Head Start, won an Oscar nomination for best documentary short. After this success she formed a production company, Screenways, with editor Muriel Balash. They make educational films for children and "Sesame Street" shorts.

JILL HULTIN, Columbus, Ohio, switched from writing to the visual communication of filmmaking because of "pure frustration with *words!*" Her first film was *El Teatro Campesino: The Farmworkers' Theater* (1968, 30 minutes), which she directed and co-produced with Viki Hochberg. It is a documentary about the theatrical group that was formed during the grape strike and then broadened to communicate the culture and history of La Raza. In 1971 she directed *Sisters* (21 minutes), a surrealistic drama exploring some of the roles available to women in contemporary society. A young woman tries to warn her little sister of some of the traps awaiting women (all of which are neatly stylized):

domesticity, in the form of homelike car interiors; unceasing attempts to achieve beauty (we see two old women cajoled into beauty treatments by a white-uniformed attendant who could be a beautician—or deathbed nurse); and false "liberation" (glamour girl popping birth-control pills). In the last scene the older sister realizes that she is part of the social web that both of the sisters must try to break through.

In early 1971 Hultin and some friends established the Women's Film Co-op in New Haven, where she was living at the time. The co-op grew out of a need "to consolidate information on films about women and by women with specific data on where the films are available and how much they cost." It's now located in Northampton, Massachusetts. (See our directory of distributors.)

MARIAN HUNTER, New York, heads Herstory Films, Inc., a 16mm film production company specializing in films about women made by all-women crews. Among the films produced by the company are: *Just Married* (1974, 30 minutes), which focuses on the romantic myths and harsh realities of marriage; *Roll Over* (1974, 10 minutes), about sex-role stereotyping in employment; *Women for Women* (1972, 30 minutes), a view of the women's movement; and *The Feminist Party Streetwalks* (1972, 6 minutes).

Herstory Films was founded in 1972 by several women as a production cooperative. Marian Hunter and Pat Bertozzi were among the founders, and they produced and directed some of the films together. The company is no longer a collective, but "a corporation of one" with Hunter in charge.

LOUVA ELIZABETH IRVINE, New York, studied art, graphics and theater at the Art Students League and the School of Visual Arts, then went on to get her B.A. in filmmaking from the Hans Richter Institute at City College in New York. While still in school she wrote, directed and produced *Dig We Must* (10 minutes), about an artist's attempt to overcome Con Edison and find his inner light. It was shown on NET.

Her first film job was as script consultant to Charles Gordone on his feature, *From These Ashes* (1966). She continued to work with Gordone on the play "No Place to Be Somebody," as script consultant, production manager, and costume and set designer. The play won a Pulitzer Prize and several Obies. Irvine comments:

"I then began using all the talents I had acquired in the theater to make films. Every week I would buy film and shoot. I made 200 short films which are studies of time as a spatial element."

Notable among her films are *Rain* (10 minutes), a pixilated live animation film. "I shot from an overhead angle on the corner of 33rd and 3rd, choreographing in the rain. I worked with 11- and 22-frame counts to see what kind of energy I could get. The result was a happy, energetic film." *Elegy for My Sister* (10 minutes) "is a very slowed-down tone poem for my sister who died in 1972. I photographed sun, sand, and people on the beach in winter trying to understand what my sister's leaving this plane was all about."

Irvine's other film projects include *Three Lives* (1971, 70 minutes), a documentary made with an all-female crew, revealing the consciousness of three women; and *Circus* (1972, 20 minutes), a triple-screen fantasy circus made with 100 children in collaboration with John Daryl Clegg.

"I feel responsible about communications," Irvine says. "I think of it as an art, not an industry. The artist is in touch with something universal which she wants to translate into a vision and the work is an attempt to perfect that translated vision. One reason for working independently is that I don't want that vision watered down, having to hassle with the needs of unions and producers. In some respects it's easier as a woman because no one knows what to expect. I work a lot on my intuition and trust it. As a woman I can get away with saying that's how I feel, while a man would have to intellectualize his feelings to have them accepted."

Advice to young filmmakers: "The best way to learn is by doing—make films. Get yourself a camera you can afford and start shooting. Even if you work for others you have to understand what they're doing and that comes from attempting it yourself. Get in touch with your ideal. Stay with it. Keep that vision."

BARBARA ISAACS, New York, is moving from documentary to dramatic films. *Marie and Henry* (1966, 20 minutes), one of her first films, is a documentary of four seasons in the lives of an elderly couple in the rural Midwest. *Fifteen Women* (18 minutes) is an intimate visual description of women who lead disparate professional lives (including NBC's Barbara Walters). In *Revolution for Two* (10 minutes), two young people drift around, engaging in trivial talk as they pass through a peace rally, a riot, and an atomic attack, illustrating that not all young people are as responsible or concerned as they should be.

LINDA JASSIM, Santa Monica, California, has done camera and editing on a variety of independent films. Her most interesting film, made in 1971, is only 10 minutes long but has great impact. Called *Cycles,* it is a dance film that transforms a vicious rape into an agonizing rebirth. Another film, *The Tub,* is a short abstract study of femaleness, as a woman (never seen totally) mutely scrubs. She also directed and edited *Venice ½ and ½,* and has received a $5,000 grant from the American Film Institute for a documentary on a prostitute. In 1973-74 she held an AFI directing fellowship, with a $1,000 James Cagney Scholarship living stipend.

KAREN JOHNSON, Northridge, California, first summoned attention to her work in 1969 with her voluptuous 3-minute short, *Orange.* Enormous closeups of the dripping, squirting orange being dug into by insistent fingers made the film a sure winner at the Erotic Film Festival in San Francisco. In 1971 she turned out *Lizard Mozaic* (3 minutes), a lush study of a chameleon changing colors, and followed that with *Hands* (3 minutes), an imaginative exploration of the movements of fingers.

Johnson tells of the problems of getting started: "I think it ought to be easier for women to get into the unions so we can learn about the equipment on the job. I was fortunate and got a real editing job right after school and managed to learn all the little tricks and techniques without a lot of hassle, but there are a lot of college graduates in film who just can't get jobs. Film companies know that universities do little teaching. This, by the way, is a common complaint of both male and female filmmakers fresh from college. But, you know, most of the guys manage to make good because it is a male-dominated medium. Clients and employers don't trust you, and you have to work twice as hard as a man to prove yourself competent. People are amazed when I say I'm a filmmaker. 'Oh, what do you do? Do you edit?' they most often ask. 'No,' I say, 'I do edit to make a living, but I also make my own films entirely on my own.' Or they ask, 'Did you do the camera work *too*?' Well, why not? Admittedly, I am not strong enough to carry an Eclair around all day, but I know a lot of women who are— and why should that be out of the question? Perhaps, as percentages go, there are more *good* women filmmakers around than good male filmmakers, simply because the challenge is so great."

Despite the problems, Johnson's advice to women considering careers in film is: "Do it! Most of the obstacles are ridiculous, and if we persevere we can get rid of them. If film is in your blood, you won't be happy until you're making films."

Suzanne Johnston, Princeton, New Jersey, and her husband, Hugh, are partners in making educational films and documentaries. She does the writing, directing, and sound recording; he does the camerawork and editing. They have been making films for about ten years. *Parents Are Teachers Too* won a Chris statuette, the Oscar of educational films. Another prize-winner (certificate of honor at the Columbus, Ohio, film festival) was *A Different Childhood*, the study of a shy three-and-a-half year old boy living in poverty. According to the Johnstons, the film is designed to "orient those who are not poor to the emotional and psychological effects of an impoverished environment on the pre-school age child." It is used as a training tool for teachers and volunteers in urban schools and Operation Head Start programs. Suzanne Johnston made these suggestions about filmmaking:

"There's a great need for talent in the field. Anyone planning to go into it should get the best possible background in liberal arts, and some visual training. Filmmaking is more sophisticated visually now than it was ten years ago. Anyone who can get a 16mm or 8mm camera and a hand editor can learn a lot by herself. And it's good to have samples of your work to show. I learned a lot writing scripts for advertising—a good chance to experiment while someone else was footing the bill. I did some photography, too. But a big commercial studio hires a series of different people to do different jobs. It's fragmented. I like our way of life better."

ANNA-LENA KEATING, Evanston, Illinois, is an animator who became so adept at the use of stop-motion photography that her film *The Bedroom* (8½ minutes) won first prize for Film as Art in the 1971 Chicago International Film Festival. In the film, Keating brings an ordinary bedroom to life through thousands of single-frame exposures that have the effect of animating all the objects in the room. Rugs, chairs and even the wallpaper seem to dance in synchronization to an electronic score.

Keating has been a filmmaker since 1968, specializing in

3-D animation. As she describes it, "This is animation of real three-dimensional objects as opposed to cell animation." She opened her own studio early in 1974 so that she could have complete control over her projects. The result? "It has been most profitable," she says.

Keating's very brief animated film, *School* (1 minute), which she made for "Sesame Street," won second prize in 1974 at the Chicago International Film Festival in the category of Films for Children (network). Her *New Ball in Town* (2 minutes) was also made for "Sesame Street." Among her other animated films are *The Kitchen* (5 minutes) and *The Chair* (2 minutes). On all of these films she was producer, director, camerawoman and editor, as well as animator.

A number of Keating's films have been produced for specific clients. These films include *Munchers, a fable* (10 minutes), for the American Dental Association; *Cow* (15 minutes), for the National Dairy Association; and *Six Men and an Elephant* (6 minutes), for the Encyclopedia Brittanica. In addition, she has done television commercials for such products as Lipton tea and Meadow Gold cottage cheese.

"But I find that the films I'm most satisfied with are the ones I made without clients or a product to sell," she says. "In the future, I see myself moving toward feature films."

MARY PAT KELLY, New York, was a consultant to the producer of "The American Dream Machine" series on National Educational Television, and was the director of programming for the *Festival de Films Underground* held in Paris. She wrote the feature *Heaven*, a satire of the showgirl films of the forties. The film starred Andy Warhol superstars Ondine, Holly Woodlawn, and Ruby Lynn Rainer. A current project is *Ready*, also a feature, which she is writing and directing. It is a dramatic narrative set in Chicago's black community.

Other recent projects include *Austin: Community in Tran-*

sition (60 minutes), on which she is associate director; and *Beside the Singing River* (30 minutes), which she is writing.

NANCY KENDALL, New York, like many filmmakers, began as a still photographer and actress in underground films. She was in Storm De Hirsch's *The Tattooed Man*. To learn about films and to gain a financial foothold she has been everything from script girl and film librarian to associate filmmaker for the Ann Arbor Dance Theater. Like many other women in film, she has had to spread herself thin. Her first film, *Almira* (1970, 20 minutes), took four years to complete. In this film a young woman, painfully laced in an old woman's clothes, is carried, in a dance of pain, toward death. But her suicide is viewed as a fleeing from men into the female image of the ocean, and is hence also a rebirth. Kendall has been working on a 45-minute film, *Journal I*.

BARBARA KOPPLE, New York, a producer, director and sound editor, took her film crew into the coal mines of Appalachia during production of *The Miners Film*, a full-length color documentary scheduled for completion in 1975. The film explores the history of the coal industry, the day-to-day lives of the miners and their families, problems of mine safety, and—particularly—conflicts within the United Mine Workers Union. It was partially financed by a $10,000 grant in 1973 from the American Film Institute.

As project director, Kopple heads a small crew consisting of Anne Lewis, co-editor, camera assistant and assistant to the director; and Hart Perry and Kevin Keating, photographers. They began their mining film with the help of an unconditional loan from a labor historian, then sought additional funding when they decided to expand the scope of the film. The crew shot several days' footage a mile underground where they interviewed miners at work.

Kopple made her first film at Medfield State Hospital in Massachusetts, as a project for her degree in clinical psychology. She worked as assistant editor to the Maysles brothers on their 1969 documentary, *Salesman;* edited and did sound for *Living Off the Land* (1972, 32 minutes) and *Wild Orange* (1972, 90 minutes); and directed, produced, edited and did the sound for *Winter Soldier* (1972, 92 minutes).

Kopple and Lewis are founders of the Cabin Creek Center for Work and Environmental Studies, a cooperative that produces films on political and social issues such as labor problems, unemployment and industrial sabotage.

RENA KOSERSKY, New York, is a music editor. She researches and selects pre-recorded music for films, occasionally writing or improvising the music herself. She transfers the music, cuts it to the film, and directs the final mix. Her major efforts include the hour-long films *The Slave Coast, The Congo,* and *The Bend of The Niger,* for which she did the sound. Soundwomen, whether in the field or in the lab, on feature productions or documentaries, are very rare. Kosersky comments:

"I got into the field indirectly. Although I studied music at college, my first job was as a secretary. Then I became an assistant and started to learn about the film process and putting sound to film. I have often thought that there is opposition to women working in sound, though I have not yet met another woman to compare notes with. When I first began my work as a music editor, men had difficulty in trusting me with their films. If it weren't for the support of my employer (male) they would never have trusted me until after the final mix. I used to feel that I was in a constant state of proving myself to men.

"When I was working on the series of four one-hour specials on Africa I told the producer-director-writer that I didn't believe it was right to have only men as narrators for all four films. 'Why not have at least one woman do a film?' I asked. I was subjected to an attack of male supremacy which I hope never to experience again. I was laughed at, jeered at, by all

the men involved in the film. The production manager said
these films weren't for women. I asked him if he thought
films about music, art, and dance are not for women. He
responded with a laugh. But I persevered. The result of all
this appeared on television: the film *The Slave Coast*, narrated by Maya Angelou."

HELEN LEVITT, New York, who in 1949 made an instant
and stunning impact with her film *The Quiet One*, can only
be described as the most casual of filmmakers. Before she
made this sensitive study of a rootless Harlem boy, Levitt
was a still photographer, and a most gifted one. She still is.
Movies, she insists, are only a sometimes thing.

Levitt's filmmaking began in a tentative way in the late
forties when she joined Janice Loeb and the late James Agee
in two years of sporadic and random shooting in the streets
of New York as an experimental exercise. When they were
done, the film was just "put away" and wasn't looked at
again until 1952, when Levitt cut it for an 18-minute movie
that critic Richard Griffith described as "an advance inquiry
into the nature of motion picture photography and a unique
revelation of the human countenance unmasked."

The Quiet One, on which she worked again with Loeb
and Agee, won first prize and the critics award at the Venice
Film Festival, and took every other award in sight. She later
produced a half-hour documentary on the problems of the
aging, *The Steps of Age*, which was nominated for an Academy Award. She directed *Another Light*, a 20-minute documentary for the U. S. Department of Health, and has done
editorial work on many other documentaries. She has also
been involved with several features, including *The Savage
Eye* (camera), *The Balcony* (special assistant to the director),
and *An Affair of the Skin* (assistant to the producer).

What problems has she faced as a woman? Levitt says "I
never had any problems except that I couldn't carry as much
as a man." She holds that "anybody who really has something

to say can find a way to say it—if you have the money and the time to do it."

LYNNE LITTMAN, Los Angeles, has a closet full of Emmys for her work on television documentaries. In 1974 she received a local Emmy Award for Individual Achievement as producer-reporter for two film reports—*In the Matter of Kenneth* and *Wanted: Operadoras*—that she made for the Los Angeles Collective on KCET-TV. Her films for the collective also earned her the Los Angeles Press Club Award for Best TV Documentary in 1974, and a Golden Mike Award for investigative reporting in 1973.

In addition to her individual films, she is also the producer of the collective's weekly TV news programs, which won local Emmy Awards in 1972 and 1973.

Recalling her early attempts to break into film, Littman says: "I started as a secretary in the publicity department at WNDT (Channel 13) in New York. The job had *nothing* to do with film. Two hundred freelance research jobs later, I came to meet and work with NET Journal producer Mort Silverstein. His commitment to Murrow-style journalism affected me permanently."

Littman became associate producer on the NET Journal series, and was involved with several hard-hitting documentaries, including Silverstein's "What Harvest for the Reaper" which "allowed us to live alongside the migrant labor camps of Long Island and share in the lives of the farmers and their 'slaves.'"

Later she went to California as assistant to director Agnes Varda on a feature film, *Lion's Love;* was associate producer for Wolper Productions on *Drugs and the Mind;* produced two documentaries on drugs for the UCLA media center; and then joined KCET-TV as associate producer on its current events series. A year later she was made producer of the station's Los Angeles Collective.

Littman received all her training in the field rather than

in the classroom, and tends to be "less than enthusiastic about college film training." She says, "I need to be in the middle of a 'real' situation and find it difficult to simulate that in school. I think people should do whatever they can to get directly into the industry."

It is important to her to be identified as a *woman* filmmaker because women who are conscious of feminism inscribe their feelings and ideas onto their work, she believes. "It's funny and sad to me when a woman says, 'I'm not a woman. I'm a director.' Baloney!"

JUDITH MACDOUGALL, Houston, Texas, is an ethnographic filmmaker. Ethnographic films are studies of various cultures, documentaries meant to record rather than to evaluate. MacDougall says of her work:

"For the past several years my husband and I have been working together, functioning as a complete production unit, making ethnographic films. A few years ago we shot three films in Africa, one of which, *Nawi,* is in distribution. We have our own Moviola and editing set-up and produced these films ourselves with the assistance of UCLA equipment and grants. We went into the field with an Eclair-Nagro set-up, lived (in a tent) with a pastoral tribe in northeastern Uganda, and filmed over a period of eight months. David did the shooting, I did the sound. Although it was a collaborative effort, he necessarily did all the photography, as there were only two of us, plus an African assistant. We plan to return to Africa and then I will do the photography on a picture (or several pictures) concerning attitudes and events dealing with childbirth. Since many of the things involved in this subject are kept from men, I will probably train an African woman to do my sound recording and the only male involved will be my two-year-old son, who will build rapport, get fingermarks on the lens, and help generally."

MacDougall does not feel she has been held back because she is a woman. "In documentary situations people do not get so uptight with a woman doing the filming. They don't believe you will do them harm. Or they don't take you seriously. Either way you can get right in there—fast. Somehow they don't feel so threatened."

CAROLE MARNER, Reseda, California, was working as a painting and crafts instructor with Mobilization for Youth (1963–64), when she and her husband, Gene, decided to make films about children. They borrowed equipment and taught themselves. Since then the Marners have made more than a dozen films of 30 minutes or longer. She generally does sound and co-editing and co-producing, and he directs. Their films include *Isaac Stern* (60 minutes), a documentary about the violinist, and *Phyllis and Terry* (35 minutes), about two black teenage girls who are close friends. Carole Marner also co-produced and did sound on segments of *Africa* (4 hours) for NBC. Asked about her partnership with her husband, Marner said:

"My husband and I work very closely together. We feel we have in our long relationship—thirteen years—enriched each other's sensibility. I doubt that I would have stayed in film without my husband. I love the medium, I love doing *cinéma-vérité*, but I hate the business. Oddly enough, my husband would give it up tomorrow to farm, but I would still like to work in *cinéma-vérité*."

The Marners also do freelance work for television, and industrial films. "Television," she says, "is a bureaucracy impossible to deal with if you are a man—worse than impossible if you are a woman. As I said, I enjoy the work, shooting, so I've not cared about having to play a subordinate role with TV producers."

DINITIA SMITH MCCARTHY, New York, was an Associated Press reporter after graduating from Smith College, later worked at Bobwin Associates as producer, director and writer, and since 1972 has been working freelance. Her major work in fiction film is *Passing Quietly Through* (30 minutes), which she wrote and directed in 1971. The film, starring Lou Gilbert and Janet Ward, is an intense study of an old man examining the meaning of his life as he lies dying. Richard Roud, director of the New York Film Festival, where it was shown, called it "one of the finest American short films." Among her many documentaries are two which she produced and wrote for WNBC-TV in 1974: *Rape*, a film about victim and rapist, dealing with some of the myths and little known aspects of the crime, and *Does Parole Work?*, an examination of the New York State parole system. McCarthy also has done a number of first-rate educational films and several commercials.

McCarthy has some firm views about women filmmakers. "Now that many of us are working as producers, writers and technicians," she says, "it is important to go beyond a mere consolidation of our identity as *women* filmmakers. Many films that deal with so-called women's issues have the predictability and clichéd rhetoric that often accompanies the emergence of oppressed groups into freedom. It is important for us to go beyond this narrow concern with women's issues. Good art is really androgynous, and the concerns of good art are for the condition of all human beings."

MUFFIE MEYER, New York, was an English major at Grinnell College who began making a few films for fun. Then she took an MFA at the New York University Institute of Film and Television and began her career as an editor. *Expressway to Your Heart* (1968) won first prize at the National Student Association Film Festival. She was an editor on *Woodstock*, several shorter films, and a feature-length musical promotion film for Simon and Garfunkel. She has also edited *An Essay on Loneliness* (30 minutes) for NET; *The Grand Funk Railroad Documentary* for the Maysles brothers; *Groove Tube*, and *The Lords of Flatbush*.

KATE MILLETT, New York, artist and author of the widely known, controversial book "Sexual Politics," has made one film, *Three Lives* (1970, 70 minutes). She is credited as "filmmaker"; Robin Mide, Susan Kleckner, and Louva Irvine are credited as "co-directors." This is a documentary portrait of three women of different ages, backgrounds, and lifestyles. One of them, Mallory, had to fight hard to achieve responsibility as an adult and now won't accept help from anyone. Lillian, an older woman, tells placid, humorous stories about growing up female in an Italian family, where a college education was only for boys. Robin speaks from within a cage, radiating an aggressively irresponsible attitude toward life. And she has humor: "I go to bed with women, my mother doesn't like that. I go to bed with men, my grandmother doesn't like that!"

JANE MOYNIHAN, Milwaukee, Wisconsin, spent about ten years as a feature writer for a newspaper before joining her husband, Paul, in Moynihan Associates in 1967. They make sponsored films—short films for business, government agencies, and large corporations. *How Many Lifetimes?*, a film about theosophy which she wrote, produced, and directed, won a gold medal from the Atlanta International Film Festival and was chosen by Business Screen Magazine as one of the fifty best sponsored films of 1970. Other films include *Leading to Learning*, a five-part series on training the disadvantaged; many product promotional films; and films on teaching machines, unwed parents, drug abuse, reincarnation, school buses, and fishing in the Canadian wilderness.

GUNVOR NELSON, a painter, and DOROTHY WILEY, a teacher, who both live in Muir Beach, California, worked as a team on the film *Schmeerguntz* (1965, 15 minutes), an enjoyable, disenchanted view of marriage (they are both married and mothers). *Schmeerguntz* is a collage of the fantasies women have about marriage and babies—and what really happens. An enormously pregnant woman reads a fairy tale about a princess; other women scrub greasy pans, change messy diapers, and struggle with clogged sinks, while magazine pictures of fine housekeeping obscure the reality of what it means to be female. The collaboration by Nelson and Wiley began with *Fog Pumas* (1962, 25 minutes), a surreal study of a woman's mind, and continued with *Five Marin Artists* (1971), a documentary. Nelson has made *My Name is Oona* (1970, 10 minutes), a portrait of her daughter; *Kirsa Nicholina* (1970), a documentary about natural childbirth; *Take Off* (10 minutes); and *Moons Pool* (15 minutes).

YOKO ONO, New York, made her first film in 1964, a 3-minute survey of an assortment of behinds provided by friends. She called it *Film No. 4*, and it won prizes at festivals at Ann Arbor and the University of Cincinnati.

Subsequently she was approached in London by an apparently wealthy man who offered to put up money for a feature film. Gathering together friends, equipment, an apartment, and out of date film (which she got for free), she began production on a feature length "bottoms" film. The level of enthusiasm was high, the publicity was fantastic, but the money never materialized. The feature was produced on about $100 of Ono's own money—but the film was never shown in this country because customs didn't let it in.

Her next film ventures were with husband John Lennon. The films they made together include *Fly* (20 minutes), showing a fly crawling on a nude female body; *Erection* (20 minutes), about a hotel being built; *Apotheosis* (25 minutes), abstractions shot through a balloon; and *Rape II* (20 minutes), about a German girl visiting London.

"John and I made films together because we both felt it was important to work with someone who really understood the spirit of the project. Our cooperation was a very important part of the films as far as the creative energy was concerned. Since the world wasn't as much in love with our films as we were, working together gave me incentive."

But Ono feels no overwhelming inspiration to devote herself to films. She is also a poet, a painter, a composer. As the spirit moves her, she will write poetry, paint or compose music. Or make more films.

SHEILA PAIGE and ARIEL DOUGHERTY, New York, are co-directors of Women Make Movies, Inc., a non-profit, educational corporation formed in the spring of 1972. Women Make Movies operates Chelsea Picture Station, a community film and video workshop which opened in July, 1972, and works with Chelsea residents of all ages producing movies, videotapes and radio plays. The workshop has also been involved in several independent film productions, among them Judith Shaw Acuna's *For Better or Worse* (1973, 7 minutes); Barbara Brown and Nancy Greiner's *Katie Kelly* (1973, 5 minutes); and Jean Shaw's *Fear* (1973, 7 minutes).

Paige and Dougherty have been full-time film teachers and independent filmmakers since 1969. Their films include *Mother America* (1970, 25 minutes), cooperatively made with Dolores Bargowski, a documentary on the dynamics of four mother-daughter relationships; *The Trials of Alice Crimmins* (1971, 6 minutes), which argues that Crimmins was convicted of the murder of her two children because of her lifestyle, not for evidence brought against her; *Sweet Bananas* (1972, 30 minutes), a documentary about the working lives and ambitions of a dancer, weaver, and writer; and *The Women's Happy Time Commune* (1972, 50 minutes). This is an all-woman Western (cast and crew), the characters clothed in nineteenth century garb but speaking unabashed New Yorkese.

Paige and Dougherty have extensive backgrounds as teachers. They have taught children and oldsters, Spanish-speaking, white, black and Chinese people. Their insights into girls and boys as filmmakers are particularly interesting:

"Our presence attracted girls into hitherto male-dominated workshops and our encouragement enabled them to complete their first movies. Still, scarcely a fifth of our students were girls.

"Young girls need to learn the enthusiasm for technical equipment which boys possess. Girls need to be encouraged specifically to load projectors, to carry equipment, to do the camerawork for their movies instead of asking the boy who is 'good at it.' Unless girls become involved with the technical process of moviemaking, they remain actresses, spectators, accessories to, instead of prime agents in, the creation of their own movies.

"Young girls find it harder than young boys to assume active technical and creative control over their movies because they make more personal films than boys. Boys tend to make action pictures involving cops, muggers, cowboys, bankers, soldiers, and detectives. Girls' movies deal with very personal situations: one or two heroines who get lost in the park, friends who quarrel and make up, a girl who finds a boyfriend. These types of films are more subtle and more difficult to make.

"After puberty, the number of girls involved in film workshops drops. At best, Young Filmmakers' Super 8 Film Club may have thirty-five percent girls; in teenage 16mm workshops, like the Henry Street Movie Club, girls are one in twenty. At adolescence, film becomes more an individual activity than the group activity typical of eight- to twelve-year-olds, and girl filmmakers get increasingly wary of making movies. While young girls never make movies about boys, older teenage girls will often make their first movie about a boy. The boy hero acts as a filter for the filmmaker's feelings, saving her from the exposure of expressing herself directly.

"Because girls make such personal movies and are so often deeply involved in roles that require passivity of them, teachers must prod and encourage girls to step outside of themselves enough to become involved with directing, with camerawork and editing—with a joyous sense of new skills and powers."

PAT POWELL, Brooklyn, New York, began her film career in 1960 at Bob Drew Associates, where she became a film editor and later general manager. In 1963, after leaving Drew, she took freelance assignments from Time-Life, which included the Birmingham riots (*Crisis Behind a Presidential Decision*) and Vietnam combat (*The American Commitment*). "They didn't want a woman to go to Vietnam," she recalls, "but I take excellent sound, so they let me."

With the hope of becoming a producer, she took a job at WABC-TV in 1965 as a researcher for news and public affairs. The plan worked—after a fashion. She got a chance to produce, as well as research, a variety of shows, including an hour-long documentary on mental retardation. This film, *Who Will Tie My Shoe?*, won a New York Emmy, two Sigma Delta Chi awards, and the Lasker Award in medical journalism, but when the smoke cleared she was still on the payroll as a $125-a-week researcher. Back to freelancing, she produced, directed, and edited films for a fair number of clients. Some of her freelance films: *John Von Neumann* (1966, 60 minutes), a biography of the mathematician; *Well I Got a Job, Ain't I?* (1968, 55 minutes), a survey of programs for the hardcore unemployed; *Veronica* (1969, 27 minutes), a portrait of a black teenager accused of being an uncle tom; *Zookeeper* (1971, 15 minutes), a portrait of a sensitive zookeeper who talks to animals; *Sigaboy* (1971, 60 minutes), a close-up look at life in a small Philippine village; and a series of fourteen mini-documentaries for children which won another Emmy. In 1974 she joined the ABC network as field producer and editor.

MYRNA RAVITZ, Chicago, formed her own film production company—Cinepac, Inc.—in 1972 after working for several Chicago film producers. Her company does feature film work,

commercial films and sales films, and clients include Quaker
Oats, Sears Roebuck, Brunswick, and Alberto-Culver. One
of the first women to head a commercially successful operation of this scale, she has made a reputation for her mana-
gerial skill in bringing films in on schedule and on-budget.
Ravitz began her film work at Ryerson Institute in Toronto
and later studied at Chicago's Goodman Theatre School.

JULIA REICHERT, Dayton, Ohio, and Jim Klein made the
documentary about women, *Growing Up Female: As 6 Become I* (1971, 50 minutes). This film examines the social
forces that shape women's self-concept as they grow up,
from nursery school through high school and become middle-
aged housewives. Parents, guidance counselors, employers,
and advertisers all insist on a path of traditional femininity.
Reichert and Klein have also done *Methadone: An American
Way of Dealing* (60 minutes), a documentary showing the
drawbacks of methadone treatment programs.

Reichert began her career by using still photography to
express her political ideas. She recalls, "I took pictures of
workers on picketlines, women working, confrontations between police and demonstrators. Film appealed to me partly
because of its ability to reach more people than photographs,
partly because it was great fun and really adventurous for a
female. My first filmmaking was in the underground style,
sort of imagist, inner-documentary. I learned to make films
by doing them, since there were no courses or experts around.
Almost no women, either."

Faced with the usual problems of distributing independently made films, Reichert and Klein joined with Amalie
Rothschild, Liane Brandon, and others to form the distribution cooperative New Day Films. The co-op's brochure raps
commercial distribution companies for their profit motive,
frequent discrimination against new filmmakers and women,
and their reluctance to handle controversial topics, then explains:

"We found these conditions unacceptable, and have set out to create an alternative for ourselves and for other filmmakers.

"We make films because we have discovered certain ideas, facts, or situations that are important to us. We want to share these with others. Therefore, our work does not stop when a film is completed; this is only half the task. The sharing of ideas (via distribution) is to us an integral part of the process of producing films. Our films are our contribution to what we see as progressive forces in society. A responsibility to share these ideas is our primary concern, not the accumulation of personal monetary profit.

"However, we face difficult financial realities. Survival as a filmmaker depends a great deal on money. Producing and distributing films is extremely expensive. It involves taking many risks and expending tremendous energy. Each filmmaker must personally raise her/his own funds. It is reasonable that we be repaid adequately so as to allow us to continue to make films. For this reason, basically all money a film earns goes directly to its creators. We ask fees that are fair, yet we wish to be responsive to the needs of all audiences, whether they be college classrooms, storefronts, high schools, union halls, or livingrooms.

"Although we produce our films independently, we have common goals. Those involved in New Day share ideas, resources, and energy, because we believe in the importance of cooperative action in bringing social change. We hope our experiment will grow to make available many films about women."

BARBARA ROOS, Milwaukee, Wisconsin, is a producer-writer who often does sound, camera, and editing. *Silent Heritage* is a series of ten 30-minute shows, partly filmed on location and partly videotaped in the studio. Each show covers an aspect of the history of an Indian nation, followed by filmed segments of current life on the reservation. *We*

Came to Stay (15 minutes) is about people in the Mississippi Delta who are active in the freedom movement. It was sponsored and distributed by the National Council of Churches. *Lisa's World* (30 minutes) describes the life of a seven-year-old mentally retarded girl. *Everybody's Eagle* (1972, 29 minutes) was written, produced, edited, filmed, and directed with George Allez. It is an ironic account of the decline of the bald eagle set against the proliferation of eagle iconography on tissue boxes, toilet seats, lampshades, and cocktail glasses.

Roos describes how her involvment with film has changed over the years:

"A major reason I got into film (though I didn't intend to stay) was the opportunity to travel. This was in the early sixties, and I'd been brought up to be a good academic (MA in anthropology, Phi Beta Kappa, etc.). I was rather ashamed to go into 'show biz'—but the freshness, movement, and involvement with other people that film offered could not be argued with. I also went into film because I thought it was a way to tell my side of the story, as it were. I used to think I could convince audiences to change their values to fit my own. I've changed a lot. I'm still in film because it gives me pleasure to just plain do it, to juggle all the visual and audio problems, to play with techniques and ideas. As for travel and changing the world, well, those things are still important to me, even now that I'm gray-haired (well, a few) and cynical."

Although as a woman she has encountered some discrimination, she says, "The only real resistance I've found so far is to female cameramen. You can talk your way into writing, producing, directing, and editing. I even know one woman TV engineer. But men guard that Arriflex with their lives."

AMALIE ROTHSCHILD, New York, partner in the New Day Films distribution cooperative, and a still photographer, received her MFA in film in 1969 from New York University. She photographed and edited *The Center* (45 minutes), a documentary about the leader of a Lower East Side community center, then wrote, directed, and edited *Woo Who? May Wilson* (1970, 33 minutes). May Wilson is an artist who, after years of marriage in suburban Maryland, is told by her husband that he no longer wants to live with her. When she arrives in New York City she is so accustomed to dependence on her husband that she does not know how to use an elevator or close the bathtub drain at her hotel. Slowly creating a new life for herself, she builds up a circle of acquaintances and ultimately achieves professional success with her "junk-assemblage sculptures." A hilarious rather than mournful story, the film is a record of a unique and determined woman's struggle to express a side of herself that had long been dormant.

A later Rothschild film is *It Happens to Us* (1972, 30 minutes), a color documentary on abortion, shot by an all-woman crew. Unlike many commercial educational films about unwanted pregnancies, which rely on charts, graphs, or statistics, and an occasional shot of a remorseful young woman, *It Happens to Us* lets the women speak for themselves. Their stories, often horrifying, occasionally amusing, point out the contradictions in morality that produce unwanted children.

Rothschild's *Nana, Mom and Me* (1974, 45 minutes), portrays the interaction among three women of different generations—a daughter, a mother, and a grandmother. Other Rothschild films are: *It's All Right to Be Woman* (1972, 50 minutes), and *Safari* (1970, 13 minutes). At this writing she was working on a script for a short fiction film.

HOPE RYDEN, New York, was once an airline stewardess with an interest in photographing unusual sights on her journeys. This interest broadened into a profession that has brought her considerable recognition. Working with Drew Associates, she has written, directed, and produced more than thirty documentaries for ABC and CBS television. *Mis-*

sion to Malaya (1964, 60 minutes) is the story of a Peace
Corps nurse; *Operation Gwamba* (1965, 30 minutes), shows
the rescue of wild animals in a flooded African jungle; *To
Love a Child* (1969, 30 minutes) is a study of adoption; and
Strangers in Their Own Land: The Chicanos (1971, 30 minutes) explores the problems of Mexican-Americans. In addition to her filmmaking career, she has completed a book
about wild horses of the West, illustrated with her own stills.

NINA SCHULMAN, New York, started in publishing, then
went to work for Leacock-Pennebaker for a year and learned
sound and editing. In addition to working on several commercials and documentaries, she has edited a Bell Telephone
film, *Van Cliburn* (60 minutes); worked on *Monterey Pop*
(80 minutes) and *Twiggy Why* (60 minutes); and did sound
recording for two Norman Mailer features, *Beyond the Law*
and *Maidstone*. Schulman also did sound recording on an
F.T.A. documentary featuring Jane Fonda and Donald Sutherland, and was producer of *Werewolf of Washington* (1974),
a feature film starring Dean Stockwell that was written and
directed by Milton Ginsberg. She was associate producer of
Funny Car, a segment about black drag racers for NET's
"Great American Dream Machine."

DIANA SEIDEL, Chicago, is a film producer for Sears,
Roebuck and Company. Her background was in commercial
art, but she "fell into the field when a filmmaking unit at
Iowa State University at Ames needed an editor.

"I learned by doing, under the direction of the head of the
unit, and had the opportunity to get familiar with all the
technical areas of filmmaking by actually doing the work of
the technician. I had no idea that such a field existed until
that episode."

Seidel edits and produces most of the Sears films, and
occasionally writes them as well. They include: *Scroll Saw*
(7 minutes), *Best Dressed Man in Town* (17 minutes), and

Every Inch a Lady (22 minutes). She has also done educational films about grouse hunting, tarpon fishing, and basketball.

AVIVA SLESIN, New York, started as a graphic artist, then switched to film editing. She edited two 90-minute specials for NET, *Gertrude Stein: When This You See Remember Me* and *The Great Radio Comedians.* She also edited Shirley MacLaine's *China Memoir: The Other Half of the Sky.*

After editing other people's films for several years, Slesin produced her own work, *Fat Film,* a study of a woman's compulsion to overeat. Slesin financed the film with money she saved working as an editor, and found that "professional people of the highest caliber—particularly women—were willing to help me with this film and lend me equipment. I think they enjoyed being involved because they know everyone needs help getting started."

BARBARA L. SMITH, New York, got into film, she says, "through the love and respect of a male filmmaker and also through my concern for the condition of the black community." She was animation editor for *Something to Build On* (25 minutes), a documentary on blacks in academic institutions. She was production assistant and assistant editor for *Kick* (22 minutes), a dramatic film about a drug addict trying to kick the habit, and for *The Folks* (45 minutes), a documentary on Bedford-Stuyvesant and Harlem. She is currently editing shorts for "Sesame Street."

LELA SMITH, Mill Valley, California, runs Franciscan Films in San Francisco. After college she married a photographer, became interested in cinema, and in 1948 organized a distribution company, Gateway Productions. She co-produced one of the first film series for television, *Piro the Puppet.* Later she worked for other film companies in jobs ranging from laboratory timer and printer to editor and assistant director. After the birth of her daughter in 1954, she did freelance editing and negative cutting at home and freelance commercial still photography, until she founded Franciscan Films and was once again working full-time as a producer. She edits and often produces and distributes films on a wide variety of subjects: *You Got What?* (20 minutes), on venereal disease; *Thermal Power* (20 minutes); and *Science on a Small Planet*, a series of 30-minute shows for instructional television; as well as the Paulist telespots (1 minute each).

PENNY SPHEERIS, Venice, California, studied film at UCLA. Her dramatic documentary, *I Don't Know* (1970, 20 minutes) is a story of love between a lesbian and a boy who is physically and emotionally part female. This is a rare paradox: a gentle and serious film that succeeds by making fun of itself. The film is especially appealing because it deals sensitively with people who are usually not portrayed as fully human in films. It has won nearly a dozen prizes in festivals across the country. Her other films include *Synthesis* (1968, 12 minutes), a science-fiction film; *The National Rehabilitation Center*, a pseudo-documentary on the McCarran Act, which introduced detention camps in the United States; *Hats Off to Hollywood* (1972, 26 minutes), a dramatic documentary on the lifestyle of young people in Hollywood's underground; and *Foghat Energized* (24 minutes).

Spheeris supported herself during her early years in film by working "as a waitress in coffee-shops and cocktail lounges, culminating my career in that line of work with a job in Hollywood's Pink Pussycat. When I hung up my black net stockings I hung up my waitress career. Anyway, by that time I had enough status and background to get a job as a teaching assistant in UCLA's beginning film-production classes. For two years I earned my living as a teacher and somehow managed to scrape together enough money to put several films together. After one of my films received some recognition in national and international competition, I asked for one of the motion-picture division's grants, but on three separate occasions the money was given instead to men students. In place of a grant, I got assurances that I was a person with a lot of drive and initiative and could make it on my own."

KATHERINE STENHOLM, Greenville, South Carolina, is a former instructor of speech and drama and the first woman producer-director to hold membership in the University Film Producers Association and the Society of Motion Picture and Television Engineers. In 1950 she founded Unusual Films, the motion-picture unit of Bob Jones University. She has directed and produced many sermon films featuring Bob Jones, Sr.; a half-hour documentary on the Holy Land; a film version of *Macbeth;* and a documentary called *Shadow Over Italy*. Her feature films, all on religious topics, include *Wine of Morning* (1955), *Red Runs the River* (1963), and *Flame in the Wind* (1971), the story of persecution in the Spanish Inquisition. She has also directed numerous other educational, documentary, industrial, commercial, and missionary films.

JANET STERNBURG, New York, is a filmmaker, writer and feminist who has been active in many areas. While working for NET, she produced and directed *Virginia Woolf: The Moment Whole* (10 minutes), a Cine Golden Eagle award winner; *El Teatro Campesino*, a 90-minute documentary about the Chicano street theater troupe that grew out of the farm workers grape strike, and *The Movie Crazy Years: Films of the Thirties* (90 minutes).

As a feminist, Sternburg has been trying to get her views across to children through her "Me, Myself and I Movie Matinee," a 70-minute program of non-sexist children's films that have been shown at New York City theaters under the sponsorship of the Center for Understanding Media. Sternburg did not make any of these films herself, but selected them from among dozens of children's movies. In trying to find films that were free of sex-role stereotyping, she encountered many difficulties, not least of which was her discovery that few children's films focus on girls; as in books, the central characters are usually boys.

Sternburg writes poetry and critical essays on film for Aphra, the feminist literary magazine. Her articles have also appeared in Film Library Quarterly, and she has reviewed children's books on film and poetry for the New York Times Sunday Book Review.

After leaving NET, Sternburg formed her own company, Clea Films. Under a grant from the Center for Understanding Media, she is involved in a project that utilizes films to stimulate creative writing among elementary school children.

CHICK STRAND, Los Angeles, is Coordinator of Educational Media and a film instructor at Occidental College, and a freelance filmmaker as well. Her interest in film began in 1960 when she was asked to co-direct Canyon Cinema in Berkeley, the first West Coast theater to have experimental film showings. She also began the Canyon Cinema News, along with underground filmmaker Bruce Baillie and Ernest Callenbach, editor of Film Quarterly, and helped run a small cooperative film workshop. Her short films include several experimental works: *Eric and the Monsters* (1963, 4 minutes), *Angel Blue Sweet Wings, Anselmo* (1968, 4 minutes), *Kulu Se Mama* (1968, 1 minute), and *Waterfall* (1968, 4 minutes). In *Anselmo*, a Mexican man plays the trombone as evocative images of dancing women, fireworks, and a shadowy airplane are solarized across the screen. *Waterfall* was done entirely on a contact printer, using original and stock footage of everything from iceskaters to Eisenstein and Busby Berkeley movies set in time to koto music. Strand has also made *Orfano* (25 minutes) and *Elasticity* (20 minutes).

Her longest film, *Mosori Monika* (1970, 20 minutes), springs from her anthropology background. It is an ethnographic film dealing with acculturation in the lives of the South American Warao Indians as they are exposed to Christian missionaries. It was made at UCLA under a Ford Foundation grant. Strand says, "One of my most interesting experiences was a complete and immediate rapport with the Warao Indians, even though their culture was strange to us. Men always seem to have to go through a lot of male macho games before there is any communication. I found, not knowing the language and hardly anything of the culture, that I could make friends right away with both men and women. I found this true in Mexico as well.

"For one thing, women have that universal bond of being mothers. There seems to be some sort of secret acknowledgment of womanhood, a communication without words. And as for the men (at least I found this to be true in other cultures), they see no threat from a woman. Women don't play the male game, and we'll get right in there on a very personal basis right away."

ELAINE SUMMERS, New York, founded and heads Experimental Intermedia, a nonprofit center that provides space and equipment for research by dancers, composers, artists, and filmmakers. In most of Summers' own work, film and projected images are part of an event in space rather than simply a projection on a flat surface.

A typical intermedia work of hers is *Walking Dance for Any Number*, which uses from two to ten dancers and four 10-minute films that run simultaneously. The dancers, dressed in white, perform in front of the projection screen, becoming moving screens themselves. Her other intermedia projects include *Interchange, Black and White* (5 minutes), *Les Illuminations* (25 minutes), *Kinetic Athletic Frenzy* (20 minutes), *Another Pilgrim* (42 minutes), and *City People Moving* (15 minutes). Experimental Intermedia sends out films and scores in one neat package with instructions for the performance of film and dance. About this mixing of media, Summers says:

"For me, film is primarily a dance medium. Editing is a fantastic choreographic process. Filming dances as a record holds no interest for me whatever. You cannot design a dance to happen in space and then expect to translate it onto film and have anything but the most limited remainder of the actual dance, primarily because film is a flat medium, with space suggestions always a *trompe-l'oeil*. However, this particular quality of film plus the other possibilities peculiar to film in kinetic action give choreographers great dance possibilities, not available in 'real space.' And of course film offers the choreographer a work of art that does not vanish after the performance."

Summers feels that although it is hard to avoid vestiges of male and female chauvinism throughout the film industry, people in the art-film area tend to be very supportive of other artists. "The early support and understanding of my work by Jonas Mekas, for example, was a source of strength to me during times of discouragement. Stan Vanderbeek and Phil Niblock have both been very helpful over the years. The commercial world, of course, is much different, and the complexities of male chauvinist putdowns are an entire book in themselves. But even in that competitive world there are exceptions."

PAT THOMSON, Cambridge, Massachusetts, is an editor whose work includes *Sketches of a Man* (45 minutes), a TV pilot about black involvements in the United States; *Children Reborn* (30 minutes), a documentary she also co-produced about a children's center for psychiatric problems; and *Nightmare's Child* (45 minutes) and *The Inventory* (30 minutes), both for the Maryland History series on ETV. About problems women encounter, Thomson says:

"Men are often given opportunities because they are expected to work in all aspects of filmmaking. But women are expected to do only one phase—editing is most accepted. I was turned down for membership in the National Association of Broadcast Employees and Technicians because one man on the membership committee was against a woman member on principle. The other six men thought it was a great idea. When I showed up, check in hand, for membership—no. The one dissenter had his way. Sometimes the social upbringing plays a role; my tradition says that women do quiet things, like writing and painting."

DOROTHY TOD, Warren, Vermont, has worked as a freelance editor and soundwoman since 1967. She learned the basics of documentary filmmaking while doing research, handling sound, and editing films for Drew Associates. She has edited everything from "Captain Kangaroo" to a feature film on Leonard Bernstein in Israel after the Six Day War (*Journey to Jerusalem*). She has directed and co-edited (with Margaret Murphy) over 100 short films for the Children's Television Workshop, traveling to locations at the San Diego Zoo, Sea World, and Africa. She is currently working on films for "Sesame Street."

CARLA VALENTINE, Weston, Massachusetts, grew up in a film studio, where her mother put together travelogues and film lectures. She "started playing with films as soon as I was big enough to reach the crank on the rewind." She has been art director on several films, and also works as editor and animator on a freelance basis. She wrote and directed a 30-minute videotape on *Gamma Scintillation Spectrography* and a 30-minute film on *Cardiac Catheterization* (which she also edited).

"I think it's fair to say that women have equal chances in editing, graphics, maybe sound," she says, "but as far as running camera or direction, it's still a man's world. There are exceptions to this, of course. If a woman can find backing as an independent producer, she can write her own ticket.

"If you want an opportunity, you'll have to make your own. The marketplace isn't hungry enough to gobble up every aspiring film person as soon as he or she emerges from the woodwork. It takes a lot of effort to find a job."

JUDITH VOGELSANG, Haverford, Pennsylvania, made several films for local television when she lived in Kansas, as well as short films on her own. The latter include *Blow Up* (1968, 3 minutes), *Cigarette* (1968, 3 minutes), *Underground Movie* (1968, 3 minutes), *Roxanna* (1970, 8½ minutes), *Friendly Document* (1971, 10 minutes), and *Wichita Go Go* (1972, 25 minutes).

Film jobs were difficult for anyone to come by in Kansas, she says, but it was especially difficult for women. She ran into discrimination when she applied to film school, and still remembers her interview with the director:

"He informed me that I had excellent qualifications and academic background, better than most of the applicants he was considering. But, he said, there was little or no chance that they would admit a married woman into the program. I asked him if they were going to admit married men into the program. He looked surprised and then replied, 'Yes, of course.' I asked him in that case why he wouldn't consider married women. He made some reference to pregnancy. I told him I was taking birth-control pills. He ignored my comment. I was never notified one way or the other about admission until after classes had begun. I received a letter from the director's secretary informing me that I had been placed on a 'waiting list.' Five years have passed and I've heard nothing."

In the meantime, she went on to master film technique with her short films and applied for jobs at local television stations. She recalls: "I was told when I applied for a production job, 'Well, we don't have a specifically women's show.' When I replied that I was not particularly interested in producing a specifically women's show, the interviewer, a vice-president of the station, looked at me blankly and seemed not to understand." She has since become producer-director and writer for Philadelphia's WCAV-TV.

JULIANA WANG, New York, as far as can be determined, is the first female member of a cinematographers' union in the United States. Her credits for camerawork include several ABC specials, a Bell Telephone Hour, many commercials, and films for Holiday Magazine, American Motors, and other companies, as well as four short features. She heads Smiling Cat Productions, Inc., in New York. Her philosophy might be summed up in her comment: "I get kicked out one door, I go in the other door."

Her first job was in Switzerland, doing animation. When she came to the United States she got a job with the Paramount cartoon studio and worked there five years. "As a sideline I was doing still photography. But my closeups were all out of focus, so I traded in my camera for a better one—then another and another and another. When I decided that I'd like to make movies I bought my first Bolex. Then I got offers from people who needed stock shots—Wall Street at noon, clouds, that kind of stuff. One day someone called me saying he needed some stock shots of sunsets in 35mm. He asked me if I knew how to use a 35mm camera, and I said 'Yeah, yeah, I know how to use it.' So I rented a 35mm Arriflex and took it home—and learned how to use it that night! This is how I learned to use a lot of different cameras.

"After a while I wanted to take on more camerawork, but I found that companies would hire only union people. I put in an application with IATSE [International Alliance of Theatrical Stage Employees and Motion Picture Machine Operators], but soon I realized they were reluctant to take me in. So I joined NABET [National Association of Broadcast Employees and Technicians], a new, young union that was looking for members. When the people from IATSE asked why I had joined the other union, I said 'Because they didn't make a fuss. If you'll take me in, I'll leave NABET.' So they took me in. It's very slow for a woman to get into the unions. When you want something you have to keep after it, but I think there are very few women who are really trying.

"My first assignment when I got into the union was a big job. There was this forty-foot Chapman crane, a big 35mm Mitchell camera, and the big tripod head with wheels. It was only the second time I had ever used that. Inside, I panicked. I had to do a big crane shot with this tripod head—and I couldn't move it! Finally I said I'd do it hand-held. Everybody laughed at me sitting up there on the crane with a hand-held camera. But I got the shot.

"When I'm trying to get a job doing camera for people, they always say, 'You can't lift all that heavy equipment. You're a girl.' At one company that uses Auricons, the man said to me, 'Oh, you can't—we do all hand-held. The camera's too heavy for you.' So I said 'Show me.' He handed me the camera and—no problems. It was so light.

"Now I would like to do a feature, but that's hard to get because it seems that the same cameramen and the same crews get all the features. It's like a little club."

SUSAN WAYNE, New York, began working for Gotham Film Productions in the early 1950s while "at liberty" between engagements as a professional singer. Today, with her singing career just a memory, she owns Gotham Film Productions.

Wayne started out by scoring background music for the industrial films produced by Gotham. Then she branched out into other areas, doing "anything and everything people were willing to let me do," she recalls. In 1954, she was put in charge of a film for the first time, and immediately ran into trouble with the client. "He called up my boss and said

'What do you mean, sending over a woman?' But my boss was very firm and told him, 'I put Susan on it because I think she's the best person for the job. Take it or leave it.' Well, we are still doing films for this client today."

Equality for women was not a burning issue in those days, and the main reason Wayne got that first assignment was because the film was directed at salespeople—mainly a "women's audience." Her boss felt a feminine approach was needed for the film, "and I was the only woman around." After producing and directing a number of films, she was made a partner and vice president of Gotham in the early 1960s, and became sole owner in 1965 when her partner died.

In doing films for some of the large corporations, such as J.C. Penney, First National City Bank, Renault, W.T. Grant, AT&T and the Celanese Corporation, Wayne has come across many capable, talented businesswomen who somehow never get promoted. "It's really a shame," she says. "I think the problem is not so bad in my field because film types and other showbusiness types are always different. For my staff, I don't particularly seek out women; I seek out anyone who is efficient and imaginative."

She believes that on-the-job training is probably more important than film school, noting that she herself never received any formal education in film. "I was in showbusiness from the age of five," she says. "My parents were both opera singers, and when I was singing I did my own arrangements. In London I appeared in repertory and directed some plays, and later on I just drifted into film work."

Of the many hundreds of films she has produced and directed over the years, a few stand out in her memory. Among them are *The Good Guys Are Faster*, which was awarded a prize by the National Visual Presentation Association in 1968, and is still being shown in movie houses; *Showdown at Pretty Pass*, a Western satire dealing with waste; *Just a Secretary*, a motivational film that attempts to upgrade the job; and *Safe or Sorry*, a film on safety that was made for the

New York Telephone Company and is also being used by the Atomic Energy Commission.

CLAUDIA WEILL, New York, has her own production company, Cyclops Films, with her partner, Eliot Noyes. Weill's early work was as a production assistant and assistant editor to Carl Lerner on the feature documentary, *Revolution* (1967). She followed this with independent work, *Fran* (*Radcliffe Blues*), a 25-minute film on an SDS-womens' lib radical; and *Metropole,* a 4-minute film on go-go dancers at the Metropole Cafe. Films made with Noyes include a documentary on the *Putney School* in Vermont (1969, 23 minutes), one on the *Aspen Design Conference* (1971, 20 minutes), and fifteen for "Sesame Street." Their film *This is the Home of Mrs. Levant Graham* (1970, 15 minutes) is about a black family from South Carolina, living in the North. Though the family's house is cramped and life is hard, a strong spirit shines through.

Weill has done much freelance camerawork on political spots, network television specials, and such feature documentaries as Sandra Hochman's *Year of the Woman*. She also produced and directed short films about the quality of life in New York for WNET's "The 51st State." Topics included cockroaches, a marriage license bureau, yoga classes, and a commuter train that carries white executives from Scarsdale to New York and black maids from New York to Scarsdale. She co-directed, with Joyce Chopra, the much-viewed *Joyce at 34,* about Chopra's experiences in having her first child at the age of 34. Weill also directed, shot and co-edited, with Aviva Slesin, a documentary produced by Shirley MacLaine on the first American women's delegation to the People's Republic of China, *The Other Half of the Sky: A China Memoir* (74 minutes).

MIRIAM WEINSTEIN, Concord, Massachusetts, learned the basics of filmmaking at film school. A film she did as a stu-

dent, *Liberate the Ladies* (6 minutes), shows some of the
"lunatic fringe" of the women's rights movement. Later she
filmed *Not Me Alone* (30 minutes) and *How to Make a
Woman* (60 minutes) with co-filmmaker Al Fiering. *Not Me
Alone* shows a woman and her husband preparing for natural
childbirth. It dispels the myth that suffering is an inevitable
part of childbirth, and concentrates on the preparatory exer-
cises and the birth itself as a shared experience for the
couple. *How to Make a Woman* is a film of a women's liberation play. It dramatizes how men attempt to "create" women
in images that please men, grossly padding them and im-
prisoning them in Peter Pumpkin-Eater domesticity. Weinstein has made a film in support of day-care facilities, *Day
Care Today*, and three other short films, *My Father the
Doctor* (18 minutes), *Living With Peter* (22 minutes), and
We Get Married Twice (22 minutes). She is one of the
founders of a professional filmmakers association, Filmwomen
of Boston.

RUTH WHITE, Los Angeles, a producer-composer for Angel
Records and head of the educational record company
Rhythm Productions, also does sound for independent films.
A self-taught electronics expert, she works with a roomful of
intricate electronic machinery, all of it modified to make
music: two synthesizers, a reverb unit, amplifiers, oscillators,
speed changers, and tape recorders, as well as a piano, guitar,
and harpsichord. She built one of the synthesizers herself
before the Moog came on the market. In 1970 she did the
music for Computer Image's short film *Steel*, matching electronic music to the computer's version of the various uses of
steel. She has also worked on promotional films and short
films for television. More recently she has made four educational pilots, to be released on video cassettes. One is on
paper sculptures, another is on a space trip. The third is an
electronic arrangement of folk songs, *Hush Little Baby*, and
the last, *Adventures in Underland*, is the story of a dog who

digs down so far he reaches a land where the law of relativity has gone wild. She wrote, directed, and conceived the sound effects for all these pilots.

JEAN L. WILLIAMS, Venice, Florida, whose specialty is scientific and industrial animation, belies the enduring notion that women can't grasp complex technical concepts. Her 30-minute film for the American Heart Association, *Functional Anatomy of the Aortic Valve,* which she directed, supervised and animated, was judged the best scientific film of the year by the American College of Chest Physicians and won several other prestigious awards. Some of her other award-winning films: *The Development of the Human Tooth* (25 minutes) for the American Society of Dentistry; *Symmetry* (11 minutes) for the National Science Foundation, and *Shapes* (six 10-minute films) for Xerox. She also has done a number of technical films for pharmaceutical manufacturers, industrial firms and the U.S. Army, all of them marked by a high degree of precision and a mastery of the mechanics of motion picture production. Williams worked for several production studios beginning in 1950, and in 1971 struck out on her own. Now based in Florida, she travels wherever her work takes her.

JEANNIE YOUNGSON, New York, has a graduate degree in fine arts and has conducted classes on underground and experimental film techniques for several years. Her early short films include *Alphabet, Shapes, Happiness Is a Rolls Royce, The Diamond Lady,* and *Trilogy.* More recent short films include *Eleanor's Cake Which Ate Her; An Egg Named Sam; Fun Village* (subtitled: *If You Like Cops*); *I Never Promised You a Garden, Rose; I'll Drink to That;* and *It's a Wise Man Who Knows What's Biting Him!* She recently produced and directed *My Name Is Debbie,* a documentary on a transsexual father of a fifteen-year-old girl, who became a female after a sex-change operation. Other films include the 3-minute animated *Maude in Her Hat*, a comic film about an old lady who has a habit of collecting funny sounds; *Water* (1 minute), about pollution; and *The Snow Fairy* (2½ minutes), an animated film about the director's childhood. Youngson says:

"Since I have been working alone for the most part, I have not run into any bias against women in films. Nearly all women I've met who are totally immersed in the women's liberation movement have turned out in the long run to be frustrated—sometimes they were held down by their fathers or were unhappily married. I think most of the women's liberation movement is a drag! I started to make movies because I *wanted* to make movies, and I've never been happier or busier."

Coni Beeson

Kristina Nordstrom

Juliana Wang

Jill Godmilow

Deborah Shaffer and Bonnie Freedman

Marian Hunter, Patricia Bertozzi and Yvonne Young

Deedee Halleck   Elaine Summers

Lynn Connor Fischer, directing an industrial film.

Mary Pat Kelly, writer and co-producer of *Beside the Singing River*, with actors Dennis Mulligan and Brian Doyle Murray.

Yvonne Andersen, with a student.   Phyllis Chinlund

PART THREE

DIRECTORY

A LISTING OF WOMEN FILMMAKERS
THROUGHOUT THE UNITED STATES

There is nothing connected with the making of a motion picture that a woman cannot do as easily as a man, and there is no reason why she cannot master every technicality of the art.

Alice Guy Blaché wrote this in 1914, but only now is the breakthrough taking place. Women in increasing numbers are making films and forcefully insisting that they be judged by their talents. A clear expression of what this new determination has already produced was the Festival of Women's Films held in New York in June, 1972. Organized by Kristina Nordstrom and a group of friends, the festival presented 120 films to large audiences of women who found in the films and in each other a heightened sense of purpose and solidarity. Since that time there have been other gatherings of women filmmakers and other events underscoring their achievements, and each of these has illuminated the way ahead. The best films are yet to be made—films that enrich the mind, ennoble the human spirit, and offer new revelations of beauty—and many of these films will be made by women.

(About the directory: This is by no means a complete compilation, although every effort was made to locate filmmakers in all parts of the country. A second edition of this book is planned, and I invite filmmakers who are not listed to write to me at Hopkinson and Blake, 329 Fifth Avenue, New York, N. Y. 10016. Meanwhile, I hope this directory will be helpful to women who are forming film crews and to those male employers who say they would hire women filmmakers if they knew where to find them. Sharon Smith)

Antonia: A Portrait of the Woman, by Judy Collins and Jill Godmilow, was one of the outstanding documentaries of 1974. The film about conductor Antonia Brica was nominated for an Academy Award.

ABBOUND, PHYLLIS, Chicago Audiovisual Services, 533 E. Ontario St., Chicago, Ill. 60610. Producer.

ACUNA, JUDITH SHAW, % Women Make Movies, 257 W. 19th St., New York, N. Y. 10011. Her short film, *For Better or Worse* (7 min.), is about a young woman pediatrician with husband trouble.

ADATO, PERRY MILLER, 3 Fraser Rd., Westport, Conn. 06880. Producer-director, WNET-13. Feature documentary films include *Dylan Thomas: The World I Breathe* (Emmy Award); *Gertrude Stein: When This You See, Remember Me; The Great Radio Comedians; The Film Generation and Dance.* Short films include *Untitled* (a film of a radio performance), and *Eames at Moma.* (See p. 146)

AINGE, SUSAN M., 1557 York Ave., New York, N. Y. 10028. Educational production, direction, scriptwriting and cinematography for Behavioral Research Labs and other firms.

ALAIMO, LOUISE, 11248 Emelita St., #4, North Hollywood, Cal. 91601. Directs; some sound, camera, writing and editing. Films include *The Woman's Film* (45 min.).

ALBERTANO, LINDA, 11 Wavecrest Ave., Venice, Cal. 90291. One-woman films, including *Overdose* (20 min.).

ALDAN, DAISY, 325 E. 57th St., New York, N. Y. 10022. One-woman films including *Once Upon an El*, about tearing down the Third Avenue El, and *The Racial Question.*

ALEMANN, JOHANNA, % Alemann Films, P.O. Box 76244, Los Angeles, Cal. 90076. Veteran filmmaker, educational films; production, writing, editing, camera. Series include: "Changing Environment U.S.A.," "History Through Art," "Inspirations from Nature," and others.

ALENIKOFF, FRANCES, 68 Hog Creek Rd., East Hampton, N. Y. 11937. Creates and produces short films for multimedia dance theater works.

ALLEN, DEDE. (See p. 75)

ALLEN, GLORIA, 240 E. 28th St., New York, N. Y. 10016. Documentaries; *City Scenes #1* and *City Scenes #2* (both 10 min.).

ALLEN, NORMA, % Bald Eagle Films, 1520 New Hampshire Ave., N.W., Washington, D.C. 20036. Documentary filmmaker. Films include *A Song for Dead Warriors* (26 min.), distributed by Tricontinental Film Center, and *The Lawmakers* (80 min.).

AMATNIEK, KATHIE, 169 Sullivan St., New York, N. Y. 10012. Associate/assistant editor for many films, including *If You Give a Dance You Gotta Pay the Band* (90 min. TV special produced by David Susskind for ABC), *Doc* (feature produced by Frank Perry), *Crushproof* (independent feature), and other feature, documentary, educational and industrial films.

ANDERSEN, YVONNE, Director of the Yellow Ball Workshop, 62 Tarbell Ave., Lexington, Mass. 02173. Animator, teacher, author. Films include *Let's Make a Film* (13 min.), and *Fat Feet* (19 min., camera). Distributes prize-winning animated films made by children. (See p. 146)

ANDERSON, AMELIA, 2105 N. Beverly Glen Blvd., W. Los Angeles, Cal. 90023. One-woman films, including *Revelation* (4 min.), about a young woman facing and resolving a dilemma.

ANDERSON, ERICA, % Albert Schweitzer Friendship House, Hurlburt Rd., Great Barrington, Mass. 01230. Promotes Albert Schweitzer's philosophy. Films include *Henry Moore, Grandma Moses, Albert Schweitzer, A Clearing in the Jungle, A Village Is Waiting.*

ANDERSON, MADELINE, % Children's TV Workshop, 1 Lincoln Plaza, New York, N. Y. 10023. Professor, Columbia University School of the Arts. Veteran producer, also director and editor. Films include *I Am Somebody* (28 min.), *Tribute to Malcolm X* (14 min.), "Sesame Street" shorts and "Electric Company" shorts. (See p. 147)

ARENS, RUTH, 1957 Palmerston Pl., #3, Los Angeles, Cal. 90027. Films include *The Landlady* (10 min.), *Strangers Lost* (7 min.), and *Through Glasses Darkly* (13 min.).

ARMSTRONG, SUZANNE, % Women Make Movies, 257 W. 19th St., New York, N. Y. 10011. Retired. Her short film, *Just Looking* (6 min.), is about the loneliness of an older woman.

ARNOLD, EVE, % Richard Price Associates, 314 W. 56th St., New York, N. Y. 10019. Film: *Behind the Veil* (50 min.). (See p. 147)

ARTHUR, KAREN, Arthur Productions, 7018 Woodrow Wilson Dr., Los Angeles, Cal. 90068. Producer/director. Films include *Legacy* (110 min., producer/director), *Segue* (20 min., producer/director), *Eileen* (30 min., filmmaker), and *Her's* (15 min., filmmaker).

ARZNER, DOROTHY. (See p. 19)

ASHLEY, MARTA, % Femedia, 2286 Great Highway, San Francisco, Cal. 94116. Producer of feminist films, including *Teach Your Children Well* (30 min.).

ASHUR, GERI, 33-35 Greene St., New York, N. Y. 10013. Director of feminist films, including *Janie's Janie* (24 min.).

AVILES, VICENTA, 12 W. 19th St., New York, N. Y. 10011. One-woman films on Puerto Ricans, such as *Coney Island* (60 min.).

BABBIN, JACQUELINE, % Pyramid Films, Box 1048, Santa Monica, Cal. 90406. Films include *J.T.* (1970, 51 min.), a drama of a young boy from Harlem and the alley cat he adopts.

BACH, MARGARET LESSER, 140 Hollister Ave., Santa Monica, Cal. 90405. Documentary film production. Films include *Sam* (17 min.), *The Good Life* (27 min.).

BACHAND, TREVA, 1205 Sherwin, Chicago, Ill. 60626. Editor.

BACHNER, ANNETTE, 360 First Ave., New York, N. Y. 10010. Veteran director and producer, mostly 35mm, but also 16mm and videotape. Commercials, industrials, documentaries. (See p. 148)

BACHRACH, DORO, 51 E. 93rd St., New York, N. Y. 10028. Writer, director, and producer of documentaries, theatrical shorts and feature films. Films include *David: Off and On* (42 min.; producer), *The Victors* (22 min.; writer and director), *The Waiting Room* (100 min.; co-producer). *The Waiting Room*, directed by Karen Sperling, is the first 35mm theatrical feature to be produced by an all-woman technical crew. (See p. 83)

BADZIAN, TERESA, % McGraw-Hill, 1221 Ave. of the Americas, New York, N. Y. 10020. Films include *The Little Giraffe* (8 min.).

BAGLEY, EUGENIE, 75 Perry St., New York, N. Y. 10014. Editing, sound. Was sound editor for *America, America* (1964), *The Boys in the Band* (1970), and Bob Fosse's *Lenny* (1974). Editor of TV documentaries including *The Individualist* on NET, and one of several editors of NBC's *Vietnam Hindsight*, a two-part program. Also edits TV series including ABC's "Wide World of Sports" and "The American Sportsman."

BAILEY, ELIZABETH, Box 3J, NMSU, University Park, Las Cruces, N. Mex. 88003. General manager, TV station; writer, director. Films include *Malnutrición* (28½ min., producer, director, co-writer), *Toward Peaceful Revolution* (28½ min., producer, director, writer, editor), and many television programs.

BAKALINSKY, ADAH, 3765 Wright Pl., Palo Alto, Cal. 94306. Film teacher. One-woman short films include *A Bit of Whifflery* (7 min.), *Hercules* (7 min.), *Time Out* (7 min.), and *Random Shapes Aloft* (8 min.).

BAKER, LAURETTA, % Youth Film Distribution Center, 43 W. 16th St., New York, N. Y. 10011. Short films, including *Office Cinderella* (3 min.).

BALFOUR-FRAZER, ANNE, % Phoenix Films, Inc., 470 Park Ave. S., New York, N. Y. 10016. Films include *Women of the Toubou* (25 min.), documenting the lives of the women of this ancient, matriarchal, nomadic tribe in which men and women share equally in every aspect of life.

BALTER, DIANE ROBB, 198 Ely Rd., Petaluma, Cal. 94952. One-woman films; animation.

BANK, MIRRA, Apt. 4A, 108 W. 15th St., New York, N. Y. 10001. Veteran editor. Films include *Metro: People in Transit*. (See p. 148)

BAREY, PAT, 6124 N. Winthrop Ave., Chicago, Ill. 60660. Documentary films with Gloria Callaci include *Until I Die* (30 min.), a documentary on the stages of dying with Dr. Kubler-Ross, *To Be Free: Jane Kennedy*, about a 45-year-old nurse who went to prison for destroying memory banks in protest against the Vietnam war. On her own Barey made *And Baby Makes Two*, a short about a single parent and an adopted child, and *Wheelies*, an impressionistic film on cars and their effect on the ecology.

BARNES, CHRISTINA, 96 Greene St., New York, N. Y. 10012. Camera, editor, director; documentaries. Films include *The Urban Lab: Boston Model Cities* (60 min., camera, editor), and *The Group School* (60 min., camera, editor, director).

BAROSS, JAN, % Ramona Productions, 740 S.W. 17th St., Corvallis, Ore. 97330. Animation; one-woman shorts; writer and director of documentary and promotional films.

BARRY, DIANE, % Center Cinema Co-op, % School of the Art Institute, Michigan at Adams, Chicago, Ill. 60603. Short films include *Dear Diary*, shot at sporadic intervals capturing the fragments of a day in the filmmaker's life.

BARTLETT, FREUDE, % Serious Business Co., 1927 Marin Ave., Berkeley, Cal. 94707. One-woman short films, including *Promise Her Anything but Give Her the Kitchen Sink* (3 min.), *Women and Children at Large* (10 min.). Also distributor.

BASS, BARBARA DeJONG, % Directors Guild of America, 7950 Sunset Blvd., Hollywood, Cal. 90046. Second assistant director. Films include *Honky Tonk* (MGM), *Little House on the Prairie* (NBC and Ed Friendly), *Heavy Traffic* (Steve Krantz Productions), *The Supercops* (MGM), *The Exorcist* (Warner Bros.), and *Jaws* (Zanuck/Brown and Universal).

BASS, ELAINE, % Pyramid Films, Box 1048, Santa Monica, Cal. 90406. Films include *From Here to There* (1964, 9 min.), about the human experience of travel, and *The Searching Eye* (1964, 18 min.), in which a 10-year-old boy sees what he can see at the beach. Co-filmmaker, Saul Bass.

BATCHELOR, JOY, % Pyramid Films, Box 1048, Santa Monica, Cal. 90406. Films include *Automania 2000* (1964, 10 min.), an animated look at traffic congestion in the future. Co-filmmaker, John Halas.

BAUMAN, SUZANNE, 25 Grove St., New York, N.Y. 10012. Entertainment films, including *The Cabinet* (14 min.), available from Carousel Films; *Button, Button* (13 min.); *Why the Sun & Moon Live in the Sky* (12 min., animated), available from ACI Films.

BAUMBACH, JO ANN, 1431½ Barry Ave., Los Angeles, Cal. 90025.

BEAMS, MARY, 83 N. Beacon St., Watertown, Mass. 02172. One-woman films, including *Aunt Mary* (5 min.), *Class of '75* (5 min.), and *Zoo Story* (30 min.).

BEEKMAN, BERNADETTE, 109-65 198th St., Hollis, N. Y. 11412. Film: *3 in the Park* (7 min.), distributed by Youth Films.

BEESON, CONI, Box 590, Belvedere, Cal. 94920. One-woman filmmaker; prize-winning shorts on sexuality, identity, dance. Films include *Unfolding* (17 min.); *Thenow* (14 min.); *Holding* (13 min.); *Watercress* (13 min.); *Ann, A Portrait* (19 min.); *Stamen* (6 min.); *Women* (12 min.); *Firefly* (6 min.). Video tapes include *Fast Therapy* and *Dancer's Workshop*. Films available from her or Radim Films. (See p. 148)

BEH, SIEW HWA, 2802 Arizona Ave., Santa Monica, Cal. 90404. Editor, Women & Film magazine. Two-woman shorts, including *The Stripper, The Dinner.*

BELLE, ANNE, Box 413, Remsenburg, N. Y. 11960. Director, editor, writer. Films include *Henry* (10 min.) and *August T* (25 min.). Awarded grants by National Endowment for the Arts and Creative Artists Program to film *Bayman,* a documentary of the men who harvest shellfish on eastern Long Island.

BELNIAK, SUSAN LOUISE, 4532 N. Major, Chicago, Ill. 60630. Writer, producer, director; short films.

BELSON, JANE, % Creative Film Society, 7237 Canby Ave., Reseda, Cal. 91335. Short films, including *Logos* (3 min.) and *Odds & Ends* (4 min.).

BENSON, CAROL, 2717 Rutledge Way, Stockton, Cal. 95207. Films include *It Only Hurts When I Laugh* (over two hundred slides documenting the sexual stereotypes in cartoons which degrade the image of women).

BENSON, LILLIAN, 11 Rivington St., New York, N. Y. 10002. Film teacher; one-woman shorts.

BEN-VENISTE, LORRAINE, 285 Ave. C, New York, N. Y. 10009. Writer, researcher, producer, teacher. Educational videotapes include *A Layman's Voyage to the Stars,* hour-long documentary on Kohoutek Comet watch.

BERTOZZI, PATRICIA, 32 Cooper Sq., New York, N. Y. 10003. Camera and sound; feminist films for Herstory Films, including *Feminist Party Streetwalks* (15 min.), *Women for Women* (20 min.), and *Just Married,* which portrays the myth and reality of marriage.

BEUGEN, JOAN, The Creative Establishment Inc., 740 N. Rush St., Chicago, Ill. 60611. Producer.

BEVERIDGE, HORTENSE, 401 Clinton Ave., Brooklyn, N.Y. 11238. Editor. Films include *Morris, Time to Make It* (9 min.), and the feature *Honey Baby* —*Honey Baby.* (See p. 150)

BILDERBACK, CAROLYN, 26 Grove St., New York, N. Y. 10014. Directs and edits dance films, including *From the Inside Out* (13 min.), available from Film Images.

BINFORD, MIRA, 434 West Mifflin, Madison, Wis. 53703. Writer, director; educational and documentary films. Did many films in India under USIS and Indian Government auspices, including *Cross-Currents* (on India's Five Year Plans), which won Cup of Honor at Second International Film Festival of Cambodia in 1969. Now engaged in a series of films on civilization of South Asia at the University of Wisconsin.

BJORK, JEWEL, % Visual Resources, 1841 Broadway, New York, N. Y. 10023. Co-directed *Where Time is a River* with Gay Matthaei.

BLACKINO, YVETTE, 125 E. 59th Pl., Los Angeles, Cal. 90003. Directed film on Watts: *Mi Cuidad Mi Amor* (15 min.).

BLACKSTONE, VIVIAN, % Peli-Graphic Productions, 2104 Hancock St., San Diego, Cal. 92110. Director of educational films, including *Opus One* (8 min.), *Well-Springs* (30 min.), *Acupuncture* (22 min.).

BLUMENTHAL, ANN E., 315 E. 69th St., New York, N. Y. 10021. Researcher, associate producer; live, film and tape. Worked on many films for NBC, CBS, and NET, including *New York Philharmonic Young People's Concerts* with Leonard Bernstein, Peter Ustinov's *Words and Music, Michael Tilson Thomas at Tanglewood, A Copland Celebration,* and "The Great American Dream Machine," among others.

BOBCZYNSKI, MICHELE, 3155 Octavia, San Francisco, Cal. 94123. Animated films.

BODE, LENORE, 25 Fifth Ave., New York, N. Y. 10003. *Three Lives* (70 min.; camera), *The Jaguar Film* (70 min., co-producer, camera), *Between 3 & 4: Creating Freely* (20 min., producer, director, camera).

BONHAM, KATHY, 1452 Pennsylvania St., Denver, Colo. 80216. One-woman documentaries, including *Head Start and the Community* (24 min.).

BOOKER, SUE, 1645½ Lyman Place, Los Angeles, Cal. 90027. Producer, director, writer; Emmy Award winner specializing in films for television. (See p. 151)

BOOTH, SHEILA, % Lawrence Booth Films, Box 907, Half Moon Bay, Cal. 94019. Composer, motion picture sound recordist. Has completed 60 film scores and sound tracks, 22 "sound paintings," including *The Wheel* (7 min.), *Pulse* (16 min.), and *God's House* (30 min.). (See p. 152)

BORO, SUSAN, 3420 Louisa St., Pittsburgh, Pa. 15213. Writer, editor, some camera; short films.

BOTTNER, BARBARA, 812 Broadway, New York, N. Y. 10003. One-woman animated films. Short films include *A Goat in a Boat,* seven animated films for "The Electric Company," and one live-action film, *God Bless America* (6 min.). Winner, International Animation Festival in Annecy, France.

BOYER, ELEANOR ANDERSON, % Center Cinema Co-op, % Columbia College, 540 N. Lake Shore Dr., Chicago, Ill. 60611. Films include *Corita's Ice Man Bar* (5½ min.), a collage of the old times in a southwestern town.

BRADLEY, CLAIRE, 107 W. 82nd St., New York, N. Y. 10024. Production coordinator, associate producer, unit manager.

BRADLEY, SANDRA WENTWORTH, 1611 Connecticut Ave., N.W., Suite 1, Washington, D.C. 20009. Film editor, sound recordist mixer, assistant camera operator, second camera operator. Work includes commercials, documentaries for foreign (USIA) and domestic release, occasional news coverage, sales films, political spots.

BRANDON, LIANE, % New Day Films, Box 315, Franklin Lakes, N. J. 07417. Feminist shorts; *Betty Tells Her Story* (20 min.), *Sometimes I Wonder Who I Am* (5 min.), *Anything You Want to Be* (8 min.), and *Not So Young Now as Then* (18 min.). (See p. 153)

BRIGGS, NORMA, % Department of Apprenticeship Training, 310 Price Pl., Dept. of Labor, Madison, Wis. 53705. Films include government-sponsored *Never Underestimate the Power of a Woman* (15 min.), showing women doing work which is often male defined.

BROCKMAN, SUSAN, 138 Duane St., New York, N. Y. 10013. Filmmaker. Member, Women Artists/Filmmakers.

BROOKS, VIRGINIA (HOCHBERG), 460 Riverside Dr., New York, N. Y. 10027. Director, camera, editor; primarily dance films, including *School of American Ballet* (43 min.).

BROWN, BARBARA, 413 W. 21st St., New York, N. Y. 10011. Films include *Weaving* (4½ min.), *Lady Blue* (3 min.), *Morris the Misfit* (2 min., distributed by B. E. Brown), and *Katie Kelly* (5 min., distributed by Women Make Movies).

BROWN, GWEN, 41 King St., New York, N. Y. 10014. Films include *My Name Is Children* (60 min.), *Four Children* (30 min.), *Goodbye—Goodluck* (30 min.), about a black G.I. returning from Vietnam, and *Where the People Are* (30 min.), about a divinity student who struggles with his conscience about the war in Vietnam.

BROWN, JEAN PATRICIA, 77 Chittenden Ave., Columbus, O. 43201. One-woman short films: theatrical and animated.

BROWN, MARCIA, 3915 Coco Ave., Los Angeles, Cal. 90008.

BUCHANNAN, PATRICIA, 131 Alvarado Road, Berkeley, Cal. 94705. One-woman films; camera; ass't professor of film history and animation at the University of California at San Francisco. Short films: *The Day We Seized the Streets in Oakland* (12 min.), *The Spirit of the People Is Greater Than the Man's Technology* (3 min., clay animation) and *Autopsy of a Queen* (30 min., financed by an American Film Institute grant).

BUCKNER, BARBARA, 254 W. 15th St., New York, N. Y. 10011. Films include *Erotica Extenda*, shown at the Whitney Museum.

BURGUND, ANN, 412 West End Ave., New York, N. Y. 10024. Editor, writer; children's educational films.

BURNS, CAROL, 4311 Cooper Point Rd., N.W., Olympia, Wash. 98502. Camera, editor, writer. Films include *Huelga* (60 min., camera), *As Long as the Rivers Run* (60 min., camera, editor, writer).

BURRILL, CHRIS, 1332 Laurel Way, Beverly Hills, Cal. 90210. Camera-woman; editor. (See p. 154)

BURTON, FRANCES, % Center Cinema Co-op, School of the Art Institute, Michigan at Adams, Chicago, Ill. 60603. Short films include *March 13 to March 20* (20 min.), a diary film in which the filmmaker participates.

BUTE, MARY ELLEN. (See p. 33)

CAIN, SUGAR, % Creative Film Society, 7237 Canby Ave., Reseda, Cal. 91335. Short films, including *Rama* (16 min.).

CALAGNI, ANN CURTIS, % Film Images, 17 W. 60th St., New York, N. Y. 10023. Films include *The Search* (13 min.), a blending of poetry, sculpture, and music with the sounds of a river bank.

CALHOON, BARBARA, 2150 Concord Blvd., Concord, Cal. 94520. Producer, director, some editing and camera. Films include *The Creative Kindergarten* (40 min., producer, director), *Visualization: A Key to Reading* (25 min., producer and special effects), *A Child Creates* (7 min., producer and director).

CALLACI, GLORIA, 561 Stratford Pl., Chicago, Ill. 60657. Co-directed with Pat Barey *Until I Die* (30 min.), a documentary on the stages of dying with Dr. Kubler-Ross, and *To Be Free: Jane Kennedy*, about a 45-year-old nurse who went to prison for destroying memory banks in protest against the Vietnam war.

CANTOW, ROBERTA, 353 E. 15th St., New York, N. Y. 10003. Writer, director, editor. Short films include *Autostop* (15 min.).

CARTER, DIXIE, 220 E. 63rd St., Chicago, Ill. 60637. Editor.

CAUFIELD, MARIE CELENE, % Women Make Movies, 257 W. 19th St., New York, N. Y. 10011. Films include *It's a Miracle* (1973, 7 min.), about a girl's work and the boy she wants to love her.

CAVALLARO, JEANNE FISHER, 38 E. 75th St., New York, N. Y. 10021. Veteran writer, producer, editor; documentaries and commercials.

CHAFFEE, JOAN, 176 W. 82nd St., New York, N. Y. 10024. Edits features, commercials, educationals, industrials, and art films.

CHANGAR, MYRNA HARRISON, 61 South Lilburn Dr., Garnerville, N. Y. 10923. Directs short films, including *The Neighborhood* (18 min.), available from Filmmakers' Co-op.

CHANGAS, ESTELLE, 455 Westmount Dr., Los Angeles, Cal. 90048.

CHAPELLE, POLA, 29 W. 89th St., New York, N. Y. 10024. Feature films: *Windflowers* (64 min., "an elegy for a draft dodger") and *Going Home* (60 min.; co-filmmaker Adolfas Mekas; distributed by New Yorker Films). Short films include *An Interview With the Ambassador from Lapland* (6 min.), *Those Memory Years* (8 min., "a woman in search of fulfillment"), and *How to Draw a Cat* (2½ min.). Distributed by Filmmakers' Co-op.

CHAPPLE, WENDY WOOD, Hanks Hill Rd., Storrs, Conn. 06268. Writer, director, camera, editor; documentaries. Films directed and written include *Yankee Craftsman* (20 min.; prizes include Cine Award), *Promises to Keep* (28 min.; award winner), *Teaching the One and the Many* (28 min.), *Alcoholism: Industry's Hangover* (28 min.), *America at Sea* (20 min.). (See p. 154)

CHARLTON, MARYETTE, Box 15, Schooley's Mountain, N. J. 07870. Director, camera, editor, producer, painter; films on American artists, including *Loren MacIver* (two parts, 23 min. each).

CHASE, DORIS, 222 W. 23rd St., New York, N. Y. 10011. Filmmaker, painter, sculptor. Films, all in color with sound, include *Circles I* (7 min.), *Circles I Variation II* (7 min.), *Circles II* (14 min.), *Circles II Variation II* (8 min., available from Perspective Films), *Squares* (7 min., available from Pictura Films), *Full Circle—The Work of Doris Chase* (10½ min., produced by Elizabeth Wood, available from Perspective Films).

CHEN, BETTY, % Serious Business Co., 1927 Marin Ave., Berkeley, Cal. 94707. Director of short films, including *Marguerite* (3 min.).

CHENIS, PATTI-LEE, % Filmmakers' Co-op, 175 Lexington Ave., New York, N. Y. 10016. Short experimental films including *Sumleo* (2 min.), *Yogurt Culture* (11½ min.), *Texture Study* (15 min.); all sound-on-tape.

CHICAGO, JUDY, % California Institute of the Arts, McBean Pkwy., Valencia, Cal. 91355. Artist; collaborated on *Womanhouse* (18 min.).

CHILD, ABIGAIL, 114 E. 13th St., New York, N. Y. 10003. Director; also editor, some camera and sound. Films include *Game* (38 min.), *Except the People* (20 min.), *Mother Marries a Man of Mellow Mien* (7 min.), *Will You Still Be a Mother?* (23 min.), *Savage Streets* (24 min.). (See p. 156)

CHINLUND, JENNIFER, 624½ Shotwell St., San Francisco, Cal. 94110. Editor of feature films, documentaries, educationals. Director/editor of several short films for educational TV.

CHINLUND (formerly Johnson), PHYLLIS, 2 Horatio St., New York, N. Y. 10014. Producer, director, editor; documentaries. Films include *Family Planning: More than a Method* (27 min.); *Two Worlds to Remember* (38 min.); *Robin, Peter & Darryl: 3 to the Hospital* (53 min.); *It Won't Be Easy* (34 min.); *It Began with Birds* (28 min.), and others. (See p. 157)

CHOPRA, JOYCE, 6 Follen St., Cambridge, Mass. 02138. Producer, director of many films, including *A Happy Mother's Day* (co-directed with Richard Leacock); *Room to Learn* and *Present Tense* (for NET Playhouse); *Tyrone Guthrie* (NET Creative Person Series), *Water* (for "Sesame Street"), and *Joyce at 34* (co-filmmaker Claudia Weill). Winner, Venice Film Festival. (See p. 158)

CHURCHILL, JOAN, % A. Churchill Film, 662 N. Robertson Blvd., Los Angeles, Cal. 90069. Filmmaker, camera. Films include *Sylvia, Fran and Joy* (25 min.; director), and *A 7½ Minute Film* (camera).

CICHY, THEODORA, % Filmmakers' Co-op, 175 Lexington Ave., New York, N. Y. 10016. Short films, including *Maximus to Himself* (5 min.).

CITRON, MICHELE, % Radio-TV Dept., Temple University, Philadelphia, Pa. 19122. Short films include *April 3, 1973*, in which the activities of three women are represented by different colored index cards, and *Self Defense*, an experimental film.

CLARK, SUSAN HANSEN, 450 West End Ave., New York, N. Y. 10024. Directs and edits documentaries, including *Maurice Lidchi: Auctioneer* (20 min.), *The Mayorkas Collection* (30 min.).

CLARKE, SHIRLEY. (See p. 42)

CLIFTON, MICHELLE GAMM, Avery Rd., Garrison, N. Y. 10524. Art director. Films include *Christina's World* (52 min., for television), *Not a Place* (26 min.), *In Order to Effect Change . . .* (28 min.).

COHEN, MAXI M., 71-73 Franklin St., New York, N. Y. 10013. Video and filmmaker; producer, director, editor. Films include *Nature Morte Aux Fruits* (3 min., writer, director, animator; available from Perspective Films), *Its Your Time* (10 min., director, editor), *Dedicated to Peace* (12 min., producer, director, editor), *Me and Daddy* (60 min., producer, co-director, co-editor).

COHN, JUDITH, 2829 S. Sepulveda, Los Angeles, Cal. 90064. Research director and associate producer.

COLEMAN, WILLETTE, % NET Training School, 10 Columbus Circle, New York, N. Y. 10019. Writer, director, editor; short social and racial commentaries.

COLLINS, MARY SHARACIO, % The Film School, School of Visual Arts, New York, N. Y. 10010. Short films include *Zoo* (3 min.), about a zany animal house.

COLLINS, SUSAN TRIESTE, 29012 Crags Dr., Agoura, Cal. 91301. Film editor, sound editor, associate producer, assistant director; features, shorts, commercials. Film and sound editor for *Love, Love, Love* (Hallmark TV special); *To Europe with Love* (Timex TV special); *The Blue Horn* (feature); *Secret Places, Secret Things* (feature), and others.

COMMENT, CONSTANCE, 1402 Geurerro St., San Francisco, Cal. Filmmaker, writer. Films include *Ova Express* (10 min.), *Voyage à la Lune* (10 min.), and *Yesterdays* (6 min.). Distributed by Underground Cinema 12 Group.

COMPTON, JULEEN, 474 Cuesta Way, Bel Air, Cal. 90024. Director, independent filmmaker. Films include *Stranded,* and *The Plastic Dome of Norma Jean* (producer, director, writer; awards include the Special Award at the San Francisco Film Festival and the Jury's Grand Prize at the Cannes Festival). (See p. 158)

CONRAD, BEVERLY GRANT, 111 W. 42nd St., New York, N. Y. 10036. Director. Films made with Tony Conrad include *Coming Attractions* (78 min.), about the lives and loves of an aging transsexual, *Four Screen* (1971, 18 min.), a multi-screen projection about red, the space and time, *Straight and Narrow* (1970, 10 min.), a study in subjective color and visual rhythm. The films, which have been shown widely in the U.S. and Europe, are all available from the Filmmakers' Co-op.

COOLIDGE, MARTHA, 236 E. 19th St., New York, N. Y. 10003. Producer, director; also some editing and writing. Documentaries and dramatic films including *David: Off and On* (42 min.), *More Than a School* (55 min.), *Old Fashioned Woman?* (30 min.). Distributed by Films Incorporated and the filmmaker. (See p. 159)

CORONADO, ELIDA, 311 S. Witmer St., Los Angeles, Cal. 90017. Ethnic films.

COSTA, SYLVIA, 76 Harding Rd., Red Bank, N. J. 07701. Producer; films in 16mm and 35mm.

COUZIN, SHARON, Augenlust Films, 6643 Sueno, Goleta, Cal. 93017. Educator, head of her production company, and maker of one-woman experimental films, including *Dance of Well-Spaced Teeth* (5 min.), *Nimbusodilongradiva* (7 min.), *True Flick* (4 min., shown at the Ann Arbor and Bellvue Film Festivals), and *Roseblood* (7 min., shown at many festivals including the Ann Arbor 8mm Film Festival and the Atlanta International Film Festival, where it won awards). (See p. 159)

COX, NELL, % Nell Cox Films, Inc., 109 W. 11th St., New York, N. Y. 10011. Producer, writer, editor, director of many films, including *French Lunch* (15 min.), *Operator* (15 min.), *A to B* (36 min.), and *Trial* (54 min., documentary of a murder trial). (See p. 160)

CRANDELL, L. LEE, 28 Warner Plaza, #7, Kansas City, Mo. 64111. Cinematographer, filmmaker. Films include *Tai Chi: A Way of Centering* (3 min., 16mm, sound; filmmaker). Also writes screenplays.

CRANE, SHIRLEY, 1331 44th St., San Francisco, Cal. 94122. Films include *To See To Be I* (5 min.), an analysis of a tree, *To See To Be II* (8 min.), an analysis of color and movement, and *Dance of (?)* (15 min.).

CRESAP, SALLY WILLISS, Box 723, Woodstock, N. Y. 12498. Films include *Aqua Continuance* (8 min.), *Saratoga Improvisation* (15 min.), *Shootout on Tinker Street* (12 min.).

CRUIKSHANK, SALLY, 1890 Arch St., Berkeley, Cal. 94709. Short animated films, including *Fun on Mars* (5 min.), *Chow Fun* (5 min.).

CUNNINGHAM, PHYLLIS FENN, 291 Collins St., Hartford, Conn. 06105. One-woman films including *Legend of the Cherry Tree* (15 min.) and *Life-Lines* (15 min.).

DALE, RUBE L., 6022 Dauphin Ave., Los Angeles, Cal. 90034. First black unit manager in Hollywood. In 1974 wrote, produced and directed first feature, a Western, *My Own Peacemaker*, possibly first feature made by a black woman.

DALEY, SANDY, 222 W. 23rd St., New York, N. Y. 10011. Producer, director; documentary films, including *Robert Having His Nipple Pierced* (33 min., soundtrack by Patti Smith).

DANCOFF, JUDY, % Creative Film Society, 7237 Canby Ave., Reseda, Cal. 91335. Feminist film director. Films include *Judy Chicago and the California Girls* (27 min.).

DAVENPORT, REBECCA, % New Line Cinema, 121 University Pl., New York, N. Y. 10003. Films include *The Upperville Show* (10 min.), about the oldest horse show in America.

DAVENPORT, SUZANNE, Kartemquin Films Ltd., 1901 W. Wellington, Chicago, Ill. 60657. Films include cooperatively made *Winnie Wright, Age 11* (26 min.), a portrait of an individual in a community torn by racial conflict as it changes from white to black.

DAVEY, FLORENCE, % New Line Cinema, 121 University Pl., New York, N. Y. 10003. Films include *Indian Holy Men* (28 min.), four Indian holy men explore varieties of Indian spirituality. Co-filmmaker, Satyan Shivan Sandaram. Shown at the Whitney Museum.

DAVID, MERIDITH BAR, 614 Eastwood Way, Mill Valley, Cal. 94941. Editor. Films include *Liaisons* (60 min.).

DE CASTRO, DOLORES, 1134 7th St., Santa Monica, Cal. 90403. One-woman films including *Paper Film* (10 min.).

DE HIRSCH, STORM, 136 W. 4th St., New York, N. Y. 10012. Veteran abstract and experimental filmmaker. Films include *The Color of Ritual, the Color of Thought* (26 min.) and *The Tattooed Man* (35 min.). Films available from Filmmakers' Co-op and Canyon Cinema Co-op. (See p. 161)

DE LAY, PEGGY, % Sedelmaier Film Productions, Inc., 610 N. Fairbanks Ct., Chicago, Ill. 60611. Editor.

DEEN, NEDRA, % Nedmar Productions, 1265 No. Havenhurst Dr., Los Angeles, Cal. 90046. Created, produced and performed in *A 7½ Minute Film,* a 16mm color short about women's role in society. Film has appeared in several film festivals.

DEES, SYLVIA, 6637 Franklin Ave., Hollywood, Cal. 90028. One-woman experimental films including *Superman and the Strippers* (5 min.), *Breath of Life* (2 min.), and *Turned On* (1 min.).

DEITCH, DONNA, 413 Howland Canal, Venice, Cal. 90291. Director, camera. Short films: *P.P.1.* (6 min.), *Memorabilia* (3 min.), *She Was a Visitor* (2 min.), *Berkeley: 12 to 1* (4 min.), *Portrait* (14 min.). Available from Filmmakers' Co-op and Canyon Cinema Co-op.

DEITRICH, ANGELA, % Youth Films Distribution Center, 43 W. 16th St., New York, N. Y. 10011. Director, short films, including *From the Bathroom* (7 min.).

DELL'OLIO, ANSELMA, 43 W. 54th St., New York, N. Y. 10019. Dialogue consultant for *The Leopard* and *Rocko and His Brothers* (both Visconti) and *The Tenth Victim* (Elio Petri), among others; assistant to Francesco Rosi on his latest film, *Lucky Luciano;* co-writer and assistant director, feature documentary for Canadian TV (director, Ene Riisna). Has also translated scripts, worked as associate producer for English TV series, founded her own theater group and written articles for many publications.

DELSON, SUE, Kartemquin Films Ltd., 1901 W. Wellington, Chicago, Ill. 60657. Films include cooperatively made *Now We Live on Clifton* (25 min.), about social effects of remodeling old apartments, i.e. higher rents which force out families.

DELUC, GERMAINE, % Creative Film Society, 7237 Canby Ave., Reseda, Cal. 91335. Work includes *Assault on the Eiffel Tower* (25 min.).

DEMBY, JILL, 17 W. 95th St., Apt. 1B, New York, N. Y. 10025. Editor. Also does short one-woman films.

DEMETRAKAS, JOHANNA, 6644 Valmont St., Tujunga, Cal. 91042. Editor, director, producer. Films include *Celebration at Big Sur* (feature, co-directed and edited with Baird Bryant); award-winning documentary *Womanhouse* (47 min., director and editor), and new feature *Caged Heat.* (See p. 162)

DEREN, MAYA. (See p. 34)

DICKENSON, MARGARET, % Impact Films, 144 Bleeker St., New York, N. Y. 10012. Films include *Behind the Lines* (32 min.), a close-up of life in a liberated zone in Mozambique.

DICKSON, DEBORAH, 310 W. 88th St., New York, N. Y. 10024. Films include *The Children's School* (17 min.; director, editor); *August* (25 min.; director, editor), and an experimental film, *Water's Dream* (10 min.; director, editor, camera).

DILLS, BARBARA, % Women's Film Co-op, 200 Main St., Northampton, Mass. 01060. Co-filmmaker of *Autobiography of a Woman* (20 min.), depicting the brutal and repressive forces that have kept women in their place yet given them a sense of future direction.

DOBSON, JANE, 423 E. 77th St., New York, N. Y. 10021. Films include *Shadowgraph* (10 min.), a study in form, and *Waterform* (10 min.), a slow-motion exploration of water and ice.

DONAHUE, BONNIE, % Center Cinema Co-op, School of the Art Institute, Michigan at Adams, Chicago, Ill. 60603. Animator, educator. Films include *Fly Bites*, which expresses the inner space of dreams.

DOUGHERTY, ARIEL, % Women Make Movies, 257 W. 19th St., New York, N. Y. 10011. Co-director and co-founder of this non-profit organization, which is devoted to helping women create their own film, video and radio productions. Her films include *Sweet Bananas* (30 min.; director), and *The Women's Happy Time Commune* (50 min.; camera). (See p. 195)

DOWD, NANCY ELLEN, Box 523, Topanga, Cal. 90290. Writer, filmmaker. Films include *The Gibbous Moon* (27 min.; one-woman film); *The Decay of Fiction* (one-woman film), and *Teamsters and Students on Strike* (co-filmmaker Attila Domokos). Member, Writers Guild.

DRUKS, RENATE, 26885 Via Linda, Malibu, Cal. 90265. Director, scenic designer. Films include *Painter's Journal* (12 min.) and *Space Boy*, 1973 Cannes Film Festival entry.

DUGA, IRENE VERBITSKY, % Filmmakers' Co-op, 175 Lexington Ave., New York, N. Y. 10016. Short films, including *Pesca, Pesca* (3 min.), *Turtle Soup* (5 min.), *Maze Doodles* (7 min.), *Woman* (1 min.), and *The Beginning* (1 min.).

DU LUART, YOLANDA, % New Yorker Films, 43 W. 61st St., New York, N. Y. 10023. Documentary films include *Angela Davis: Portrait of a Revolutionary* (60 min.).

DUNCAN, BEVERLY, 1564 Milvia St., Berkeley, Cal. 94709. Illustrator; animator, *Current Approach to the Hypertensive Patient.*

DUNCAN, VIRGINIA BAUER, Box 18222, San Francisco, Cal. 94118. Director, producer; video and films. Films include documentaries *Ascent* (30 min.) and *Ski Touring* (28 min.).

DYAL, SUSAN, % Creative Film Society, 7237 Canby Ave., Reseda, Cal. 91335. Short films, including *Navajo Rain Chant* (3 min.).

EDELHEIT, MARTHA, 1140 Fifth Ave., New York, N. Y. 10028. Painter, one-woman filmmaker. Films include *Camino Real* (3 min.) and *The Albino Queen and Sno-White in Triplicate* (22 min.; three screen projection).

EDELL, NANCY, % Creative Film Society, 7237 Canby Ave., Reseda, Cal. 91335. Short films, including *Black Pudding* (7 min.) and *Charlie Co.* (10 min.).

EGGAN, CAREL ROWE, 818 Reba Pl., Evanston, Ill. 60202. Writer, director, producer: *L.I.N.K.* (25 min.), *Flamethrowers* (30 min.), and others.

EHRLICH, GRETAL, 1780 Twinslope Trail, Topanga, Cal. 90290. Editor; also director, camera, producer. Films include *Chicago Picasso* (60 min.; editor), *Watts Towers Theatre Workshop* (30 min.; editor), *Jockey* (30 min.; producer, director, editor).

ELDER, SARAH, 316 Brookline St., Cambridge, Mass. 02139. Short one-woman films.

ELLIOTT, SUE, 463 West St., New York, N. Y. 10014. Editor. Films include *The Making of the President, 1972* (90 min.) and *The Hard Chargers: Riding the Stock Car Circuit* (60 min.), both TV documentaries produced by Time-Life, *911* (3½ min. experimental documentary on police violence; winner of International Short Subjects Award at 1969 Chicago Film Festival), *Planned Parenthood* (two 30-minute documentaries), *Arena* (color short produced on AFI grant).

ENGLISH, DEIDRE, % Creative Film Society, 7237 Canby Ave., Reseda, Cal. 91335. Co-filmmaker on *D.C.III* (34 min.), a documentary on anti-war activities in Washington, D.C.

ERBACHER, SHIRLEY, 5234 S. Dorchester Ave., Chicago, Ill. 60615. Short films include *Kyle and Dawn,* portraying her children in various stages of growing up. Available from Center Cinema Co-op.

ERENBERG, ELENA, 20812 Hillside Dr., Topanga, Cal. 90290. Ethnographic research videotapes and animated shorts.

ESPAR, SHERI GILLETTE, 1643 Woodland Ave., E. Palo Alto, Cal. 94303. Editor; also writer and director. Films include *Miner's Ridge* (25 min.; editor), *Tomorrow's Children* (17 min.; writer and editor).

ETKES, NADINE, 7566 De Longpre Ave., Los Angeles, Cal. 90046. Short one-woman films, including *Aquarius* (4 min.).

EVANS, PAT, 546 Magnolia Wood Ave., Baton Rouge, La. 70808. Writer, producer, editor; documentaries for television, including *St. Gabriel Prison* (28½ min.).

FAYMAN, LYNN, % Creative Film Society, 7237 Canby Ave., Reseda, Cal. 91335. Films include *Greensleeves* (4 min.), abstract film to music of "Greensleeves," and *Sophisticated Vamp* (4 min.).

FEFERMAN, LINDA, 42 Grove St., New York, N. Y. 10014. Director; also writer and editor of independent films, including *Dirty Books* (17 min.) and *Menstruation* (18 min.).

FELDHAUS-WEBER, MARY, % WGBH, 125 Western Ave., Boston, Mass. 02134. Veteran writer, producer, director; films for television. Films include *Diane* (30 min.) and *Nine Heroes* (60 min.).

FELTER, SUSAN, 171 Mt. Vernon Ave., San Francisco, Cal. 94112. Filmmaker, still photographer; teaches film and photography. Films include *Pescados Vivos* (17 min., prize winner at Ann Arbor, Yale, Kent State and other film festivals).

FERGUSON, BETTY, % Filmmakers' Co-op, 175 Lexington Ave., New York, N. Y. 10016. Films include *Barbara's Blindness* (17 min.), made with Joyce Weiland.

FIELDS, PHYLLIS, 7900 Westlawn Ave., Los Angeles, Cal. 90045. One-woman short live-action and animated experimental films, including *Variation* (3 min.) and *Inept* (2 min.).

FINCH, KAYE, % University of Wisconsin, 45 N. Charter St., Madison, Wis. 53706. Veteran writer, director, editor; educational and documentary films. Films include *Blindness Is* (28 min.) and *Quartet* (57 min.). (See p. 162)

FINCK, JOAN, % Cambridge Films, 9 Florence St., Cambridge, Mass. 02139. Camera, *Taking Our Bodies Back* (30 min. documentary on women's health).

FIRESTONE, CINDA, Attica Films, Inc., 789 West End Ave., New York, N. Y. 10025. Documentary filmmaker. Produced, directed, edited *Attica* (1973, feature), a penetrating look at the 1971 prison rebellion. (See p. 163)

FISCHER, LYNN CONNOR, 2825 North Kings Road, Virginia Beach, Va. 23452. Producer, also director, writer, editor (slide films only). (See p. 165)

FISHER, ANNE, % Kostick, 234 W. 14th St., New York, N. Y. 10011. Co-produced and costumed historical film, *Guns Over Rockport* (12 min.).

FISHER, HOLLY, % Creative Film Society, 7237 Canby Ave., Reseda, Cal. 91335. Short films including *PSSSHT* (6 min.).

FISHKO, SARA, 201 W. 16th St., New York, N. Y. 10011. Editor; features and documentaries. Films include *Sammy Somebody, Echoes of Masada,* and *The Unknown Eiffel;* also a number of commercial films.

From Julia Reichert's *Growing Up Female.*

From Faith and John Hubley's *Of Men and Demons.*

FITZGERALD, DEBORAH, Voice & Vision Productions, Inc., 1833 Kalorama Rd., N.W., Washington, D.C. 20009. Vice-president of this minority-owned firm. Writer, director, and producer of films for national non-profit organizations and government agencies. Films include *Sobre Un Volcan* (28½ min., producer), for Central American audiences; winner of Cine Golden Eagle and other awards. Also bilingual TV film *Ayuda* (30 min.) and others.

FLAUM, THEA, 734 W. Hutchinson, Chicago, Ill. 60613. Writer, producer.

FLEMING, LOUISE, 661 West End Ave., New York, N. Y. 10025. Editor, director, producer. Films include *In Here Out There* (14 min., documentary, editor); *D.C. Public Schools Federal Programs* (30 min., documentary, director); *Betty's Theme* (7 min., director), *Just Briefly* (20 min., director).

FOLLMER, PATRICIA, 204 Franklin St., Cambridge, Mass. 02139. Director, editor, writer; feature films, documentaries, theatrical shorts, promotional films. Films include *Pinetree Camp* (15 min.), *Skin* (15 min.), *The Gypsy Life* (16 min.; writer, producer, director, camera, editor).

FORMAN, JANET, 230 E. 5th St., New York, N. Y. 10003. Producer, editor, production manager. Films include *To Sandy* (17 min., producer) and *Four Ladies on Stage* (15 min., producer).

FOSTER, ZENA, 1516 N. Hobart Blvd., #307, Hollywood, Cal. 90027. Associate producer, writer, script director, story analyst, actress, composer.

FOX, BARBARA B., % Postgraduate Center for Mental Health, 124 E. 28th St., New York, N. Y. 10016. Producer and director, training films for mental health professionals.

FRANCO, DEBRA, 62 Columbia St., Brookline, Mass. 02146. Independent filmmaker, editor. Films include *Marge Piercy* (2 min., director, editor), *Don Land* (8 min., director, editor), and *Not So Young Now As Then* (18 min., assistant editor).

FRANKLIN, MARJORIE, 2214A Carleton, Berkeley, Cal. 94704. Short films, including *Last Week* (5 min.), *White Susan* (6 min.).

FRENCH, BRANDON, Dept. of English, Yale University, New Haven, Conn. 06520. Films: *Brandy in the Wilderness* (82 min.; writer-producer), *The Butcher's Art* (writer), and one-woman films, including *Penelope* (22 min.).

FRERKS, GERALDINE, Box 41, Larkspur, Cal. 94939. One-woman experimental shorts. Animation production.

FREYER, ELLEN, 112 W. 15th St., New York, N. Y. 10011. College instructor of film history and maker of feminist shorts.

FRIEDMAN, BONNIE, 200 Riverside Dr., New York, N. Y. 10025. Pandora Films; co-writer, -producer, -director, camera, sound, editor. Feminist films, including *Childcare: People's Liberation* (20 min.) and *How About You?*, a film on birth control and sexuality (24 min.). In production, *Chris and Bernie* (30 min.), a film on single mothers. (See p. 166)

FROESCHNER, DONNA ANDERSON, Box 2579, St. Louis, Mo. 63114. Curriculum developer; film. Also writer and director. Films include *Movement in Dance* (15 min., director), *Introduction to Motion* (12 min., director, writer), *Lithium* (5 min., co-director), *Steve* (17 min., co-director, camera).

FULKERSON, TAVI, 712 Oakland, Ann Arbor, Mich. 48104. Films include *In Due Time*, a short about a college woman who had a leg amputated.

GAFFORD, CHARLOTTE, % Interlock Film Studio, 1218 S. 20th St., Birmingham, Ala. 35205. Writer; industrial films, including *A New Look at the Old Address* (28 min.), *On with the Flow* (20 min.). (See p. 166)

GALE, KIRA, 1616 N. 51st St., Omaha, Neb. 68104. Filmmaker and inventor of process for developing Super-8 film at home.

GARDNER, JANET, % American Documentary Films, 379 Bay St., San Francisco, Cal. 94133. Producer of feminist films, including *Inside the Ladies Home Journal* (15 min.).

GARDNER, JOAN A., 548 Orange St., New Haven, Conn. 06511. Co-animator-filmmaker (with husband, Frank); *The Robot* (18 min.) and *Jig Jag* (5 min.). Available from filmmaker.

GARSON, ARLINE, 511 Third Ave., New York, N. Y. 10016. Editor: TV dramas, theatrical features, documentaries, industrials, including *Rivals* (feature), *House of Dark Shadows* (feature), and "The Defenders," (TV series).

GAUDIO, CHERYL, % Carlos Cortinez, Language Dept., University of Maine, Orono, Me. 04473. Films include *Apple Pie*, showing the photographing of an FDS ad.

GERBER, DAISY, 2310 Midvale Ave., Los Angeles, Cal. 90069. Assistant director; Hollywood features. Films include *The Killing of Sister George, Whatever Happened to Aunt Alice, Bunny O'Hare, Steelyard Blues.* Member, Directors Guild of America.

GERSTEIN, CASSANDRA, 1227 Quartier le Pioulier, Vence 06 140 France. One-woman short films. Also *Tales* (70 min.).

GILL, ELIZABETH, 1234½ 6th St., Santa Monica, Cal. 90401. Screenwriter: *Girls of Huntington House* and *She Lives* (ABC Movie of the Week).

GILLIGAN, SONJA CARL, Indian Brook Rd., Garrison, N. Y. 10524. Director, writer. Films include *Christina's World* (52 min., for television), *Not a Place* (26 min.), *In Order to Effect Change . . .* (28 min.).

GIRITLIAN, VIRGINIA, % Serious Business Co., 1927 Marin Ave., Berkeley, Cal. 94707. Films include *Cumulus Nimbus* (6 min.).

GLASSMAN, JUDITH, % WEDH-TV, 24 Summit St., Hartford, Conn. 06106. Director, associate director, producer; television and film. Member, Directors Guild of America. Specialist in dance films and videotapes.

GLOBUS, DIANE, 21 Greenwich St., North Bennington, Vt. 05257. One-woman films; camera, writer.

GODMILOW, JILL, 480 West Broadway, New York, N. Y. 10012. Director, editor. Films include *La Nueva Vida* (85 min., writer, director, editor), *Tales* (70 min., co-director, editor), *Traveling* (30 min., writer, editor), *Antonia: A Portrait of The Woman* (57 min., co-director, editor; Special Jury Recommendation, Ann Arbor Film Festival, 1974). *Antonia* is available from Rocky Mountain Productions. (See p. 167)

GOLDBERG, JENNY, % Third World Newsreel, 26 W. 20th St., New York, N. Y. 10011. Produced *Homefront* (25 min.), portraying the life of tenants in New York City and their struggles to get decent housing for their community.

GOLDBERG, SHARON, 42 Horatio St., New York, N. Y. 10014. Assistant editor; writer, director, editor.

GOLDBERGER-JACOBY, SUSAN, 912 Fifth Ave., New York, N. Y. 10021. Short one-woman films, animation.

GOLDMAN, MICHAL, 8543 Lookout Mountain Ave., Los Angeles, Cal. 90046. Editor. Films include *Caged Heat* (85 min., feature), *Isaac Bashevis Singer and Mrs. Pupko's Beard* (27 min., documentary), *Panola* (23 min., documentary), and *The Exorcist* (121 min., feature, assistant editor).

GOLDSHOLL, MILLIE, 420 Frontage Rd., Northfield, Ill. 60093. Documentary, educational, and industrial films, including *From A to Z* (27 min.); *Operation Head Start* (35 min.); *Up Is Down; Out of Sight; Black Youth; To Reason Why; Summer Harvest; Soil for Growth* and many others.

GOLDSMITH, SILVIANNA, 151 W. 18th St., New York, N. Y. 10011. Filmed, wrote, directed, edited *Orpheus Underground* (55 min.).

GOLDSTEIN, KAY, 3233 48th Ave., Minneapolis, Minn. 55406. Films include *Welcome To The Beltless, Pinless Generation*, a short animated compilation film.

GOODMAN, PEARLYN, % Filmmakers' Co-op, 175 Lexington Ave., New York, N. Y. 10016. Experimental films including *Richard's Bath* (14 min.).

GOODRICH, DIANE, % Magic Theater Company, 110 W. Kinzie St., Chicago, Ill. 60610. Animator.

GORDON, BARBARA, New York, N. Y. Producer, writer.

GORDON, BETTE, % Communication Arts, Speech Dept., University of Wisconsin, Madison, Wisc. 53706. Films include *Go Go*, showing a woman auditioning for a job as strip teaser while she discusses her feeling about the job.

GOTTLIEB, LINDA, % Omaha Orange, 211 Central Park W., New York, N. Y. 10024. Producer. Films include *Limbo* (feature), *The Immigrant Experience: The Long Long Journey* (30 min.), and *The Fur Coat Club* and *The Case of the Elevator Duck* (shorts).

GOULD, DIANA, 2486 Cheremoya Ave., Los Angeles, Cal. 90028. Screenwriter: *Jenny* (feature). (See p. 169)

GRAHAM, DIANE T., 1936 Aberdeen Dr., Columbus, O. 43220. Psychological documentaries on the filmmaker's state-of-mind at the time the films were conceived, including *Act of Contrition* (5 min.), and *Barbara* (15 min.).

GRANT, ANNE, 617 49th St., Brooklyn, N. Y. 11220. Films include *Our North American Foremothers* (75 min.), a documentary of women's history.

GRAVENSON, ANNE W., 101 74th St., N. Bergen, N. J. 07047. Assistant film editor, writer, director.

GRAVES, NANCY, 69 Wooster St., New York, N. Y. 10013. Artist; producer, director, animal films. Films include *Flight Motion* (60 min.), *Izy Boukir* (20 min.). Latter is available from Filmmakers' Co-op.

GREENE, NANCY ELLEN, 231 S. Alexandria, Los Angeles, Cal. 90004. One-woman shorts.

GREENFIELD, AMY, 27 Bellis Circle, Cambridge, Mass. 02140; also % Filmmakers' Co-op, 175 Lexington Ave., New York, N. Y. 10016. Dancer, dance-film director. Films include *Element* (12½ min.) and *Transport* (6 min.). (See p. 169)

GREENFIELD, LOIS, % Holly Hartley, Children's Cultural Foundation, Inc., 325 E. 57th St., New York, N. Y. 10022. Films include *Mais Mois* (8 min.).

GREGORY, ANNE, 4103 43rd N.E., Seattle, Wash. 98105. Graphics, animation; films for U. of Washington, Seattle schools and Seattle Dept. of Health.

GREGORY, MOLLIE, % Thunderbird Film Enterprises, 325 Flint St., Reno, Nev. 89501. Producer, director, writer; documentary films. Films include *Welfare: Exploding the Myths* (18 min.), *Shores* (14 min.), *Cities Are for People* (25 min.), and *ERA and the American Way* (20 min.). (See p. 170)

GREINER, NANCY, % Women Make Movies, 257 W. 19th St., New York, N. Y. 10011. Assistant director, Media Equipment Resources Center. Films include cooperative film *Katie Kelly* (5 min.).

GROSKLOS, BETSY, 46 Longfellow Rd., Mill Valley, Cal. 94941. Animation, camera; one-woman films. Films include *The Puppet Man* (10 min.), *The Liberators* (7 min.), *Football for Mothers* (3½ min.).

GROSSMAN, REDA, 438 N. Sycamore Ave., Los Angeles, Cal. 90036. Writer, director. Films include *Set-up* (31 min.), a fictionalized documentary about an aging provacateur, and *Stacy is a Girl's Name* (feature), about a female photographer in the Caribbean and Cuba.

GUNTER, PATRICIA, 1500 National Blvd., Los Angeles, Cal. 90034. Writer.

GURIEVITCH, GRANIA, % Togg Films, 630 Ninth Ave., New York, N. Y. 10036. Producer. Films include *Rehabilitation: A Patient's Perspective* (26 min., producer, director), *Foxfire* (26 min., co-producer), *A New Perspective* (26 min., associate producer).

HAAG, JAN, 1215 N. Hayworth, Los Angeles, Cal. 90046. Writer, director.

HACKERMAN, NANCY, 8415 Bellona Lane, Towson, Md. 21204. Editor; educational films for television. Films include *The 50-Hour Day* (28 min.), *The Salvation of Gideon Crocker* (28 min.).

HALAS, SUSAN, 690 Arkansas, San Francisco, Cal. 94107. Producer, writer. Films include *Miss Pacifica 1971* (14 min., producer), *A Simple Heart* (14 min., producer).

HALEFF, MAXINE, % Halproductions, 85 Barrow St., New York, N. Y. 10014. Producer, director, editor. Films include *The Forbidden Playground* (11 min.). Available from Filmmakers' Co-op.

HALL, SHARON, 327 W. Malvern, Fullerton, Cal. 92632. Director, writer.

HALLECK, DEEDEE, Gate Hill Co-op, Stony Point, N. Y. 10980. Director, film teacher, video artist. Films include *Minimoviemakers* (10 min., director), *Mural on Our Street* (17 min., co-director; 1965 Academy Award nominee), *Mr. Story* (28 min., co-producer/director), and *Jaraslawa* (10 min., producer/director). NEA artist-in-residence, Texas and Nebraska. NEA Public Media Grant, 1974. (See p. 171)

HALLET, JUDITH, % Film Images, 17 W. 60th St., New York, N. Y. 10023. Directs short films. Films include *Child of Dance* (9 min., co-directed with husband, Stanley).

HAMMER, BARBARA, 1931 McGee St., Berkeley, Cal. 94703. Filmmaker. Films include *Menses* (3 min.), about menstruation, *Sisters!* (12 min.), a celebration of lesbian women, *X* (9 min.), about one woman's despair *A Gay Day* (3 min.), a satire on lesbian monogamy, *I Was/I Am* (6½ min.), a woman's fantasy of death, *Jane Brakhage* (10 min.), an expressionistic documentary of the influential and pioneer spirit in women, *Markets* (10 min.), a study of women in the economic situation in Mexico, *Women's Rights* (15 min.), women on a country weekend with complications, and *"Y"* (15 min.), the sub-personalities of one woman's psyche.

HANI, SUSUMI, % New Yorker Films, 43 W. 61st St., New York, N. Y. 10023. Films include *A Full Life* (102 min.), about a woman in the traditionally male-dominated society of modern Japan.

HANLEY, LINDA, 4 McAlpine, Carrboro, N. C. 27510. Writer, director, editor. Films include *Forest and the Child* (6 min.), *Ceasefire* (7 min.) and *Conversation with a Friend* (25 min.).

HANNEMANN, YVONNE, 228 E. 22nd St., New York, N. Y. 10010. Documentary films, including *Muruga* (23 min.), about the Hindus' pilgrimage to the Muruga Festival; *Vesak* (17 min.), Lord Buddha's birthday; and *The Work of Gomis* (50 min.), focusing on the rich living traditions in Ceylon and India.

HARMS, VALERIE, 10 Sunset Hill, Norwalk, Conn. 06851. Writer, photographer, editor, one-woman filmmaker. Films include *Boing* (90 min., assistant producer, editor), *Hands* (20 min., one-woman film), *This Long Disease, My Wife* (writer, editor).

HARRIS, SUSAN K., 29C Escondido Village, Stanford University, Palo Alto, Cal. 94305. Film teacher, writer.

HARRISON, JEANNE, 16 W. 46th St., New York, N. Y. 10036. Veteran director and producer; commercials and industrials.

HARRITON, MARIA, Maria Harriton Films, 463 West St., New York, N. Y. 10014. Filmmaker and editor; theatrical shorts, documentary, educational, industrial films. Films include *The Island* (7 min.), *Work, Seafall* (15 min.), *The Draft Card Burners* (7 min.), *9 Variations on a Dance Theme* (13 min.), and *At Your Fingertips* (10 min.). Films have been shown at New York, San Francisco, and various international festivals. (See p. 172)

HARTLEY, ELDA, Cat Rock Rd., Cos Cob, Conn. 06807. Producer, camera, editor; educational films on Eastern thought, parapsychology, world religions, art, and Indian cultures of the Americas. Films include *Requiem for a Faith* (28 min.), *Psychics, Saints, and Scientists* (33 min.), and six films on Zen with the late Alan Watts. (See p. 177)

HARVEY, STEPHANIE, % Canyon Cinema Co-op, Industrial Center Bldg., Sausalito, Cal. 94965. Short films include *Wheat Hearts* (3 min.), an animated collage.

HARWOOD, RAVEN, 9046 Phyllis Ave., Los Angeles, Cal. 90069. Writer, producer, director. Films include *Jungles of the Soul* (35 min.).

HASLANGER, MARTHA, 1200 E. University, Ann Arbor, Mich. 48104. Photographer, filmmaker. Short films include *June* (8 min.), *Your Home Is You* (15 min.), *Focus* (3 min.). Award winner, Ann Arbor Film Festival.

HEESTAND, DIANE, R.R. #3, Tiffin, O. 44883. Short one-woman films.

HEICK, SUSAN, 722 Palms Blvd., Venice, Cal. 90291. Director, editor, camera, documentaries, commercials, and theatrical shorts. Films include *Narrow House* (8 min., director, camera, editor), *Lost It At the Movies* (15 min., camera), *Aquatic Locomotion* (15 min., director, editor).

HEILWEIL, SAMANTHA LEE, 32 Cornelia St., New York, N. Y. 10014. Filmmaker and film technician; dramatic shorts, documentaries, commercials. Films include *The Daughter* (dramatic short; sound), *The Meaning of Our Experience* (documentary; sound), *Voices* (60 min.; assistant camera/gaffer), *Module* (film for AT&T), short subjects for "Sesame Street" (sound), and others. Member, NABET sound department.

HEINS, MARJORIE, 8 St. Mary's St., Watertown, Mass. 02172. Director of short films, *Firearms* and *Places*. Had to sell Bolex during hard times and has since turned to more economical art form, writing.

HENDRICKS, CATHY, % Department of English; University of Washington, Seattle, Wash. 98105. Short films, including *Hands* (8 min.).

HENNESSEY, SHARON, % Serious Business Co., 1927 Marin Ave., Berkeley, Cal. 94707. Short films, including *What I Want* (1971, 10 min.) and *Bird* (1 min.).

HERMAN, WANDA, Biddle Hall, Ohio University, Athens, O. 45701. Director and producer; feature and documentary films for television.

HERRICK, ABBIE, 28 South Portland Ave., Brooklyn, N. Y. 11217. Filmmaker-director of short films, including *Regeneration* (6 min.), *Prey* (5 min.), *Ghosts* (15 min., filmmaker), *Caged* (3½ min., director). Also soundperson on Alexis Krasilovsky's *La Belle Dame Sans Merci* (8 min., shown at the Whitney Museum), and production assistant on the Dinsmore Foundation's Human Resources School films shown on TV as one-minute spots. A full-length feature script, *The Children of the Night*, has just been completed.

HICKS, BRENDA, 26 Prentice Rd., Newton Centre, Mass. 02159. Camera and editing.

HILL, MARY, % ACI Films, 35 W. 45th St., New York, N. Y. 10036. Films include *Barrier Beach* (1971, 20 min.), a study of the changes in a beach barrier over a year.

HILL, PAMELA, % Phoenix Films, Inc., 470 Park Ave. S., New York, N. Y. 10016. Films include ABC News' *Close-up on Fire* (54 min.), investigating the failure of government and industry to adequately protect us from death and injury by fire. A 1974 Blue Ribbon winner at the American Film Festival.

HILTON, MINNA, 208 Grayson Pl., Teaneck, N. J. 07666. Teacher, producer, co-directors of films, including *This Is a School* (13 min.), *Harlem Prep* (20 min.), *Four Women* (5 min.), *We Shall Survive* (15 min.), and *The Weaving Studio at Peters Valley* (15 min.).

HO, LAURA, Box 550, 308 Westwood Plaza, Los Angeles, Cal. 90024. One-woman films.

HOBAN, TANA, 2219 Delancey Pl., Philadelphia, Penn. 19103. Writer, producer, director; educational films for children.

HOCHBERG, VICTORIA, 154 Eighth Ave., New York, N. Y. 10011. Director, editor, producer; documentaries and dramatic features. Films include *Hollywood: You Must Remember This* (90 min., producer, director), *El Teatro Campesino* (60 min., producer), *To Be Young, Gifted and Black* (90 min., editor). Member, Directors Guild of America.

HOCHMAN, SANDRA, 180 E. 79th St., New York, N. Y. 10021. Director of feminist films, including *The Year of the Woman* (feature, camera work by Claudia Weill and Juliana Wang). In preparation: *All in a Day's Killing.*

HODES, ROBERTA, 420 E. 23rd St., New York, N. Y. 10010. Producer, editor, director of *The Game* (20 min.). Script supervisor for feature films including *On the Waterfront, Rachel, Rachel,* and *Where's Poppa?* (See p. 178)

HOELCL, GISELA, 51 Prentiss St., Cambridge, Mass. 02138. Filmmaker and photographer. Films include *Living the Good Life,* distributed by Daylight Films.

HOELSCHER, JEAN, Austin, Texas. Co-producer, co-editor, sound, director; educational films, including *The Great Depression: A Human Diary* (52 min.), *Next Time: No Brains* (15 min.), *War in the Crimea* (28 min.), *Before Gutenberg* (20 min.). (See p. 178)

HOFFMAN, RONI, 3732 Oceanic Ave., Brooklyn, N. Y. 11224. Producer, director, camerawoman for *Gumby's Adventures on the Moon.* Camerawoman for some segments of *Bogus Boxing Trash* (produced and directed by Richard Meltzer), animatics for several advertising campaigns, animator for *Menstruation* (New York State Council on the Arts).

HOLMES, DOLORIS, 30 Catlin Ave., Staten Island, N. Y. 10304. Filmmaker, playwright, stage director. Films include *Room of the White Mask* (15 min.).

HOLT, NANCY, 799 Greenwich St., New York, N. Y. 10014. Films include *Swamp* (6 min.), shown at the Whitney Museum. Co-filmmaker, Robert Smithson.

HORNISHER, CHRISTINA, % Creative Film Society, 7237 Canby Ave., Reseda, Cal. 91335. Short films, including *And on the Sixth Day* (5 min.) and *4 × 8 = 16* (3 min.).

HORVATH, JOAN. (See p. 179)

HOVDE, ELLEN GIFFARD, 140 Sullivan St., New York, N. Y. 10012. Editor: *Christo's Valley Curtain* (Academy Award nominee, 1974), *Gimme Shelter* (90 min.), *Songs of America* (60 min.), and others.

HOWE, SYLVIA, 90 Dean Rd., Weston, Mass. 02193. Short one-woman films.

HUBLEY, FAITH. (See p. 59)

HUGHES, JANN, 1892 Market St., San Francisco, Cal. 94103. Camera, producer, director, editor. Member of the Santa Cruz Women's Media Collective.

HULTIN, JILL, 258 Winthrop Rd., Columbus, O. 43214. Director, producer, writer, editor. Films include *Sisters* (21 min.), *El Teatro Campesino: The Farmworkers' Theater* (30 min.). (See p. 179)

HUNTER, MARIAN, % Herstory Films, Inc., 137 E. 13th St., New York, N. Y. 10003. Feminist films include, among others, *The Feminist Party Streetwalkers* (6 min.), *Roll Over* (10 min.), and *Just Married* (30 min.), about the myth and reality of marriage. (See p. 180)

HUNTER, REBECCA L., % Distaff Media Productions, 411 Lathrop, River Forest, Ill. 60305. Short one-woman films and videotapes dealing with women and their behavior, including *Rocktop* (3 min.) and *Chicago Gay Pride Parade 1973* (10 min.).

HUSH, LISBETH, 5140 Nagle Ave., Sherman Oaks, Cal. 91403. Writer.

HUSSIE, BARBARA, Washington, D.C. Executive producer, director, writer; documentary films including *Women Who Care* (30 min., executive producer), *With Music Ring* (30 min., director, producer, writer), *Pictures from New World* (36 half-hour films for television, producer).

IDEMITSU, MAKO, % Canyon Cinema Co-op, Industrial Center Bldg., Sausalito, Cal. 94965. Director of feminist films.

IRVINE, LOUVA ELIZABETH, 158 E. 30th St., New York, N. Y. 10016. Total design consultant. Documentary and experimental filmmaker. Films include *Three Lives* (70 min., co-producer, director, production manager, music; Impact Films), *Birth Film* (35 min., sound, interviews; New Yorker), and *Rain* (5 min., filmmaker; Filmmakers' Co-op). Film instructor, Guggenheim Museum, Board of Education, and Women's Interart Center. (See p. 180)

IRVING, ANN, 311 Almar, Santa Cruz, Cal. 95060. One-woman filmmaker. Member of the Santa Cruz Women's Media Collective.

ISAACS, BARBARA, 333 E. 43rd St., New York, N. Y. 10017. Writer, director, producer; documentary films and theatrical shorts. Films include *Marie and Henry* (20 min.), *Fifteen Women* (18 min.), *Revolution for Two* (10 min.). (See p. 182)

JACKSON, BABS, 959 W. 17th St., Costa Mesa, Cal. 92627. Artist. Films include *Threshold* (10 min.), *Delta Wave* (5 min.), *Oxherding* (10 min.) and the *Mindpower* series.

JACKSON, GLENNA, % University of Minnesota, Dept. of Studio Arts, Duluth, Minn. 55812. Short films of social comment include *Make-up* and *Reunion*.

JACKSON, LISA, % MIT Film Section, Cambridge, Mass. 02139. Writer, director, editor; films include *Girl Watching* (12 min.), *Charm School* (8 min.), *Ceci and Pam* (18 min.).

JACOBS, DOROTHY, 784 Columbus Ave., New York, N. Y. 10025. Writer, educator, artist, dancer. One-woman film *Focus on Movement* (20 min.).

JACOBS, ELAINE, % Perennial Education, Inc., 1825 Willow La. N., Chicago, Ill. 60648. Documentary filmmaker. Films include *Lavender* (13 min.), which records the intimate thoughts and feelings of two lesbians. Co-filmmaker, Colleen Monahan.

JACOBSON, DENISE, 134 S.E. Ninth Ave., Portland, Ore. 97214. Teacher. One-woman films on classroom methods.

JACOUPY, JACQUELINE, % Film Images, 17 W. 60th St., New York, N. Y. 10023. Films include *Assault on the Eiffel Tower* (23 min.).

JAFFE, PAT, 1148 Fifth Ave., New York, N. Y. 10028. Editor of feature films; co-filmmaker of short films. Films include *For Love of Ivy* (editor), *Jenny* (editor), *Journey Through Rosebud* (editor), *Friends of Eddie Coyle* (editor), *Anatomy of Cindy Fink* (12 min.; co-filmmaker), *Who Does She Think She Is?* (co-filmmaker).

JANUS, DIANNE ROCK, % Distaff Media Productions, 411 Lathrop, River Forest, Ill. 60305. Short one-woman films for and about women, including *Narcissia* (8 min.), *X-Retaining Valve* (5 min.), *An Experience in Learning* (8 min.). Winner, Columbia Film Festival Award and others.

JARVIS, BARBARA A., % ARICA, 9916 Santa Monica Blvd., Los Angeles, Cal. Editor. Films include *Winter Soldier* (90 min. feature documentary), *Gimme Shelter* (feature, associate editor), *Christopher Discovers America* (60 min., editor), *Hawthorne Circle* (40 min., filmmaker), *Lambing* (30 min. documentary, filmmaker).

JASPER, SUZANNE, 218 Thompson St., New York, N. Y. 10012. Documentary filmmaker and editor.

JASSIM, LINDA, 921-A Lincoln Blvd., Santa Monica, Cal. 90405. Filmmaker, editor, camera. Films include *Cycles* (10 min., director, editor), *Womanhouse* (18 min., camera), *Venice ½ and ½* (director, editor), and others. Award winning *Cycles* is distributed by Creative Film Society, *Venice ½ and ½* available from filmmaker. (See p. 182)

JELINEK, MILENA, Adams Rd., Ossining, N. Y. 10562. Director, writer, editor; short films including *D.C. al Fine* (15 min.), *Convention* (14 min.), *Collusion: Chapter 8* (24 min.). Also script for *Easy Life* (feature produced in Czechoslovakia).

JENKINS, JOYCE, 112-44 209th St., Queens Village, N. Y. 11429. Films include *The Emergence of Fascism in the United States.*

JERSEY, GWEN, 630 Ninth Ave., New York 10036. Producer, director, writer, editor. Documentary films including *Good-bye and Good Luck* (30 min., director), *Emergency: The Living Theatre* (30 min., producer and director), and many others.

JOHNSON, DONNA LEE, 822 Webster Ave., Chicago, Ill. 60614. Still photography and filmmaking, including educational, medical, industrial and sales films. Johnson is currently self-employed as producer, and has handled all aspects of production for film companies in the past. Also served as judge on panel of New York and Chicago Industrial Film Festivals.

JOHNSON, KAREN, 10118 Aldea Ave., Northridge, Cal. 91324. One-woman filmmaker and film editor. Films include *Orange* (3 min.), *Lizard Mosiac* (3 min.), *Hands* (3 min.). (See p. 182)

JOHNSON, PAMELA, Box 182, Hiram, O. 44234. Films include *An I.S. Soap Opera*, showing the mother on an Ivory Soap box with a tear running down her face.

JOHNSTON, SUZANNE. (See p. 183)

JOKEL, LANA TSE PING, 55 E. 76th St., New York, N. Y. 10021. Filmmaker and editor. Films include *Heat* (feature, editor), *L'Amour* (feature, editor), *American Art in the Sixties* (60 min., editor), *Maidstone* (feature, editor), *Beyond the Law* (feature, editor), *Andy Warhol* (60 min., director, editor). Films have been shown at many festivals including Cannes, Venice and the American Film Festival.

JOLTIN, JAN, % Blue Bus, Box 6212, Cherry Creek Station, Denver, Col. 80206. Co-producer, co-editor. Documentary films including *Away with All Pests* (57 min.), *Researching the Health System* (45 min.).

JONAS, JOAN, 66 Grand St., New York, N. Y. 10013. Short films including *Left Side, Right Side* (7 min.).

JONES, ELINOR, 7 W. 96th St., New York, N. Y. 10025. Writer, producer. Films include *A Texas Romance, 1909* (22 min., producer).

JONES, JACQUELINE, 4330 Olympiad Dr., Los Angeles, Cal. 90049. Director, writer, camera; documentaries and theatrical films. Films include *Soledad Brother* (30 min., one-woman film), *Jelordie* (90 min., director), *Dark Night* (90 min., director, writer), *Students '71* (60 min., camera), and others.

JUDICE, PATRICIA, 656 West Tam O'Shanter, Las Vegas, Nev. 89109. Producer-director at PBS. Documentary; animation; one-woman short films. Short films include *Fairy Dust* (12 min.), *Alleydust* (10 min.), *Testament of Eurydice* (8 min.), and *Skate* (25 min.).

KAARRESALO-KASARA, ELIA, 134 W. 58th St., New York, N. Y. 10019. Director, producer, production co-ordinator; theatrical shorts, features, commercials. Films include *Finnish Frustrations* (7 min., director, producer; available from Filmmakers' Co-op); *Would Momma Allow* (2¼ min., director, producer; available from Finnish Filmmakers' Co-op); *Finland: My Sweet Home* (15 min., director, producer; available from Finnish AA-Organization), and others. Awards include Jussi Award of Finnish Film Critics, among others.

KALER, DORIS, 1857 Fox Hills Dr., Los Angeles, Cal. 90025. Publicist, writer.

KAPLAN, BARBARA, 1825 N. Lincoln Plaza, Chicago, Ill. 60614. Editor, writer; educational films and documentaries. Films include 80 or more educational films for Coronet (10 to 25 minutes each, editor), *Home on 15th Street* (35 min., editor), *Multiple Choice* (90 min., editor).

KAPLAN, HELENE G., 316 W. 94th St., New York, N. Y. 10025. One-woman films including *Monstera Deliciosa* (15 min.), *Vestal Theatre* (13 min.), *Untitled Dale and Stephie Film* (15 min.), *Conveyor Belt: Left and Right* (20 min.), *24 Eggs* (3 min.).

KAPROW, VAUGHAN RACHEL, 270 Wigmore Dr., Pasadena, Cal. 91105. Filmmaker; short Super-8 films, including *California Landscape, Bridge, Knees,* and *A Pretty Picture*.

KARKOWSKY, NANCY, % Phoenix Films, Inc., 470 Park Ave. S., New York, N. Y. 10016. Films include *Clay, The Puppets of Jiri Trnka, Sand, Clay,* and *The First Moving Picture Show* (7 min.), introducing children to motion picture theory.

KARLIN, ELISABETH J., Goddard College, Plainfield, Vt. 05664. One-woman film: *Katy and Suzie* (9 min.), about life in suburbia.

KARP, SHARON, Kartemquin Films Ltd., 1901 W. Wellington, Chicago, Ill. 60657. Films include cooperatively made *Now We Live on Clifton* (25 min.), about social effects of remodeling old apartments, i.e. higher rents which force out families, and *Viva la Causa* (12 min.), which documents the Chicano aspect of the mural movement in Chicago.

KASICH, JOAN, % Creative Film Society, 7237 Canby Ave., Reseda, Cal. 91335. One-woman films, including *Dreams and Ashes* (9 min.).

KASTER, BARBARA, % Florida-Atlantic University, Boca Raton, Fla. 33432. Film series about women in politics.

KATONIK, CAROL, 834 Collingwood Ave., Maywood, N. J. 07607. Films include *Centering* (7 min.), using a potter to symbolize the more important aspects of a woman's competence and confidence.

KAY, ELIZABETH C., 3145 Sandhill Rd., Mason, Mich. 48854. Educational and instructional films, including *Creating with Cartons*.

KEATING, ANNA-LENA, Animated Films Co., 907 Sherman Ave., Evanston, Ill. 60202. Films include *The Bedroom* (1971, 10 min.), winner of the Gold Hugo Award, among others. (See p. 184)

KEDZIERZAWSKA, JADWIGA, % Contemporary Films, McGraw-Hill, Princeton Rd., Hightstown, N. J. 08520. Films include *Little Joys, Little Sorrows* (10 min.).

KELLER, MARTHA ROCK, 1603 E. Stadium Blvd., Ann Arbor, Mich. 48104. Printmaker, photographer; one-woman films. Films include *Concert 1971* (30 min.).

KELLY, ELIZABETH, 68-29 Nansen St., Forest Hills, N. Y. 11375. Short films include *Ball* (7 min., writer, director, producer).

KELLY, MARY PAT, 340 W. 86th St., New York, N. Y. 10024. Film consultant, director, writer. Films include *Tryin' to Make it Real* (10 min., director, editor); *Ready* (90 min., director, writer); *Austin: A Community in Transition* (60 min., associate director); *Beside the Singing River* (30 min., writer). (See p. 185)

KEMPE, KARIN, Box 59, Rhode Island School of Design, 2 College St., Providence, R. I. 02903. Camera and sound.

KENDALL, NANCY, 325 E. Fifth St., New York, N. Y. 10003. One-woman films including *Almira 38*. (See p. 186)

KENNEDY, MARGARET FAIRLIE, 63 Hickory Circle, Ithaca, N. Y. 14850. Composer, sound, one-woman films. Films include *Demons and Dancers of Ceylon* (30 min.), *The Healing Hill* (9 min.), sound track for *African Sculpture* (10 min.), sound track for *Take My Hand* (20 min.).

KERANS, BARBARA KAY, 260 Vicksburg Drive, Lansing, Mich. 48897. Short one-woman films, including *A City Tree* (15 min.).

KERNOCHAN, SARAH. (See p. 67)

KERRY, LUCYANN, Blue Ridge Films, 9003 Glenbrook Rd., Fairfax, Va. 22030. Films include *Making It* (11 min.), about the drastic changes in a woman's life including divorce and assuming economic responsibility for her daughters; and *Woman Candidate* (13 min.), which contains a lot of practical information on campaigning, and has been called an "excellent film on women in politics." Her film *Basket Builder* (12 min.) won a Cine Golden Eagle award in 1974.

KESHEN, AMY, 2425 N.E. 194th St., Miami, Fla. 33160. Assistant director; features, shorts, industrials, documentaries, and commercials.

KILDUFF, MICHAL C., Design Center Inc., 1611 Connecticut Ave. N.W., Washington, D.C. 20009. Animator, artist, designer. Films include *One in 16 Million* (17 min.), *Native American Arts* (18 min.), *Curious Alice* (12 min.), *We* (27 min.), *Smoking and Health* (30 min.), *Messages* (12 min.), EPA commercial *Blackout*.

KIRSH, ESTELLE, 3977-F Sedgwick Ave., Bronx, N. Y. 10463. Non-narrative cinema, personal films.

KISH, ANNE, % Canyon Cinema Co-op, Industrial Center Bldg., Sausalito, Cal. 94965. Films include *Can Anybody Hear the Birds?* (10 min.) and *Umatilla '68* (37 min.).

KLASSEN, RUTH, 1263 N. Paulina, Chicago, Ill. 60622. Films composed of animated footage on self-constructed three-dimensional satin and plastic screens.

KLECKNER, SUSAN, 117 Waverly Pl., New York, N. Y. 10011. Film teacher, director. Films include *Three Lives* (70 min., co-director), *Birth Film* (45 min., director, camera, editor), and others.

KLEIN, BONNIE SHERR, 225 Edgerton St., Rochester, N. Y. 14607. Director, producer, editor; documentaries. Films include *For All My Students* (30 min., director), *Organizing for Power: The Alinsky Approach* (five films ranging from 14 to 45 min. each; director), *VTR-St. Jacques* (30 min., producer, director).

KLINGMAN, LYNZEE, 595 West End Ave., New York, N. Y. 10024. Editor; documentaries, commercials, industrials, multi-media, and features. Films include *Year of the Pig* (100 min.), *Charge and Countercharge* (52 min.).

KLOSKY, LINDA, 1521 10th Ave. S., Minneapolis, Minn. 55404. Animator, still photographer. Award-winning films, including *The Ark, Directed by Noah, Special Effects by God; And Then There Were . . .;* and *Tom's Film*.

KNOWLES, DOROTHY, % Grove Press, 53 E. 11th St., New York, N. Y. 10003. Short films including *Rabbits Are the Friends of Toads* (11 min.).

KOBEY, CLAUDIA, 11619 Ohio, Los Angeles, Cal. 90025. Teacher, animator; films include *Job #5347* (4 min.), *Antithesis* (8 min.), *Flow Control* (8 min.).

KOPPLE, BARBARA, Cabin Creek Films, 58 E. 11th St., New York, N. Y. 10003. Director, editor, producer, writer, sound. Films include *Salesman* (assistant editor), *Living Off the Land* (32 min., editor and sound), *Wild Orange* (90 min.) and *Winter Soldier* (92 min., director, producer, editor, sound). (See p. 186)

KOSERSKY, RENA, % ServiSound, Inc., 37 W. 57th St., New York, N. Y. 10019. Music editor, recording engineer. Films include *L'Chaim To Life* (85 min.); *Black African Heritage: The Congo* (60 min.); *The Bend of the Niger* (60 min.); *The Slave Coast* (60 min.); *Africa's Gift* (60 min.); *A Place for Aunt Lois* (17 min.); *Whitney M. Young, Jr.* (10 min.). (See p. 187)

KOSKI, JOAN, 201 Gunson, East Lansing, Mich. 48823. One-woman films.

KOZAK, YITKA, 1089 W. Park St., Long Beach, N. Y. 11561. Script-writer and producer.

KRANING, SUZAN PITT, Box 67, Fountain City, Wisc. 54629. Animator; films include *Crocus* (7 min.), a gentle film in which husbands and wives make love with interruptions, *City Trip* (3 min.), *Jefferson Circus Song* (19 min.). All available from Serious Business Company.

KRASÍLOVSKY, ALEXIS RAFAEL, Rafael Film, 426 W. 45th St., New York, N. Y. 10036. Director, editor, writer. Films include *End of the Art World* (35 min., director, producer, editor, camera), *Her Way to Star* (62 min., director, editor, writer), and others. *End of the Art World* available from Visual Resources, Inc.

KREPS, BONNIE, % Women's Film Co-op, 200 Main St., Northampton, Mass. 01060. Films include *After the Vote* (22 min.), a serious and comic picture of sex role stereotypes, and *Portrait of My Mother* (30 min.), a daughter's appreciation of her mother's life.

KRIEGEL, HARRIET, % Women Make Movies, 257 W. 19th St., New York, N. Y. 10011. Short film *Domestic Tranquility* (7 min.), about a woman haunted by one-time ambition to be an artist.

KRUMINS, DIANA, % Serious Business Co., 1927 Marin Ave., Berkeley, Cal. 94707. Films include *Divine Miracle* (7 min.).

KUEHL, JOAN, 47 Perry St., New York, N. Y. 10014. Editor of these documentaries: *Environmental Education . . . A Beginning* (60 min.); *Mt. Rainier; Fire and Ice* (Cine Golden Eagle Award). Associate producer, *Voices* (60 min. documentary). Associate producer and editor, "History of Man" series (nine 20 min. educational films). Editor, ABC "Discovery" series.

KUHN, SARAH, Sarsaku Productions, 8700 Skyline Dr., Los Angeles, Cal. 90046. One-woman feminist films, including *Big Bob Kuhn* (14 min.), a documentary about a 13-year-old boy, and *Rap* (8 min.), which uses role-reversal to explain sexist practices.

KURTZ, JUDITH, % Youth Films Distribution Center, 43 W. 16th St., New York, N. Y. 10011. Films include *Trio at 19* (110 min.).

KUSMIDER, LAUREN C., 6279 Crown Ave., Oakland, Cal. 94611. Director and instructor at Berkeley Film Institute. Short one-woman films include *Sight, Suicide Note,* and *Helen.* Screenwriter on productions such as *The Woodsman* (for the Canadian Film Board) and *Andrea Doria Salvage* (for Oceanic Films and NBC).

KUTAKA, GERALDINE, 113 Holladay Ave., San Francisco, Cal. 94110. Producer, director, scriptwriter. Camera, *Back on the Streets Again;* camera assistant, CBS News.

LADD, HELENA SOLBERG, 3518 35th St., N.W., Washington, D.C. 20016. Writer, director, producer; feminist films. Films include *A Entrevista* (20 min., director, producer), *Meio Dia* (5 min., writer, director, producer), *The Emerging Woman* (director).

LAIMAN, LEAH, The Great American Moving Picture Company, 36 W. 62nd St., New York, N. Y. 10023. Producer of commercials, industrials, and theatrical shorts.

LAKE, CANDACE, 10005 Reevesbury Dr., Beverly Hills, Cal. 90210. Writer, producer, director. Films include *Divorce* (30 min.).

LAMBART, EVELYN, % Creative Film Society, 7237 Canby Ave., Reseda, Cal. 91335. Short films, including *Begone Dull Care* (9 min.), *Lines Horizontal* and *Lines Vertical* (6 min. each), *Mosaic* (6 min.), and *Rhythmetic* (9 min.).

LANDWEBER, ELLEN, 11237 Lucerne Ave., Culver City, Cal. 90230. Animation; educational films. Films include $Y = X^2$ (6 min.), *Computers* (15 min.), *Electronics* (10 min.).

LANGHELD, GRETCHEN, % Dworkin, 336 E. 5th St., New York, N. Y. 10003. Director, camera, editor. Films include *Dracula* (40 min., camera) and *The Cloister* (20 min., director, camera, editor; available from Filmmakers' Co-op).

LASKOWICH, GLORIA, % Filmmakers' Co-op, 175 Lexington Ave., New York, N. Y. 10016. Short films, including *Killing Time* (11 min.).

LASSNIG, MARIA, 95 Ave. B, New York, N. Y. 10009. One-woman animated films, including *Chairs* (7 min.), *Self Portrait* (5 min.), *Couples* (9 min.). Shown widely in Europe as well as the U.S.

LAUGHLIN, KATHLEEN, 1521 10th Ave. So., Minneapolis, Minn. 55404. Short films include *A Round Feeling* (3½ min.; available from Eccentric Circle Cinema Workshop) and *Opening/Closing* (4½ min.).

LAZARUS, MARGARET, % Cambridge Films, 9 Florence St., Cambridge, Mass. 02139. Producer and sound for *Taking our Bodies Back* (30 min.), documentary on women's health.

LEAF, CAROLINE, % French Animation P36, National Film Board, Box 6100, Montreal 101, Que. Animator.

LEE, NAMMI, 293 Seventh Ave., New York, N. Y. 10001. Born in Korea, studied in Japan. One-woman films include *Dancing Gokiburi* (3½ min.), *42nd of East Broadway* (4 min.), *Doll* (4 min.). Also worked on other films with Jack Smith.

LEE, PATRICIA, 4584 Meridan Ave., Miami Beach, Florida 33140. Films include *The North End* (15 min.).

LEE, ROHAMA, % Film News, 250 W. 57th St., New York, N. Y. 10019. Writer. Feature films include *Tonight We Raid Calais* (co-credit), *We're Going to Be Rich* (co-credit), and others. Also several short subjects and documentaries.

LEFF, PHYLLIS, 10411 Hebron Lane, Los Angeles, Cal. 90024. Story editor, Hollywood features.

LENK, MARJORIE, Cellar Door Cinema, 56 Merian St., Lexington, Mass. 02173. Director of film productions by children. Films include *Clickety, Clickety, Splat* (17 min.), *Why Me?* (10 min.), *Fake It and You'll Make It* (10 min.), *Just Life* (10 min.), and *Fiction Friction* (18 min.), which has won several awards and is selling well to libraries.

LESTER, SUSAN, 14 Horatio St., New York, N. Y. 10014. Writer, producer. Films include *Woman Alive!* (60 min. special for PBS; writer, associate producer), *Franklin Books: Tehran* (30 min., writer), and *An American Family* (twelve 60 min. films for PBS, associate producer).

LEVINE, NAOMI, 463 West St., #225G, New York, N. Y. 10014. One-woman experimental films. Films include *Zero to 16* (12 min.), *Prismatic* (25 min.), *Premoonptss* (14 min.), *London Bridges Falling Down* (6 min.), *Optured Fraiken Chaitre Joe* (3 min.), *Aspects of a Hill*, and others. Available from Filmmakers' Co-op.

LEVITT, HELEN, 4 E. 12th St., New York, N. Y. 10003. Outstanding still photographer. Director, editor, filmmaker. Films include *The Quiet One* (55 min., co-filmmaker, first prize and critics award winner, Venice Film Festival, 1949); *In the Street* (18 min., co-filmmaker); *Another Light* (20 min. documentary, director); *In the Year of the Pig* (documentary, co-editor); *The Steps of Age* (30 min. documentary, producer, Academy Award nominee). (See p. 188)

LEVITZ, LINDA, 9030 Harratt St., Los Angeles, Cal. 90069. Camera, editor, producer.

LEWIS, ANN, Cabin Creek Films, 58 E. 11th St., New York, N. Y. 10003. Edited documentaries for French TV, and assisted editing *Sense of Loss*, Marcelo Phulus' film about Ireland.

LEWIS, ANN, % Ohrn, 602 E. 12th St., Bloomington, Ind. 47401. Short films include *Mrs. Richard Brand*, a portrait of an old-fashioned woman. Co-filmmaker, Karen Ohrn.

LEWIS, LAURIE, % Canyon Cinema Co-op, Industrial Center Bldg., Sausalito, Cal. 94965. Short films include *The Matchseller* and *One Way Ticket to Palookaville*.

LEWIS, SAMELLA S., 1237 Masselin Ave., Los Angeles, Cal. 90019. Writer, producer, director; films on black artists, including *John Outerbridge* (21 min.), *Bernie Casey* (21 min.), *Elizabeth Catlett* (17 min.).

LEWIS, SUSAN, R.R. 1, Box 154, West Branch, Ia. 52538. Films include *A New Film*, a witty short on university life in Iowa.

LIIKALA, ISABELLE, % Filmmakers' Co-op, 175 Lexington Ave., New York, N. Y. 10016. Experimental films include *Feels of Blue* (1969, 6 min.).

LINDE, NANCY, % Youth Film Distribution Center, 43 W. 16th St., New York, N. Y. 10011. Short films, including *Arabesque* (7 min.).

LINKEVITCH, BARBARA, 2523A Polk St., San Francisco, Cal. 94109. Short films, including *Goodman, Thought Dreams*, and *Traces*.

LINNECARE, VERA, % Pyramid Films, Box 1048, Santa Monica, Cal. 90406. Films include *Trend Setter* (6 min.).

LIPPMAN, SUSANNAH, 2 Washington Sq. Village, #6-T, New York, N. Y. 10012. Program assistant and associate director, film and television. Member, Directors Guild of America.

LITLE, ALEV, % Women's Film Co-op, 200 Main St., Northampton, Mass. 01060. Co-filmmaker of *Autobiography of a Woman* (20 min.), which depicts the brutal and repressive forces that, while keeping women in their place, have also given them a sense of future direction.

LITTLEFIELD, NANCY, 258 Riverside Dr., New York, N. Y. 10025. Assistant director, unit production manager, production manager, associate producer; industrials, commercials, feature films and TV series. Chairwoman of Directors Guild of America—the first.

LITTLEJOHN, DOROTHY, 721 San Bruno Ave., San Francisco, Cal. 94107. Camera, editor; medical films. Also short films, including *Kim and the Glass Sculptor* (10 min., camera, editor, director) and *Methadone Maintenance* (20 min., camera, editor).

LITTMAN, LYNNE, 1915 Mayview Drive, Los Angeles, Cal. 90027. Producer, writer, reporter; features, documentaries, and films for television. Member, Directors Guild of America. (See p. 189)

LLOYD, ROBIN, Wing Farm, Rochester, Vt. 05767. Short one-woman films including *Hauling Trap* (13 min.), *Dan Basen* (11 min.), *Spring Run* (4½ min.), and *Turn of the Year* (11 min.).

LODEN, BARBARA. (See p. 54)

LOEB, JANICE, Alta Lodge, Alta, Utah 84070. Producer, filmmaker. Films include *The Quiet One* (55 min., producer and co-filmmaker, winner of first prize and critics award, 1949 Venice Film Festival), *In the Street* (co-filmmaker), *Another Light* (20 min., documentary for U.S. Dept. of Health), and *Mantle of Protection* (30 min. documentary, producer).

LOIZEAUX, CHRISTINE, 7270 Pierce St., Allendale, Mich. 49401. Choreographer, director; short dance films including *Vortex* (10 min.).

LONGDON, JOAN, % CUT, 3625 Regal Pl., Los Angeles, Cal. 90068. Editor; educational, promotional, political, dramatic, and commercial films. Also film instructor.

LOPEZ, SYLVIA, 8728 Venice Blvd., Los Angeles, Cal. 90034. Production manager; one-woman films on the Chicano movement.

LOSEY, MARY (FIELD), New York, N. Y. Veteran film producer for World Health Organization and others. Directors of Film Centre International in London. Chairman of British American Film Associates. On advisory board of Flaherty Seminars. Currently special consultant to WHO.

LOTHAR, EVA, % Pyramid Films, Box 1048, Santa Monica, Cal. 90406. Documentary films including *Street of the Sardine* (21 min.), *Yesterday's Shore Tomorrow's Morning* (13 min., available from Time-Life), *With Stanley Kramer on Oklahoma Crude* (10 min., available from Columbia Pictures).

LUBOIS, MARILYN, % Texture Films, 1600 Broadway, New York, N. Y. 10019. Co-director of *How About You? A Film on Birth Control and Sexuality.*

LUEBBERT, LYNN, 3320 N. 66th Pl., Scottsdale, Ariz. 85251. Editor; educational and documentary films including *Mathematics in the Real World* (40 min.); *Junkdump* (20 min.); *Changes: P.C. Friend, Railroad Agent* (20 min); *Changes: The Farmer* (25 min.).

LUPINO, IDA, % Arthur Kennard Associates, 8776 Sunset, Los Angeles, Cal. 90069. Veteran actress and feature director. (See p. 36)

LURIE, JANE, 41 W. 16th St., New York, N. Y. 10011. One-woman films including *Gargoyles* (50 min.), *Fifth Street Women's Building* (15 min.), *Metal and Petal* (5 min.).

LUTZ, MARJORIE, 400 E. 72nd St., New York, N. Y. 10021. Program assistant; commercials and documentaries.

LYNCH, EDIE, 150 W. 58th St., New York, N. Y. 10019. Producer and director of the feature *Lost Control* (1975), about men and women in a federal drug program. Portions of the film were shot on location at a state prison in Philadelphia.

MacCULLOUGH, NANCY, % CUT, 3625 Regal Pl., Los Angeles, Cal. 90065. Editor; educational, promotional, political, dramatic, and commercial films.

MacDOUGALL, ELSPETH, % Contemporary Films/McGraw-Hill, 1221 Ave. of the Americas, New York, N. Y. 10020. Films include *Fear Woman* (27 min. documentary on women of Ghana).

MacDOUGALL, JUDITH, 1436 Branard, Houston, Tex. 77006. Ethnographic filmmaker. Films include *Nawi*, available from Churchill Films. (See p. 190)

MacINNES, MARGO, Rm. 2009C, LSA Bldg., University of Michigan, Ann Arbor, Mich. 48105. Co-director with Selma Odom of the series *Girls and Women* (ten programs of 30 min. each).

MacKENZIE, MIDGE, % Impact Films, 144 Bleecker St., New York, N. Y. 10012. Films include *A Woman's Place* (30 min.) and *Women Talking* (80 min.).

MAGUIER, VIRGINIA, 929 Gardiner Dr., Bayshore, N. Y. Educator, filmmaker. Short films include cooperatively made *Frantasia* (7½ min.), about life in New York.

MALM, LINDA, 1623 Greenfield Ave., Los Angeles, Cal. 90025. Director. Films include *Divorce* (30 min.).

MALONE, NANCY, 2808 Laurel Canyon Pl., Los Angeles, Cal. 90046. Actress, director. Films include *Run* (7½ min.).

MANGEL, SHELIA, 3023 Brighton 3rd St., Brooklyn, N. Y. 11235. Short films include *Ova* (2 min.), about creation, *City* (2 min.), *Enter Here* (2 min.), and *Coney Island* (2 min.).

MANGOLTE, BABETTE, 319 Greenwich St., New York, N. Y. 10013. Cinematographer. Films include *Lives of Performers* (1972, 90 min.) and *Film About a Woman Who . . .* (1974, 90 min.).

MARK, PHYLLIS, 801 Greenwich St., New York, N. Y. 10014. Films include *Abstraction/Refraction* (5 min.), shown at the Whitney Museum.

MARMELSTEIN, LINDA, 245 E. 35th St., New York, N. Y. 10016. Motion picture and TV producer, independent filmmaker. Films include *How Life Begins* (52 min., associate producer), *Sense of Wonder* (52 min., associate producer), *Aria for Clay* (9 min., one-woman film), *Artist in Manhattan* (9½ min., one-woman film), *Communicating Successfully* (three 25 min. films for Time-Life Films). Also co-ordinating producer for children's TV series.

MARNER, CAROLE SATRINA, % Creative Film Society, 7237 Canby Ave., Reseda, Cal. 91335. Co-producer, co-director, sound and editor; educational and documentary films. Films include *Phyllis and Terry* (35 min., co-producer, co-director, editor, sound), *World of a Teenager* (52 min., co-producer), *First Three Days* (19 min., co-director, co-producer, co-editor, sound), and many others. (See p. 191)

MARQUES, REGINA, 373 Capp St., San Francisco, Cal. 94110. Films on Third World women.

MARSHALL, LISA, 23 Seventh St., Washington, D.C. 20003. Films include *Old People* (30 min.), and *Could Tell a Whole Lot, But Ain't No Use to Tellin' It. . . .*

MARSHALL, NANCY, 367 W. 48th St., New York, N. Y. 10036. Designer; short animated films including *Are You the Cat?*

MARSHALL, SANDRA, % Canyon Cinema Co-op, Industrial Bldg., Sausalito, Cal. 94965. Films include *Standing Water* (6½ min.), *Wogged Breast* (5 min.), *Oil on the Bay* (5½ min., co-directed with Ken DeRoux).

MARTENS, BETSY, Kartemquin Films Ltd., 1901 W. Wellington, Chicago, Ill. 60657. Films include cooperatively made *Winnie Wright, Age 11* (26 min.), a portrait of an individual in a community torn by a racial conflict as it changes from white to black.

MARTIN, SUSAN, 467 Central Park W., New York, N. Y. 10025. Producer, director, writer, editor. Films include *Punishment Park* (feature, producer); also commercials.

MARX, MICHELLE, 6280 S.W. 116th St., Miami, Fla. 33156. Assistant director; commercials, industrials, features. Member, Directors Guild of America.

MARX, PATRICIA, % Creative Film Society, 7237 Canby Ave., Reseda, Cal. 91335. Short films, including *Obmaru* (4 min.) and *Things to Come* (3 min.).

MATCHINGA, CARYN, 1147 N. Clark St., Los Angeles, Cal. 90069. Writer, producer for film and TV. Films include *79 Park Avenue* (feature, screenwriter), *Ike the Tow-Trucker* (feature; screenwriter, producer), *First Touch* (feature; screenwriter), *The Prescription* (feature; screenwriter).

MATSON, DONNA, Director of Western Instructional Television, Inc., 1549 N. Vine St., Los Angeles, Cal. 90028. Lived in Africa, Asia, the Middle East, Europe and South America, working as a teacher, writer, photographer. Produced and directed nearly 500 educational television films, including the series "Exploring South America," "Exploring the World of Science," and "Lands and People of our World."

MATTHAEI, GAY, % Visual Resources, 1841 Broadway, New York, N. Y. 10023. Films include *Where Time Is a River* (18 min.).

MAY, ELAINE. (See p. 48)

MAYER, DOE, 4582 Starling Way, Los Angeles, Cal. 90065. Director, editor. Films include *3-Wheeled Fairy Tale* (20 min., director), *Wallflower* (26 min., editor).

McCARTHY, DINITIA SMITH, 29 W. 88th St., New York, N. Y. 10024. Producer, director, writer. Films include *Passing Quietly Through* (30 min., director, writer; winner of Cine Golden Eagle and other awards; distributed by Grove Press). Short documentary films for WNET-13 series "The Great American Dream Machine," "The Fifty First State," and "Behind the Lines" (producer, director). Producer and director for WNBC-TV documentaries; also educational and commercial films. (See p. 191)

McCORMACK, MARNI, Nedmar Productions, 1265 No. Havenhurst Dr., Los Angeles, Cal. 90046. Director, producer; live/tape television production. Also directed *A 7½ Minute Film,* a film about, and primarily by, women, commenting on a type of society and morality that is losing its relevance for today's young women.

McCUE, MAUREEN, 1844 Commonwealth Ave., Auburndale, Mass. 02166. One-woman films.

McLAREN, MARILYN, 165 W. 91st St., New York, N. Y. 10024. Assistant editor. Films include *Snapshots* (16mm autobiographical feature); *Miura* (35mm dramatic documentary); also commercials. Collaborating with Rose Rosenblatt on script of *Dual In the Dirt* (20 min. narrative), which she will also produce and edit. Member of Women's Film Collective.

McLAUGHLIN-GILL, FRANCES, 49 E. 86th St., New York, N. Y. 10028. Photographer, producer, director. Films include *Glamour College* (13½ min.) and *Cover Girl, New Face in Focus* (28½ min.).

McLUHAN, T. C., 241 E. 18th St., New York, N. Y. 10003. Producer, director, co-author of *The Shadow Catcher: Edward S. Curtis and the North American Indians* (1974), a documentary that recreates the years Curtis spent among the Navajo, the Hopi, the Eskimos and others, and recorded their customs.

McNEUR, LYNDA, 171 W. 79th St., New York, N. Y. 10024. Arts consultant, director, editor. Films include *Here We Are, God* (28 min.), *Now* (15 min.), *7 Ages* (28 min.).

MEHRING, MARGARET, 560 36th St., Manhattan Beach, Cal. 90266. Producer, director; documentary, industrial, and educational films.

MEYER, MUFFIE, 49 Park Ave., New York, N. Y. 10016. Editor. Films include *An Essay on Loneliness* (30 min.), *Woodstock* (feature), *Flight of Fantasy* (30 min., 3-D), *Groove Tube* (feature), *Lords of Flatbush* (feature), and others. Directed *L.A. Groupie* (17 min.). (See p. 192)

MEYERS, LAURA, 431 N. Pine, Lansing, Mich. 48933. Media specialist in education; short one-woman films, including *The Pink Religion* (10 min.), *Life Cycle* (10 min.).

MILES, BETTY, 94 Sparkill, Tappan, N. Y. 10983. Writer; children's films and documentaries, including *Elephants* (6 min.); *Special Children, Special Needs* (25 min.); *Atlanta* (5 min. segment of *Free to Be You and Me*).

MILES, JENNIFER, 4554 N.E. 16th, Seattle, Wash. 98105. Sound and animation.

MILLER, JULIA. (See p. 66)

MILLER, MARCIANNE, % Channel 11 Metromedia, KTTV, 5746 Sunset Blvd., Los Angeles, Cal. 90028. Produces feminist-oriented shows for Metromedia.

MILLETT, KATE, New York, N. Y. Author, filmmaker. Films include *Three Lives* (70 min., producer; available from Impact Films). (See p. 193)

MOBERLY, CONNIE, Box 6, Matagorda, Tex. 77457. Photographer; filmmaker. Films include *Action Angles* (3 min.), *Plea* (8 min.), and documentaries *Astrodome Indoor Track Meet* (20 min.) and *Astrodome Motorcycle Races* (15 min.).

MOBLEY, PEGGY J., 5912 60th Ave., Riverdale, Md. 20840. Editor, negative cutter; theatrical shorts, documentaries, TV and political spots, and cartoons.

MOCK, FLORA CLAR, 1551 N. Beverly Dr., Beverly Hills, Cal. 94710. Writer, director, educator. Films include *Numberline* (writer, director), *Sets* (writer, director), *How We Know the World Around Us* (director), *Cave Pantings of Baha Calis* (co-writer, director), *Waiting* (one-woman film). *Numberline, Sets,* and *Cave Paintings* available from Bailey Film Associates, *Waiting* from Grove Press.

MONAHAN, COLLEEN, % Perennial Education, Inc., 1825 Willow La. N., Chicago, Ill. 60648. Documentary filmmaker. Films include *Lavender* (13 min., co-filmmaker), about the joyous possibilities of lesbianism.

MONET, GABY, % Concepts Unlimited, 150 W. 55th St., New York, N. Y. 10028. Producer, writer; industrial and TV films including *Norman Rockwell's World* (26 min., writer), *Phone Man* (16 min., producer, writer).

MOORE, ALLYSON, 2103 Third St., Santa Monica, Cal. 90405. Editor. Films include *Binney and Smith* (25 min.), and *The Demon* (23 min.).

MOORE, GAYLEN, 304 W. 89th St., New York, N. Y. 10024. Associate producer; documentaries. Films include *Fifty Miles of Land* (60 min.) and *Forecast* (90 min., producer, writer, editor, co-director).

MORRER, CAROLE, % Filmmakers' Co-op, 175 Lexington Ave., New York, N. Y. 10016. Films include *Phyllis and Terry* (36 min., co-directed with husband, Eugene).

MOSSMAN, MERRILY, 274 W. 95th St., New York, N. Y. 10025. Associate director. On staff at WNET. Director, *Global Groove*, promos for "The Television Show," scenes for "Playhouse New York's" *Year End Report*. Associate director for series "Theater in America," including, among others, the production *Feasting with Panthers*, and for "Playhouse New York's" *Antigone* and *Particular Men*. Also work on "Soul!" (musical variety series) and news, public affairs and documentary shows. Member, Directors Guild of America.

MOTZ, JULIE, 601 Lexington Ave., New York, N. Y. 10022. Associate producer, research. Films include *Christina's World* (52 min., for television), *Not a Place* (26 min.), *In Order to Effect Change* . . . (28 min.) and others.

MOYNIHAN, JANE, % Moynihan Associates, 734 N. Jefferson St., Milwaukee, Wisc. 53202. Co-filmmaker; industrial, documentary, and educational films including *Where the Action Is* (27 min.), *His Brother's Keeper* (27 min.), *How Many Lifetimes* (27 min.), *Leading to Learning* (series of five half-hour films), and others. (See p. 193)

MUGWANA, OSHUN, 6906 S. Paxton, Chicago, Ill. 60649. Editor, camera. Films include *Jive, Morocco, Save the Children, John Sentgstacke's Visit to China, Ready, Austin: Community in Transition*, and others.

MULDOFSKY, PERI, % Youth Films Distribution Center, 43 W. 16th St., New York, N. Y. 10011. Short films, including *Aspirations* (6 min.).

MULFORD, MARILYN, 33 Greene St., New York, N. Y. 10013. Pandora Films, co-writer, -producer, -director, -editor, feminist films; including *How About You? A Film on Birth Control and Sexuality* (24 min.; available from Texture Films), and *Janie's Jane* (24 min.; available from Odeon Films).

MURPHY, BRI, 2373 Canyon Dr., Hollywood, Cal. 90068. Writer, producer, director, camera, sound. Formed own company, Sombrero Productions.

MURPHY, MARGARET, 9101 Shore Rd., Brooklyn, N. Y. 11209. Editor, producer, director; shorts for "Sesame Street."

MUSANTE, JOAN, 1157 Virginia St., Berkeley, Cal. 94702. Sound; documentary, feature, political films.

NADER, LAURA, % University of California, Dept. of Anthropology, Berkeley, Cal. 94720. Films include *To Make the Balance* (33 min.).

NELSON, HELEN, 350 E. 52nd St., New York, N. Y. 10022. Director; commercials. Member, Directors Guild of America.

NELSON, GUNVOR, Box 263 Star Route, Muir Beach, via Sausalito, Cal. 94965. One- and two-woman films including *Schmeerguntz* (15 min.), *Fog Pumas* (25 min.), *Kirsa Nicholina* (16 min.), *My Name Is Oona* (10 min.), *Take Off* (10 min.), *Moons Pool* (15 min.), and others. (See p. 193)

NEMSER, SANDY ROTHENBERG, 1305 Elizabeth St., Denver, Colo. 80206. Criminal lawyer; two-woman filmmaker, *New Vibrations: Woodstock* (15 min.).

NG, MARJORIE, One Scott St., San Francisco, Cal. 94117. One-woman films, including *After Hours, Protein Synthesis,* and *Opaque Transparency.*

NICCOLINI, DIANORA, 356 E. 78th St., New York, N. Y. 10021. Camera, editing; medical films including *Modified Radical Mastectomy* (20 min.), *External Side-to-Side Choledechoduodenostomy* (20 min.), and others.

NIGYLA, CASSANDRA, 1318 Singer Place, #2, Pittsburgh, Pa. 15221. Short films, including *Of Women* (6 min.).

NORDSTROM, KRISTINA, 1582 York Ave., New York, N. Y. 10028. Editor, writer, one-woman filmmaker. Organizer of the First International Festival of Women's Films (New York, 1972) and CINEMA FEMINA. One-woman films include *Rainbow Dance* and *Horse and Buggy;* other films include *The Journey* (editor), *Moonwalk I* (assistant editor), *George Washington Bridge,* and others.

NORTON, SUSAN, 1050 Newton Rd., Iowa City, Ia. 52240. Film student; one-woman films including *The Garden of Forking Paths* (15 min.), *From Dust to Dust* (15 min.), and others.

NOTO, CLARA B., 267 W. 11th St., New York, N. Y. 10014. Editor. Films include *Kassoundra* (30 min., director, editor), *Ten Days in Paseco* (25 min.), commercials, political spots.

NOVAS, HIMILCE, 355 E. 72nd St., New York, N. Y. 10021. Writer.

OAKES, SARAH LAWRENCE, % Tarot Films, Inc., 59 W. 12th St., New York, N. Y. 10011. Producer, editor. Films include *Coming Home* (74 min., producer and co-director), and *About Sex* (24 min., distributed by Texture Films, and winner of 1st prize, 1973 American Film Festival).

OBER, CHRISTINE, 620 Kingston Dr., Virginia Beach, Va. 23452. Writer, director, editor.

OBERHAUS, PATRICIA, % Canyon Cinema Co-op, Industrial Center Bldg., Sausalito, Cal. 94965. Films include *The Store on Telegraph* (13 min.).

ODOM, SELMA, Dept. of Dance, York University, Toronto, Ontario M4W 2X5. Dance historian and writer. Produced series on women and on dance for TV. Advised students doing experimental film and video work with dance.

O'GYLA, CASSANDRA, 5507 Margaretta St., Pittsburgh, Pa. 15206. Short films, including *Of Women* (6 min.), about the myths of womanhood and how women can overcome them.

OHRN, KAREN, 602 E. 12th St., Bloomington, Ind. 47401. Films include *Mrs. Richard Brand*, a portrait of an old-fashioned woman. Co-filmmaker, Ann Lewis.

OLIAN, HELEN, 227 E. Delaware Pl., Chicago, Ill. 60611. Animator.

OLIVE, JOAN, 765 Longhill Road, Gillette, N. J. 07933. Writer, producer, director. Works include *Labyrinth* (28 min.), and TV public service spots.

ONO, YOKO, 1 W. 72nd St., New York, N. Y. 10023. Artist, musician, poet, filmmaker. Films made with John Lennon include *Fly* (20 min.), showing a fly crawling on a nude female body; *Erection* (20 min.), the metamorphosis of a hotel being built; *Apotheosis* (25 min.), abstractions shot through a balloon, and *Rape II* (20 min.). (See p. 194)

ORENTREICH, CATHERINE, 50 E. 10th St., New York, N. Y. 10003. Films include *Nuptials* (10 min.), a critical look at marriage, documenting a bride, complete with all the trappings, including pre-marriage rituals, wedding and reception.

OSTERTAG, SANDY, 156 Gray Ave., Webster Groves, Mo. 63119. Films include *Woman Is*.

OXENBERG, JAN, 24 Breeze Ave., Venice, Cal. 90291. Short film on Lesbianism: *Home Movie* (10 min.). Available from Women's Film Co-op.

PAIGE, SHEILA, % Women Make Movies, Inc., 257 W. 19th St., New York, N. Y. 10011. Co-director and co-founder of this non-profit, tax-exempt educational organization devoted to encouraging women who would not ordinarily have the opportunity to make their own film, video, and radio productions. Films include *The Women's Happy Time Commune* (50 min.; director), and *Testing, Testing, How Do You Do?* (4 min.; director). (See p. 195)

PALETZ, DARCY, 1311 Carolina St., Durham, N. C. 27705. Producer for TV, audience services for TV; one-woman films, including *Asst. Prof.* (9½ min.), about why a man chooses a lifestyle.

PARETZKIN, BRITA, 1932 N. Larrabee St., Chicago, Ill. 60614. Editor.

PARKER, FRANCINE, 847 Alexandria Ave., Los Angeles, Cal. 90029. Director, writer, producer; features, documentaries, television, videotape. Films include *FTA* (feature; director, producer), *We Have a Melody* (30 min.; director, producer, writer), *Butterflies Don't Live in a Ghetto* (30 min.; writer, producer, director), *Fascinating Woman* from the "American Dream Machine" (6 min.; director), and others. FTA winner of 1972 Obie Award. Member, Directors Guild of America. (See p. 63)

PAUKER, LORETTA, % Khalam Productions, 820 W. 180th St., New York, N. Y. 10033. Actress, producer, director.

PAUL, MILLIE, 2103 Third St., Santa Monica, Cal. 90405. Editor. Films include *The Big Doll House* (90 min.), *The Cubist Epoch* (55 min.), *Take Two from the Sea* (27 min.), and others.

PAULETICH, AIDA, 2486 Cheremoya Ave., Los Angeles, Cal. 90068. Short one-woman films, including *Gods of Goodbye* (3 min.), *Hollywood* (3 min.), *Vitamin* (3 min.), *The Pocketbook* (3 min.), and others.

PEARL, LINDA, #6 Kings Highway, Haddon Heights, N. J. 08035. Short paint-on-film animated films, including *Garbonza* (1 min.), *Bride of Garbonza* (1 min.), and *Blood of Garbonza* (1 min.).

PEISER, JUDY, 3756 Mimosa Ave., Memphis, Tenn. 38111. Editor, documentary filmmaker, director of the Center for Southern Folklore. Films include *Gravel Springs Fife and Drum* (10 min.; editor, producer); *Ray Lum: Mule Trader* (18 min.; editor, producer), *Greene Valley Grandparents* (10 min.; editor, producer), *Black Delta Religion* (15 min.; editor), and others.

PERRY, ELEANOR, 40 Central Park So., New York, N. Y. 10019. Writer. Films include *David and Lisa* (Academy Award nomination), *Diary of a Mad Housewife, Last Summer, Man Who Loved Cat Dancing;* TV specials include *Christmas Memory* and *House Without a Christmas Tree* (both Emmy winners), *Thanksgiving Visitor,* and others. (See p. 70)

PERRY, JOYCE, 2250 N. Gower St., Los Angeles, Cal. 90068. Writer, TV and film.

PETERSON, INA MAE, 1356 N. Benton Way, Los Angeles, Cal. 90026. Writer, documentary filmmaker.

PETRAS, PEGGY, 827 Verano Dr., Glendora, Cal. 91740. Short one-woman films.

PFAFFL, CAROLYN SUE, 12 Camino Coronado, Tucson, Ariz. 85704. Teacher, maker of 8mm cine-dance films.

PHILLIPS, WENDY, 60 W. 10th St., New York, N. Y. 10003. Producer, sound. Films include *Music in the Schools* (sound recordist; documentary sponsored by the Nat'l Endowment for the Arts), *A Wonderful Construction* (associate producer; TV documentary contrasting construction workers in life and art), *Immigrants in New York* (sound recordist; ABC-TV documentary), *Louise* (feature, assistant camera), and five shorts for "The Electric Company."

PIGORSCH, PHYLLIS, 75 Bluebill Park Dr., Madison, Wisc. 53718. Short one-woman films, including *Mrs. Slattery's Stew* (10 min.), *Hunger* (23 min.), *Salmon Story, Hot Rocks,* and others.

PIHL, CHRISTINE R., 1314 Tarpon, Foster City, Cal. 94404. One-woman short films and videotapes. Films include *Hairy Kari* (9 min.), *Trance and Dental Med(itation) Center* (10 min.), and others. Films have been shown at various festivals including Cinestud International Film Festival in Amsterdam.

PIVNICK, ANITRA, 26 W. 95th St., New York, N. Y. 10025. Producer, director, editor; short films and documentaries, including *Saturday* (20 min.), a study of a girl alone.

POLON, VICKI, 14 W. 10th St., New York, N. Y. 10011. Writer, producer, director, editor. Films include *Leslie* (5 min.), *Hubert's* (5 min.), *Salon de Glas* (6 min.), "Sesame Street" shorts, and others.

PORCHOV-LYNCH, TAO, 11 Findlay Ave., Hartsdale, N. Y. 10530. Writer, director. Films include *To Light a Candle* (55 min.; writer, director), *Boy on the Ganges* (30 min.; writer), *Relentless Dunes* (20 min.; writer, producer), *Images de'Israel* (70 min.; co-director), *Face of India* (30 min.; writer, director), and others.

POWELL, PAT, 75½ Hoyt St., Brooklyn, N. Y. 11201. Producer, director, editor. Among her multi-award winning productions are *Who Will Tie My Shoe?* (1965, 60 min.; co-producer), a documentary on mental retardation for WABC News; *Well I Got a Job, Ain't I* (1968, 55 min.; producer, editor), a survey of programs for the hardcore unemployed; *Veronica* (1969, 27 min.; producer, director, editor), a portrait of a black teenager. (See p. 197)

PRISADSKY, MARJORIE, % Canyon Cinema Co-op, Industrial Center Bldg., Sausalito, Cal. 94965. Maker of short films, including *White Susan* (6 min.), on being alone and aroused, and *Last Week* (5 min.), about Apollo II.

PUGH, SALLY, % Vision Quest and Insight Exchange, 389 Ethel Ave., Mill Valley, Cal. 94941. Films include *Home Born Baby* (47 min.), showing Sally's natural home childbirth with the aid of a midwife.

RAINER, YVONNE, 92 Franklin St., New York, N. Y. 10013. Director. Films include *Volleyball* (10 min.), *Trio Film* (15 min.), *Lives of Performers* (90 min.), and *Film About a Woman Who . . .* (90 min.).

RAMSING, PAMELLA, % Canyon Cinema Co-op, Industrial Center Bldg., Sausalito, Cal. 94965. Short film, *Feathers Is a Bird If It Is A Bird* (5 min.).

RAVITZ, MYRNA, % Cinepac, Inc., 46 E. Oak St., Chicago, Ill. 60611. Owner of her own film company, Cinepac, Inc., which does feature film work, commercial films and sales films. (See p. 197)

REICHERT, JULIA, % New Day Films, P.O. Box 315, Franklin Lakes, N. J. 07417. Producer, director, camera, editor; also distributor. Films include *Growing Up Female: As 6 Become 1* (50 min.), *I Forget* (10 min.), *Methadone: An American Way of Dealing* (60 min.), and others. (See p. 198)

REID, FRANCIS, 1334 McCullum, Los Angeles, Cal. Soundwoman.

REIDEL, JUDY, 2017 Vista Del Mar, Los Angeles, Cal. 90068. Short films, including *Call It Mother's Love, EF,* and others. Available from filmmaker.

REINIGER, LOTTE, % Contemporary Films/McGraw Hill, Princeton Rd., Hightstown, N. J. 08520. Filmmaker and producer. Short films include *Three Wishes* (10 min.), and *Hansel and Gretel* (10 min.), one of the many animated films based on the live-action shadow plays Reiniger produced for BBC.

REYNOLDS, JUDY, 642 W. 34th St., Los Angeles, Cal. 90007. Producer. Films include *Renaissance* (6 min.), *A Day in the Life of Wally C.* (15 min.), and *Where Were You When the Artichoke Blew?* (40 min.).

RICCITELLI, ELIZABETH, 331 E. Sixth St., New York, N. Y. 10003. One-woman films.

RIEGLE, BARBARA, % Calico Features, 2512 Chain Ave., Anaheim, Cal. 92804. TV news editor, writer, producer; documentaries and news spots.

RIISNA, ENE, 26 Bank St., New York, N. Y. 10014. Producer, director. Films include *Indian Couples* (30 min., director, "Are You Listening" series), *Fasanella* (15 min., director/writer, CBC "Gallery" series), *Chinaman's Chance* (60 min., producer/director, documentary for WNET), *Here Come the Seventies* (30 min., documentary, director/writer; winner of Gold Medal at 1971 Atlanta International Film Festival), *A Three Letter Word for Love* (director/writer, sex education film for ghetto teenagers), *Fasten Your Seatbelts* (60 min. documentary on airline safety for NET and CBC, second-unit director), and *I Have a Dream* (60 min. documentary about Ressurrection City for CBC and US syndication), among others. Member, Directors Guild of America.

RITTER, CAROL, 100 Overlook Terr., New York, N. Y. 10040. Short experimental films, including *The Shooting on South Street* (12 min.).

RIVERA, LINDA, % Youth Films Distribution Center, 43 W. 16th St., New York, N. Y. 10011. Short films including *Young Love* (8 min.).

RIVETT-RIVER, JACKIE, % Life Style Productions, Inc., 709 W. Montrose at Marine Dr., Chicago, Ill. 60613. Writer, producer, director. Children's Films on birth, death, divorce and adoption for Encyclopaedia Britannica; TV, radio commercials and educational films for American Dental Association.

ROBERTSON, LAURI, % Youth Films Distribution Center, 43 W. 16th St., New York, N. Y. 10011. Short films, including *Still, Life* (7 min.).

ROCHLIN, DIANE, % Filmmakers' Co-op, 175 Lexington Ave., New York, N. Y. 10016. Co-director; short films, including *Diane, the Zebra Woman* (24 min.), and *Sailor Dance* (7½ min.), with husband, Sheldon.

ROECKER, DOROTHY, 2400 Archbury La., Park Ridge, Ill. 60068. Producer.

ROHMER, HARRIET, % Canyon Cinema, Co-op, Industrial Center Bldg., Sausalito, Cal. 94965. Films include *Advertisement* (16½ min.), the many sides of a Berkeley boy. Co-filmmaker, Bret Rohmer.

ROMAN, HANNA, 567 N. Windsor Blvd., Los Angeles, Cal. 90004. Co-producer, -director, -camera; short films, including *Black Windows* (16 min.), *Five Star Eggo* (5 min.), *The Vibrant Nude* (10 min.), and others. Films available from Creative Film Society.

ROOS, BARBARA, 226 E. Duffy, Norman, Okla. 73069. Producer, writer. Films include *Lisa's World* (30 min.), *Silent Heritage* (ten 30 min. films), *We Came to Stay* (15 min.), *Everybody's Eagle* (29 min.). (See p. 199)

ROSE, CARLA (VALENTINE), 132 Mason Terrace, Brookline, Mass. 02146. Writer, director, editor, animator; documentary and educational films and TV commercials. (See p. 209)

ROSENBERG, ROYANNE, 243 Elmwood, Evanston, Ill. 60202. Short one-woman films, including *The Autopsy* (4½ min.) and *Roseland* (12½ min.).

ROSENBLATT, ADRIAN, % Youth Film Distribution Center, 43 W. 16th St., New York, N. Y. 10011. Short films include *Embryonic Movement* (4 min.), expressing birth and the beginning of life through dance.

ROSENBLATT, ROSE, 165 W. 91st St., New York, N. Y. 10024. Editor. Films include *Everest* (90 min.), *Acupuncture* (30 min.), *A Study of Anais Nin* (30 min., camera), *Revolution in Modern Art* (90 min.), *Go for Broke* (90 min.) and *Noguchi: A Sculptor's World* (60 min., production assistant). Working on 20-minute experimental narrative.

ROSS, TAYLOE, 118 W. 13th St., New York, N. Y. 10011. Writer, maker of films and videotapes, including *Village Afternoon* (9 min.), *Cityscape* (15 min.), *Secretaries* (40 min.), *Moss Rose* (5 min.).

ROTHMAN, STEPHANIE, Dimension Pictures, 9000 Sunset, Los Angeles, Cal. 90069. Producer, writer, director; features. (See p. 58)

ROTHSCHILD, AMALIE R., 105 Second Ave., New York, N. Y. 10003. Writer, director, editor. Films include *Nana, Mom and Me* (1974, 45 min.), *Woo Who May Wilson* (1970, 33 min., writer, director, editor), *The Center* (45 min., camera, editor), *Safari* (13 min., producer, director, editor). *It Happens to Us* (1972, 30 min., producer, director, editor), *It's All Right to be Woman* (50 min., camera, editor). She has also made several medical films. *It Happens to Us* and *Woo Who May Wilson* available from New Day Films. (See p. 200)

ROTUNDA, MARJORIE, 3916 Riviera Drive, San Diego, Cal. 92109. Director; commercials. Member, Directors Guild of America.

RUSSELL, PAT, 80 Wooster St., New York, N. Y. 10012. Writer, director, producer, editor. Films include *Just Married* (6 min.), and others. Winner of Cine Golden Eagle and other awards.

RUSSO, LILLIAN, 9 Tulip Lane, Port Washington, N. Y. 11050. Associate director; TV and film. Member, Directors Guild of America.

RYDEN, HOPE, 345 E. 81st St., New York, N. Y. 10028. Writer, producer, director; documentaries. Films include *Mission to Malaya* (60 min.), *Operation Gwamba* (30 min.), *To Love a Child* (30 min.), *Strangers In Their Own Land: The Chicanos* (30 min.). (See p. 201)

SACHS, SHARON, J., 211 Henry St., New York, N. Y. 10002. Editor, camera. Films include *Rehabilitation* (1973, 30 min.; editor), *Kongi's Harvest* (1971, feature; editor; Ossie Davis, director), *Pound* (1970, feature; assistant director; Robert Downey, director), *The Long Awaited Guest* (1974, 15 min.; camera).

SAGER, SUE, People Reaching Productions, 1460 N. Sandburg Terr., Chicago, Ill. 60610. Producer.

SALWASSER, LYNDA BYBEE, Indian Brook Rd., Garrison, N. Y. 10524. Producer, production manager. Films include *Christina's World* (52 min., for television), *Not a Place* (26 min.), *In Order to Effect Change . . .* (28 min.).

SAMATOWICZ, D., 463 West St., New York, N. Y. 10014. Short one-woman films, including *Westbeth* (15 min.), *Secrets* (4 min.), and others.

SAMUELSON, KRISTINE, 51 Prosper, San Francisco, Cal. 94114. Producer, director, editor, sound; documentary, political, and educational films, including *Becoming*.

SANDERS, JESSICA, 525 W. 113th St., New York, N. Y. 10025. Editor, Harvest Films, Inc.

SANDERS, MARLENE, % ABC News, 7 W. 66th St., New York, N. Y. 10023. Producer, writer; TV documentaries. Films include *Population: Boom or Doom, Woman's Place,* and *The Right to Die* (60 min. each, producer, writer), *Feminism and the Church* (30 min., writer), *Children in Peril* (30 min., producer, writer), and others. (See p. 80)

SANDOVAL, CHE, 311 Almar, Santa Cruz, Cal. 95060. Member of the Santa Cruz Women's Media Collective.

SARNER, SYLVIA, 315 W. 70th St., New York, N. Y. 10023. Editor. Films include *Road Movie* (feature), *Interviews With My Lai Veterans* (22 min., Academy Award short subject, 1971), *Taking Off* (feature, assistant editor, Cannes Jury Prize, 1971), *Tropic of Cancer* (feature, co-editor), *Slaves* and *Paper Lion* (both features, assistant editor).

SAUNDERS, PAT, 685 West End Ave., New York, N. Y. 10025. Editor, director, camera; one-woman short films. Films include *Interlude* (15 min.), *Four Plus Two* (3½ min. experimental film poem), *Two* (feature; sound editor), *Vision of a City* (feature; assistant editor, sound editor), *Snake* (8 min.).

SCHARRES, BARBARA, % Center Cinema Co-op, School of the Art Institute, Michigan at Adams, Chicago, Ill. 60603. Short films include *Arrows, Handstrings, A Working Progress,* and *Self Portrait,* which is concerned with the self as body and presence.

SCHIFF, SUZANNA, % The Great American Film Factory, 961 N. La Cienega Blvd., Los Angeles, Cal. 90068. Associate producer. Member, Cinewomen.

SCHIFFMAN, SUZANNE, 311 Almar, Santa Cruz, Cal. 95060. One-woman filmmaker. Member of the Santa Cruz Women's Media Collective.

SCHMIDT, JAN, % New Line Cinema, 121 University Pl., New York, N. Y. 10003. Films include *The End of August at the Hotel Ozone* (85 min.), about nine women who survive a nuclear holocaust.

SCHNEEMANN, CAROLEE, 470 Springtown Rd., New Paltz, N. Y. 12561. Filmmaker, writer. Films include *Fuses* (26 min.), *Plumbline, Viet-Flakes* and *Waterlights? Water Needle* (all 1973). Films available from Serious Business Co.

SCHNEIDER, MARION, 301 E. 75th St., New York, N. Y. 10021. One-woman montage films: *San Francisco Montage* (11 min.), *Faces* (10 min.), *Sailing* (8 min.).

SCHNEIDER, ROSALIND, 40 Cottontail Lane, Irvington-on-Hudson, N. Y. 10533. One-woman art films. Films include *Parallax* (20 min.), *Orbitas* (10 min.), *Dream Study* (7 min.), *Abstraction* (8 min.), *Still Life* (8 min.), *Illusions on the Edge of Reality,* and others.

SCHNUR, ESTHER, 727 Park Ave., New York, N. Y. 10021. Writer.

SCHREDER, CAROL, % American Film Institute, 501 Doheny Rd., Beverly Hills, Cal. 90210. Director, editor; short films, including *The Human Sport* (10 min., director, editor), *The Editor* (20 min., editor), *Sisterhood* (32 min., director).

SCHUBERT, KATHRYN, 746 W. Belden Ave., Chicago, Ill. 60614. Editor, *My Sister's Cutting Room.*

SCHULMAN, NINA, 60 W. 57th St., New York, N. Y. 10019. Editor, producer, sound recordist. Films include *Van Cliburn* (60 min., editor), *Twiggy Way* (60 min., editor), *Monterey Pop* (80 min., editor), *Werewolf of Washington* (feature, producer), *FTA* (feature, sound recordist), *Beyond the Law* (feature, sound recordist), *Maidstone* (feature, sound recordist). (See p. 202)

SCHWARTZ, JOAN M., Rhode Island School of Design, Box 835, 2 College St., Providence, R. I. 02903. Short one-woman films, including *Garbage* (12 min.).

SCHWARTZ, LILLIAN, 524 Ridge Rd., Watchung, N. J. 07060. Art films, science films. Films include *Mutations* (7½ min.), *Apotheosis* (4½ min.), *Metamorphosis* (8¼ min.), and others.

SEARLES, BARBARA, 2950 Belden Dr., Hollywood, Cal. 90068. Writer, producer, director; TV documentaries and industrial films. Writer, TV shows. Assistant director in film and associate director/stage manager in live/tape TV. Member, Directors Guild of America.

SEEGER, JUDITH, 817 West End Ave., New York, N. Y. 10025. Writer, associate producer; educational films, promotional films.

SEIDEL, DIANA E., 6273 N. Cicero Ave., Chicago, Ill. 60646. Producer for Sears, Roebuck & Co. Films include *Duck Hunting with Ted Williams* (13½ min., producer, director, editor), *Basketball Fundamentals* (28 min., producer, editor), *Tarpon Fishing* (25 min., producer, editor), *Scroll Saw* (7 min., producer, writer, editor), and many others. (See p. 202)

SELLER, JANE, % Third World Newsreel, 26 W. 20th St., New York, N. Y. 10011. Films include *Children of the Revolution* (30 min.), about young Cubans defining themselves in their socialist society.

SELWOOD, MAUREEN, 210 W. 101st St., New York, N. Y. 10025. Animator. Films include *The Box* (5 min.), *The Six Sillies* (10 min.), and films for "Sesame Street."

SERRANO, NINA, % Impact Films, 144 Bleeker St., New York, N. Y. 10023. Filmmaker. Co-directed with Saul Landau *Que Hacer* (90 min.). Set in the political reality of Chile, the fictional story deals with the different roads to revolution.

SEVERSON, ANNE, % Serious Business Co., 1927 Marin Ave., Berkeley, Cal. 94707. Teacher, co-director short films including *Near the Big Chakra* (17 min., color), *Introduction to Humanities* (6 min.), *Riverbody* (8 min., with Shelby Kennedy).

SHACKSON, MARGO, % Ann Arbor News, Ann Arbor, Mich. Filmmaker. Worked with Selma Odom on *Girls and Women*, a series of ten programs of 30 minutes each on the physical and sociological differences between the sexes.

SHADBURNE, SUSAN, 2908 N.W. Thurman, Portland, Ore. 97210. Composer, writer. Films include *Endless Chain* (30 min., wrote poetic narrative; winner, Cine Golden Eagle), *River Where Do You Come From?* (wrote narrative ballad; certificate winner, Columbus Film Festival), *Well of Life* (30 min., writer; winner, Cine Golden Eagle), *Nature's Forge* (30 min., narrative and music).

SHAFFER, DEBORAH, 33 Greene St., New York, N. Y. 10013. Pandora Films, co-writer, -producer, -director, -editor. Feminist films including *How About You? A Film on Birth Control and Sexuality* (24 min.; available from Texture Films) and *Make-Out* (5 min.).

SHANKS, ANN ZANE, 135 Central Park W., New York, N. Y. 10023. Photographer, writer, director. Films include *Central Park* (14 min.), *Tivoli* (10 min.), *Denmark . . . A Loving Embrace* (producer, director). Producer-director of TV series "American Life Style." Winner, Cine Golden Eagle, Silver and Gold Awards, International Film and TV Festival, and many others. *Central Park* available through Columbia Pictures.

SHAW, JEAN, % Women Make Movies, 257 W. 19th St., New York, N. Y. 10011. Her first film, *Fear* (7 min.), is about a young woman's triumphant confrontation with a rapist.

SHELTON, SLOANE, 49 Grove St., New York, N. Y. 10014. Actress, producer, writer. Films include *Millay at Steepletop* (23 min., producer, screenwriter, narrator).

SHERLOCK, MAUREEN, % Third World Newsreel, 26 W. 20th St., New York, N. Y. 10011. Films include *A Space to Be Me* (30 min.), analyzing the need for daycare in terms of the positive effects on children and the possibilities it creates for mothers. Co-filmmaker David Weinkauf.

SHEVEY, SANDRA, 334 E. 53rd St., New York, N. Y. 10022. Writer; documentaries.

SHIGEKAWA, JOAN, 325 West End Ave., New York, N. Y. 10023. Producer, reporter, writer. Works include *Woman Alive!* (Public TV special for, by and about women, produced in collaboration with Ms. magazine; producer); "The 51st State" (news show, WNET, producer-reporter); "Up Against New York" (weekly series for WNET, producer, anchorperson); producer of dramatic and documentary specials for WNET; production and research staff at CBS-TV, NBC-TV and CBS News; *Ganja and Hess* (black feature film, associate producer); partner in Donnet/Shigekawa Productions (theater productions). (See p. 67)

SHUGARD, AMY V., Box 130A, Route 2, Waldorf, Md. 20601. Veteran producer and editor; documentaries and theatrical shorts. Films produced, directed and edited include *I Remember* (27 min.), *The Night Before Christmas* (10 min.), *Heritage of Freedom* (25 min.), *Chesapeake Blues* (10 min.), *Terra Maria* (23 min.), and many others.

SIDES, CAROLYN, % Sarsaku Productions, 8700 Skyline Dr., Los Angeles, Cal. 90046. Editor.

SIEDLECKI, AGNES, 17232 Kingsbury St., Granada, Hills, Cal. 91344. One-woman films, including *All Your Eggs* (20 min.) and *Drabina* (8 min.).

SIEGEL, MARIAN, 106 Enchanted Hills Rd., Owings Mills, Md. 21117. Editor, director.

SIKEVITZ, GAIL, 2250 N. Lincoln Ave., Chicago, Ill. 60614. Assistant director.

SILVER, JOAN, % Learning Corporation of America, 711 Fifth Ave., New York, N. Y. 10022. Films include *The Immigrant Experience: The Long Long Journey* (31 min.), the American dream vs. American reality for a Polish family in 1907. Co-filmmaker, Linda Gottlieb.

SIMOLA, LIISA, 35 E. 64th St., New York, N. Y. 10021. Journalist, photographer, film editor. One-woman films, including *New York City* (14 min.), *Women's Lib August 26th* (6 min.), *North African Camel Markets* (20 min.), and others.

SIMPSON, MARY K., % Dept. of Speech, West Virginia University, Morgantown, W. Va. 26505. Instructor of radio, TV, and film; producer, director, writer. Films include *A Day in the Life* (5 min.), *Prelude in Black and White* (78 min.).

SKELTON, MARLYS, 5336 26th Ave. S., Minneapolis, Minn. 55417. Short experimental films include *Willow Tree,* a winter landscape shot in negative with an electronic sound track.

SLESIN, AVIVA, 155 E. 77th St., New York, N. Y. 10021. Editor, producer. Editor *Gertrude Stein: When This You See, Remember Me* and *The Great Radio Comedians,* both 90 min. specials for NET (directed and produced by Perry Miller Adato); a segment for CBS's "60 Minutes" on tax shelters; and *China Memoir: The Other Half of the Sky* (74 min.). Produced *Fat Film,* on the nature of compulsion. (See p. 203)

SLOANE, PATRICIA, 79 Mercer St., New York, N. Y. 10012. One-woman experimental short films, including *A Knee Ad* (25 min.), *Reticulations* (4 min.).

SMITH, BARBARA L., 109 E. 45th St., Brooklyn, N. Y. 11232. Editor, animator. Films include *The Folks* (45 min., production assistant and assistant editor), *Kick* (22 min., production assistant and assistant editor), *Something to Build On* (25 min., animation editor). (See p. 203)

SMITH, JUDY, 532 W. 111th St., New York, N. Y. 10025. Films include *The Woman's Film* (45 min., co-filmmaker).

SMITH, JUNE, 7827 Church St., Millington, Tenn. 38053. Writer.

SMITH, LELA, % Franciscan Films, Box 6116, San Francisco, Cal. 94101. Editor; documentary and educational films. Films include *You Got What?* (23 min.), *San Francisco Mix* (60 min.), *Thermal Power* (25 min.). (See p. 203)

SMITH, LYNN, 30 Upland Rd., Cambridge, Mass. 02140. Animator. Films include *How Snakes Move* (1½ min.), *The Shout It Out Alphabet Film* (10 min.).

SMITH, MARY STEWART, 1334 Yale St., Santa Monica, Cal. 90404. One-woman films, including *Capri* (1 min.).

SMITH, SHARON, RFD Route 1, Hartland, Me. 04943. Writer.

SMOLLETT, MOLLY, 41-23 Hampton St., Queens, N. Y. Editor, documentaries, industrial films. Edited several segments of "Directions" for ABC-TV.

SOLOMON, MAUREEN C., 150 E. 52nd St., New York, N. Y. 10022. Writer, director, producer of *Suite Music* (7 min.), a musical narrative.

SOMMERSCHIELD, ROSE NEIDITCH, 333 E. 30th St., New York, N. Y. 10016. Short films, including *You Can* (2½ min.).

SONES, CAROL, 19 Holden Rd., W. Newton, Mass. 02165. Filmmaker.

SONTAG, SUSAN. (See p. 52)

SORRIN, ELLEN, 1234 E. 35th St., Brooklyn, N. Y. 11210. Films include *The Woman's Film* (45 min., co-filmmaker).

SPENCER, MARY ANN, 75 Creston, Tenafly, N. J. 07670. One-woman films, including *Moon* (2 min.), and *The White Cat* (1½ min.), both available from Filmmakers' Co-op.

SPERLING, KAREN, Sperling Productions, 39 W. 88th St., New York, N. Y. 10024. Director, writer, producer. Films include *Make a Face* (80 min.), about a mixed-up rich girl coming apart in her Manhattan apartment; and *Waiting Room* (feature), the first 35mm feature made with an all-woman technical crew. (See p. 83)

SPHEERIS, PENELOPE, 716 Sunset Ave., Venice, Cal. 90291. Writer, director, editor. Films include *I Don't Know* (20 min.), *National Rehabilitation Center* (15 min.), *Synthesis* (12 min.), *Bath* (5 min.), *Hats Off to Hollywood* (26 min.). (See p. 204)

SPIEGEL, OLGA, 473 W. Broadway, New York, N. Y. 10012. Animation, one-woman films. Films include *Contemplation, Charles Mingus in Japan* (both 30 min., 16mm color; camera), *Alchemy Blues* (10 min., 16mm color animation painted directly on film), and *Prince of Darkness: Miles Davis at the Fillmore* (60 min., 16mm color; camera and special effects).

SPRING, SYLVIA, 16 Laurier Ave., Toronto, Ont. M4X 1S3. Producer, director, writer, interviewer; documentaries and dramas. Films for "This Land is People," CTV series (story editor, director); "Enterprise," experimental CBC-TV series (director); "CBC Weekday" (director); "The Family of Woman," TV series in pre-production (producer, director). Also *Madeleine* (15 min., writer, director), and *Madeleine Is . . .* (90 min., feature, writer, director, producer).

SQUIRES, EMILY, % Children's TV Workshop, 1 Lincoln Plaza, New York, N. Y. 10023. Associate director, film and TV, associate producer, "Sesame Street." Member, Directors Guild of America.

STAFFORD, BARBARA, % Center Cinema Co-op, School of the Art Institute, Michigan at Adams, Chicago, Ill. 60603. Animator.

STANG, BETSY, 33 Fifth Ave., New York, N. Y. 10003. Photographer, animator, filmmaker. Films include *Spencer Supersperm* (6 min., producer, director, with Theodor Timreck), *Eggs* (production coordinator, optical effects), *Alice Cooper-Elected* (production manager, production co-ordinator, 2nd unit camera), and *The Dance of the Celestial Hare* (40 min.). Charter member, Women's Film Collective.

STEEL, JUNE MARY, 2312 Third St., Santa Monica, Cal. 90405. Director of documentary and educational films. Films include *Retirement* (10 min.), *Kienholz on Exhibit* (21 min.), *Continuum* (12 min.), "Man in Society" (30 min., BBC-TV series), *Human Animals* (26 min.).

STEIN, CAROL, 59 Gail Dr., Waterbury, Conn. 06704. Short one-woman films, including *The Gold Caboose* (4 min.).

STEIN, SARAH, 8 St. Marks Pl., New York, N. Y. 10003. Editor. Films include *Princeton: A Search for Answers* (30 min., Academy Award for best documentary short, 1973), *The Bolero* (30 min., Academy Award for best live action short, 1973) and *Woman Alive!* (60 min. magazine-format TV pilot for PBS).

STEINBERG, ROSLYN, 780 West End Ave., New York, N. Y. 10025. Films include *Coney Island* (7 min.), *Gay Liberation March* (6 min.), and others.

STEINBERG, SUSAN, 190 Riverside Dr., New York, N. Y. 10024. Film editor. Films include C.S. *Blues* (feature documentary), *Gimme Shelter* (95 min., on the Rolling Stones), *Woodstock* (feature), *Trash* (3½ min. trailer for Andy Warhol-Paul Morrissey feature; producer, editor, camera), and documentaries for TV.

STEINBRECHER, MARCIA, % Filmmakers' Co-op, 175 Lexington Ave., New York, N. Y. 10016. Short films, including *American Radiator* (10 min.).

STENHOLM, KATHERINE, Unusual Films, Bob Jones University, Greenville, S. C. 29614. Producer, director, film administrator, film professor. Films include *Wine of Morning* (120 min.), *Red Runs the River* (90 min.), *Flame in the Wind* (120 min.). (See p. 205)

STERN, JOAN KELLER, % Learning Corporation of America, 711 Fifth Ave., New York, N. Y. 10022. Films include *The Magic Machines* (14 min.), about the unconventional art and philosophy of Robert Gilvert.

STERNBURG, JANET, 514 West End Ave., New York, N. Y. 10024. Educator, writer, producer. Films include *Virginia Woolf: The Moment Whole* (10 min., producer, co-director; available from ACI Films), *El Teatro Campesino* (70 min., co-producer; available from NET Film Service), *The Movie Crazy Years* (90 min., associate producer; available from United Artists). Awards include Cine Golden Eagle and Brussels International Film Week Honors. Also, director of "The Me Myself and I Movie Matinee," a program of films for children. (See p. 205)

STEVENS, EMILY FAVELA, 11954 Moorpark St., Studio City, Cal. 91604. Writer, director, producer; documentaries, commercials; theater.

STONE, BARBARA, % Filmmakers' Co-op, 175 Lexington Ave., New York, N. Y. 10016. Films on Cuba, including *Companeras and Companeros* (90 min., with David Stone and Adolfas Mekas).

STRAND, CHICK, 1834 Canyon Dr., Los Angeles, Cal. 90028. Ethnographic and experimental films. Films include *Mosori Monika* (20 min.), *Waterfall* (4 min.), *Anselmo* (4 min.), *Orfano* (25 min.), and *Elasticity* (20 min.). (See p. 206)

STRAUB, JEAN-MARIE, % Diablo Valley College, Concord, Cal. Director. Films include *Chronicle of Anna Magdalena Bach* (90 min.), based on journals of Bach's second wife.

STRICKLAND, KATHY, % Creative Film Society, 7237 Canby Ave., Reseda, Cal. 91335. Short films including *All Come to Look for America* (3 min.).

STROUTH, PENELOPE, % Film Images, 17 W. 60th St., New York, N. Y. 10023. Films include *Ancient Art of Peru* (15 min.).

STUART, MARTHA, 66 Bank St., New York, N. Y. 10014. Producer, editor. Video tapes and films, including the series "Are You Listening" (19 tapes, each 28½ min.), "Oigamoslos" (2 tapes, each 20 min.), and "The People of World Population Year" (3 tapes, each 28½ min.). "Are You Listening" in 1974 received National Cable Television Association Award for public affairs programming. Sales and rentals from Martha Stuart Communications, address above.

STYMAN, BARBARA, 1219 Taylor St., San Francisco, Cal. 94126. Veteran producer and director, film and TV. Films include *The Long Hard Road to Success* and *The Love Gift* (available from Grove Press).

SUMMERS, ELAINE, % Filmmakers Co-op, 175 Lexington Ave., New York, N. Y. 10016. Films include *Walking Dance for Any Number* (8 min.), an intermedia/multi-projection film unit, comprised of four 8-minute silent reels —for simultaneous projection—and a dance score for two to ten dancers. (See p. 207)

SUTTON, SANDRA, % Phoenix Films, Inc., 470 Park Ave. S., New York, N. Y. 10016. Films include *Sittin' on Top of the World: At the Fiddlers' Convention* (24 min., co-filmmaker Max Kalmanowicz), documentary about the oldest and largest bluegrass festival in the U.S.

TALBOT, TOBY, 180 Riverside Dr., New York, N. Y. 10024. Writer, director, producer. Films include *Birembau* (13 min.).

TARBILL, CINDY, 6762 E. Rosewood Circle, Tucson, Ariz. 85710. Writer, director, *House Guests* (15 min.).

TAUBIN, AMY, 141 Wooster St., New York, N. Y. 10012. Short films, including *Paul's Film* (10 min.).

TAVENER, JO, 340 W. 72nd St., New York, N. Y. 10023. Short films, including *Strike* (30 min., camera, co-director), *Ladies Home Journal* (12 min., camera, editor, co-director), and others.

TAYLOR, ANNIE, 7354 Tulane, St. Louis, Mo. 63130. Films include *Before the Actor* (22 min., writer, director, editor) and *Freddy* (9½ min., writer, director, editor).

TAYLOR, LINDA, 2243 Junaluska Way, Pacific Palisades, Cal. 90272. Director; animated films. Films include *Bosses Dream* (1 min.), *Comedienne Eulogy* (3 min.), and numerous commercials.

TAYLOR, RENEE, % Creative Film Society, 7237 Canby Ave., Reseda, Cal. 91335. Short films including *Two* (10 min.).

TEREBEY, RAISA, 43 John E. Busch Ave., Somerset, N. J. 08873. Short films and screenplay adaptations.

THACHER, ANITA, 33 Second Ave., New York, N. Y. 10003. One-woman films; associate producer, editor. Films include *Mr. Story* (28 min., with Deedee Halleck), *Permanent Wave* (3 min.), *Back Track* (7 min., co-director), *Prism* (feature, associate producer). Winner, Sinking Creek Film Festival.

THETA, SHIRLEY CRANE, Big Oaks Dr., Yorkville, Cal. 95494. Multiscreen slide shows, short one-woman films, including *Next Stop* (22 min.).

THOMAS, ANNA I., 3574¾ Centinela Ave., Los Angeles, Cal. 90066. Writer, filmmaker; films include *An Old and Dear Friend* (30 min.) and *The Confessions of Amans*.

THOMSON, PAT, 19 Bernard St., Mill Valley, Cal. 94741. Writer, editor, animation. Films include *Sketches of a Man* (45 min., editor), *Child Reborn* (30 min., co-writer, co-producer), *The Gold Box* (3½ min., animator). (See p. 208)

TOD, DOROTHY, Warren, Vt. 05674. Veteran director, producer, editor, camera. (See p. 209)

TOKIEDA, TOSHIE, % Film Images, 17 W. 60th St., New York, N. Y. 10023. Documentary filmmaker. Films include *Report from China* (90 min.), showing everyday life-style in the People's Republic of China.

TOUMARKINE, DORIS, 58 Barrow St., New York, N. Y. 10012. Producer, editor.

TOURTELOT, MADELINE, % Grove Press, 53 E. 11th St., New York, N. Y. 10003. Short films, including *Music Studio: Harry Partch* (18 min.).

TRAVENER, JO, 340 W. 72nd St., New York, N. Y. 10023. Films include *Ladies' Home Journal* (112 min.), about the takeover of offices, *A Woman's Place* (30 min.), about changing roles and options for women, and *Strike* (30 min.), about a feminist strike.

TRINKAUS, MARILYN MILLER, 1107 N. Lafayette, Royal Oak, Mich. 48067. Writer, director, editor. Films include *Amusement Park* (20 min., editor) and *Woman, Woman* (3 min., one-woman film).

TUCKER, PAULA McKINNEY, 20542 Oldham Rd., Southfield, Mich. 48076. Producer, director; industrial films, documentaries. Assistant director, unit manager, TV and film documentaries and commercials. Member, Directors Guild of America.

TUPPER, LOIS ANN, 60 Chilton St., Cambridge, Mass. 02138. Short films, including *Genesis 3:16* (17 min., co-directed with Maureen McCue), *Biofeedback* (10 min.), *Marian Lincoln, City Counsellor* (3 min., co-directed with Gail Rheinlander), *Fine Times at Our House* (27 min., co-directed with Maureen McCue).

UNDERHILL, GEORGIANA, 114 Durland Ave., Elmira, N. Y. 14905. Editor. Films include *The Elementary Guidance Counselor* (30 min.), *A Kindergarten Day* (30 min.), *Community Schools Program* (30 min.), *Emergency Call Box* (5 min.).

VALENTINE, CARLA. (See p. 209)

VAN HULSTEYN, JEANNINE, 5640-A Roche Dr., Columbus, O. 43229. Short films, including *Confrontation* (3 min.) and *Our Day is Spring* (2 min.).

VINCENZ, LILLI, 5411 S. Eighth Pl., Arlington, Va. 22204. Editor, documentaries. Also one-woman films.

VIVAS, MARTA, 17 E. 97th St., New York, N. Y. 10029. Producer, director. Films include *Women for Women* (co-filmmaker).

VOGELSANG, JUDITH, 519 Montgomery Ave., Haverford, Pa. 19041. Director, producer, writer for film and TV. (See p. 210)

WALKER, GERTRUDE, 9213 Alden Dr., Beverly Hills, Cal. 90210. Veteran writer; 15 screenplays, 12 TV credits, three produced plays, three published novels. Member, Writers Guild of America, Dramatists Guild, Authors League.

WALLACE, LINDA, 16438 Gilmore St., Van Nuys, Cal. 91406. One-woman films, including *The People* (30 min.).

WALSH, ALIDA, 121 Prince St., New York, N. Y. 10012. Artist, filmmaker. One-woman films, including *Wake Dream* (10 min.) and *The Martyrdom of Marilyn Monroe* (30 min.).

WALSH, DEIRDRE, 95 Beekman Ave., North Tarrytown, N. Y. 10591. Documentary films and videotapes, including *Sykes* (13 min.) and *Evolving Towards Woman* (55 min.).

WALTER, ANNE B., 2106 Benjamin La., Bloomington, Ill. 61701. Artist, filmmaker; one-woman experimental films. Films include *Reflections* (5 min.), *Raymond* (6 min.), *Telegraph Ave.* (6 min.), *Dance Energia* (8 min.), *California Artist: Robert Hausen* (7 min.), *Our Bubbles, Our Boxes* (5 min.).

WANG, JULIANA, % Smiling Cat Productions, 234 E. Fifth St., New York, N. Y. 10003. Cinematographer; commercials, documentaries, theatrical shorts, etc. (See p. 211)

From Amalie Rothschild's *Woo Who? May Wilson.*

WARD, JUDITH JONES, 1601 Alaca Pl., Tuscaloosa, Ala. 35401. Producer, director; educational television. Films include *The Way We See It* (29 min.), on the American economic situation as seen by teenagers.

WARDWELL, JUDITH, 198 Ely Rd., Petaluma, Cal. 94952. Camera, animation; one-woman films. Films include *Flimfly* (1 min.), *Plastic Blag* (7 min.). Available from Canyon Cinema Co-op.

WARRENBRAND, JANE, % Women Make Movies, 257 W. 19th St., New York, N. Y. 10011. Short film *Paranoia Blues* (6 min.), about a woman's fear of city life.

WARSHAW, MIMI, % Pyramid Films, Box 1048, Santa Monica, Cal. 90406. Short films, including *Smoke Screen* (5 min., co-directed with Michael Warshaw) and *How to Make a Movie Without a Camera* (4 min., written and co-directed with Warshaw).

WASHBURN, GLADYS, 9 E. 32nd St., New York, N. Y. 10016. Veteran distributor and consultant. Films include *The Swing* (7 min., producer, camera, co-editor), *House of Dust* (17 min., producer, director, editor).

WATANABE, SUMIE, 124 E. 4th St., New York, N. Y. 10003. Films include *Louis* (8 min., documentary) and *Flip Stick* (15 min.).

WATSON, NUBRA, 23 Chestnut Hill Rd., Holden, Mass. 01520. Short films, including *Year One* (15 min.) and *War* (10 min.).

WAYNE, SUSAN, Gotham Films, 11 E. 44th St., New York, N. Y. 10017. Produces and directs industrial films for large corporations including W.T. Grant, J.C. Penney, First National City Bank, the Celanese Corporation and others. (See p. 212)

WEBB, TEENA, Kartemquin Films Ltd., 1901 W. Wellington, Chicago, Ill. 60657. Films include cooperatively made *Winnie Wright, Age 11* (26 min.), a portrait of an individual in a community torn by racial conflict as it changes from white to black, and *Viva la Causa* (12 min.), which documents the Chicano aspect of the mural movement in Chicago.

WECKER, MARLENE, Rivendell Films, 913 Hanover St., Fredericksburg, Va. 22401. Writer, producer; owner of Rivendell Films, makers of industrial and educational films.

WEGNER, SHAREN, 8741 Shoreham Dr., Los Angeles, Cal. 90069. Documentaries, animation and dramatic shorts.

WEIDMAN, JOAN, % Sarsaku Productions, 8700 Skyline Dr., Los Angeles, Cal. 90046. Filmmaker, camerawoman.

WEILAND, JOYCE, Box 190, Church Street Station, New York, N. Y. 10008. Experimental filmmaker. Films include *Barbara's Blindness* (5 min.), a collage film; *Dripping Water* (10½ min.), co-maker Michael Snow; *La Raison Avant La Passion* (80 min.), about the pain and joy of living on a continent; *1933* (4 min.), a glimpse of the year; *Sailboat* (3 min.); and *Water Sark* (14 min.), about Weiland making the film.

WEILL, CLAUDIA, % Cyclops Films, 1697 Broadway, New York, N. Y. 10019. Films include *The Other Half of the Sky: A China Memoir* (74 min.), *Joyce at 34* (28 min.), *Yoga* (7 min.), *Commuters* (4 min.), *This is the Home of Mrs. Leviant Graham* (15 min.), *Radcliffe Blues: Fran* (20 min.) and *Metropole* (4 min.). (See p. 214)

WEINBAUM, BATYA, 187 Forest Hill St., Jamaica Plain, Mass. 02130. Short feminist films.

WEINBERG, JEAN, % Women's Film Co-op, 200 Main St., Northampton, Mass. 01060. Co-filmmaker of *Autobiography of a Woman* (20 min.), which depicts the brutal and repressive forces that, while keeping women in their place, have also given them a sense of future direction.

WEINSTEIN, HANNAH, 250 E. 65th St., New York, N. Y. 10021. Cofounder (with Brock Peters, James Earl Jones and Diana Sands) of Third World Cinema, which provides on-the-job technical training for Blacks and Puerto Ricans. Produced *Claudine* (1974, feature); *Escapade* (1954, feature); and British and American TV series "Adventures of Robin Hood," "Buccaneers," and "Four Just Men." (See p. 65)

WEINSTEIN, KIT, % Women's Film Co-op, 200 Main St., Northampton, Mass. 01060. Films include *First National Women's Poetry Festival*, a visual anthology of some of the finest poets of our time. The film also raises some very complex issues with the juxtaposition of art and politics.

WEINSTEIN, MIRIAM, 27 Seymour St., Concord, Mass. 01742. Filmmaker, photographer, educator. Films include *My Father the Doctor* (18 min.), *Living with Peter* (22 min.), *We Get Married Twice* (22 min.), *Day Care Today* (27 min.), and many others. First three available from filmmaker, *Day Care Today* from Polymorph Films. Prizes include Midwest Film Festival and Sinking Creek Festival. (See p. 214)

WEISS, RUTH, % Canyon Cinema Co-op, Industrial Center Bldg., Sausalito, Cal. 94965. Films include *The Bunk* (40 min.).

WEST, ELEANOR, % Film Images, 17 W. 60th St., New York, N. Y. 10023. Films include *The Art of Rolf Nesch, Give and Take,* and *A Search for Ecological Balance* (co-directed with husband, Clifford).

WHITE, RUTH, % Ruth White Films, Box 34485, Los Angeles, Cal. 90034. Composer and producer. (See p. 215)

WICHMAN, ADALIN, Deepwood Dr., Lexington, Ky. 40505. Producer, director; commercials and documentaries.

WIECHEC, M. ELIZABETH, 18261 Huntley Square N., Birmingham, Mich. 48009. Editor, director. Films include *Get Off* (23 min., editor and interviewer), *Match* (15 min., director, co-writer, editor).

WIENER, ELIZABETH, 371 Prospect St., Cambridge, Mass. 02139. Films include *Document of a Painting* (24 min., editor, producer, camera), about an artist's theories of motion and his creation of a three-dimensional painting, *Peace Now* (7 min., editor, director), about the high school peace movement in New York City, and *Light at Night*, depicting light forms in the city. Films distributed by the filmmaker.

WILLIAMS, JEAN L., % General Delivery, Venice, Fla. 33595 or % The Cartoon Co., 1154 Second Ave., New York, N. Y. 10027. Direction, supervision, animation. Films include *Functional Anatomy of the Aortic Valve* (30 min., for American Heart Association), and *Symmetry* (11 min., for National Science Foundation), both multi-award winners, including American Film Festival, Cine Golden Eagle. Also *Shapes* (six 10-minute films for Xerox Corporation), "Sesame Street" films, animation for TV commercials and industrial, educational and medical films. (See p. 216)

WITT, ILANGA, % Youth Film Distribution Center, 43 W. 16th St., New York, N. Y. 10011. Films include a dance interpretation of Nina Simone's song, *Four Women* (5 min.), by students of Harlem Preparatory School.

WOOD, ELIZABETH M., 102 Western Ave., Cambridge, Mass. 02139, or 1 Sheridan Sq., New York, N. Y. 10014. Producer, director, editor. Films include documentaries such as *Full Circle* (10 min., on life and work of artist Doris Chase), *Karl Hess* (10 min., for "The Great American Dream Machine"), *Gypsies* (11 min., about the life style of Russian gypsies), *Roller Hockey* (6 min.), *Clinton* (10 min.). Also, theater work as director and designer, lecturer in film at Harvard's Visual Arts Center.

WOOLF, PEGGY, % Sarsaku Productions, 8700 Skyline Dr., Los Angeles, Cal. 90046. Filmmaker, script supervisor, production manager.

WORTH, EDITH, % Filmmakers' Co-op, 175 Lexington Ave., New York, N. Y. 10016. Documentary films and theatrical shorts. Films include *Seeds of Tomorrow* (27 min.) and *Name of the Game* (30 min.), both co-directed with husband, Robert.

WUNDERLICH, RENNER, % Cambridge Films, 9 Florence St., Cambridge, Mass. 02139. Films include *Taking Our Bodies Back* (30 min.), a documentary on women's health.

YEAGER, BUNNY, 7228 Biscayne Blvd., Miami, Fla. 33138. Writer, director, producer.

YOUNGSON, JEANNIE, 29 Washington Square W., New York, N. Y. 10011. One-woman filmmaker. Films include *Post-Op Transsexual M/F*, presenting a transsexual telling her life story, and animated films, *Maude in Her Hat* (3 min.), *Water* (1 min.), *The Snow Fairy* (2½ min.), and others. (See p. 216)

YURTIS, BEVERLY, 311 W. 11th St., Denver, Colo. 80204, Animator; one-woman films. Films include *Mother* (13 min.).

ZABRISKIE, SHERRY, % Film Images, 17 W. 60th St., New York, N. Y. 10023. Films include *The Secret Squint* (9 min., co-directed with husband, George).

ZHEUTLIN, CATHY, 237 Windward Ave., Venice, Cal. 90291. Producer, director, editor, camera; film and video. Member of the Santa Cruz Women's Media Collective.

ZIMMERMAN, ELYN, 1025 N. Kings Rd., Los Angeles, Cal. 90069. One-woman experimental films.

ZINNEGRABE, SUE, % Center Cinema Co-op, Industrial Center Bldg., Sausalito, Cal. 94965. Films include *The Actress* (1968, 6 min.), a woman starting to find herself through her art; *Response* (1968, 3½ min.), non-violent reactions to violence at the 1968 Chicago convention; *Tursiops* (7 min.), an underwater study of porpoises' motion.

ZWERIN, CHARLOTTE, 43 Morton St., New York, N. Y. 10014. Director of major feature-length documentaries, including *Gimme Shelter, Salesman, Robert Frost* (Academy Award, 1973), and *Meet Marlon Brando*.

Martha Coolidge

Rosalind Schneider

Johanna Demetrakas

Maria Harriton

Members of New Day Films: Amalie Rothschild, Julia Reichert,
Liane Brandon (bottom), Jim Klein, Joyce Chopra and Claudia Weill.

Dinitia Smith McCarthy   Eila Kaarresalo-Kasari

Anne Severson, as she appeared in her film, *Riverbodies*.

Naomi Levine

Donna Deitch

Nell Cox, with cameraman Vic Losick, during break in filming of *Kentucky Murder Trial*, an hour-long documentary. Cox received rare permission to bring her cameras into the courtroom.

Elda Hartley

Doris Chase   Sue Booker

Organizations

Association of Independent Video and Filmmakers, 81 Leonard St., New York, N.Y. 10013. A trade organization with more than 275 members, at least half of whom are women. Holds public and private screenings of members' films, and offers informal assistance in such matters as writing grant proposals, film distribution problems, legal questions and job referrals. Also does lobbying in Washington on bills affecting independent filmmakers. Officers: Martha Coolidge, chairperson of the board; Ed Lynch, president; Mark Weiss, vice president, and Amalie Rothschild, treasurer.

Cabin Creek Center for Work and Environmental Studies, % Barbara Kopple, 58 E. 11th St., New York, N.Y. 10003. A production cooperative that concentrates on films about social, political and economic issues.

Cambridge Documentary Films, Inc., 9 Florence St., Cambridge, Mass. 02139. A non-profit collective organization that produces documentaries on social problems, such as sexism and racism. The group also distributes its own films.

Cinema Femina, 250 W. 57th St., New York, N.Y. 10019. Issues catalogs of feminist films that are available for rental, and books speaking engagements for women filmmakers, film teachers and critics.

Cinewomen, 2269 La Granada, Los Angeles, Cal. 90668. Sponsors periodic exhibits of women's films (promoted the first animated Women's Film Festival), and holds monthly screenings that deal with cinematography, direction and production. The organization has about 150 members and is open to anyone interested in film.

Distaff Media Productions, 411 Lathrop, River Forest, Ill. 60305. A women's cooperative whose members work in film, videotape, still photography, graphics, journalism and creative writing. Each member has her own specialty, but works in other fields as well.

Femedia III, 2286 Great Highway, San Francisco, Cal. 94116. A collective of Third World women that provides technique workshops in cinematography and television production.

Film-Makers' Cooperative, 175 Lexington Ave., New York, N.Y. 10016. A non-profit film rental library open to any filmmaker who wishes to place a film on deposit. Rental fees are set by the individual filmmakers, who receive seventy-five percent of all rentals collected in their behalf. Periodically, the cooperative publishes a catalog of the films in its library, with descriptions and commentary provided by each filmmaker. The cooperative itself does not evaluate the films, nor does it acquire any rights to them.

Filmwomen of Boston, Box 275, Cambridge, Mass. 02138. A resource and information center for camerawomen, editors, soundwomen, writers, and women working in television, as well as critics and educators. The organization has a job referral service for its members, sponsors workshops in film and video techniques, and helps arrange screenings and festivals. Membership is open to women only.

Kartemquin Films Ltd., 1901 W. Wellington, Chicago, Ill. 60657. A production cooperative that makes films dealing with various social, political and economic issues.

New Day Films, P.O. Box 315, Franklin Lakes, N.J. 07417. A distribution collective formed by women filmmakers who had explicitly feminist films that they couldn't get distributed through traditional commercial channels.

Pandora Films, 200 Riverside Dr., New York, N.Y. 10025. A production collective that concentrates on films dealing with women's changing role in society. Pandora's films have been financed by small grants, while members support themselves through jobs in the film industry.

Santa Cruz Women's Media Collective, % Cathy Zheutlin, 237 Windward Ave., Venice, Cal. 90291. A group of women filmmakers who produce films and videotapes on feminist subjects.

Third World Newsreel, 26 W. 20th St., New York, N.Y. 10011. A collective that produces and distributes films about the struggles of Third World people and political movements. The organization is involved in a training program with Third World Cinema, which provides a stipend while it trains people for work in any area of film.

Tomato Productions, 7121 Pershing, St. Louis, Mo. 63130. A group of women filmmakers who produce films about women.

Twin Cities Women's Film Collective, 3815 Bryant Ave., South Minneapolis, Minn. 55409. Founded its own production and distribution company, Circle One, to put out films that explore women's role in the social structure.

Women/Artist/Filmmakers, % Silvianna Goldsmith, 151 W. 18th St., New York, N.Y. 10011. A collective of professional painters, sculptors, dancers, musicians, and poets who have expanded their work into film.

Women Make Movies, 257 W. 19th St., New York, N.Y. 10011. A non-profit educational organization designed to bring more women into film production. The organization distributes women's films and operates a neighborhood media center, the Chelsea Picture Station, which creates educational films and video productions.

Women's Film Co-op, 200 Main St., Northampton, Mass. 01060. Issues catalogs of women's films that are available for rental through the co-op. Members are feminists and socialists whose goal is to attain wide distribution for feminist films.

Women's Interart Center, 549 W. 52nd St., New York, N.Y. 10019. Operates workshops in film, video, photography, mime, ceramics, and other arts. The Center has its own theater where it holds film and video festivals. Approximately 300 women are members.

From Liliana Cavani's *The Year of the Cannibals.*

From Sarah Maldoror's *Sambizanga.*

Distributors

The following is a partial list of film distributors from whom many films mentioned in the Directory may be available:

ABC-TV, 1330 Ave. of the Americas, New York, N.Y. 10019.

ACI Films, 35 W. 45th St., New York, N.Y. 10036.

American Educational Films, 331 N. Maple Dr., Beverly Hills, Cal. 90201.

American International Pictures, 165 W. 46th St., New York, N.Y. 10036.

Anomaly Films, 105 Second Ave., New York, N.Y. 10003.

Association Sterling Films, 600 Grand Ave., Ridgefield, N.J. 07657.

Audio Film Center, Inc. (Audio Brandon), 34 MacQuesten Pkwy. So., Mt. Vernon, N.Y. 10550.

  512 Burlington Ave., La Grange, Ill. 60525.

  3868 Piedmont, Oakland, Cal. 94611.

  8615 Director's Row, Dallas, Tex. 75247.

AV-ED Films, 7934 Santa Monica Blvd, Hollywood, Cal. 90046.

Bailey Film Associates (BFA Educational Media), 2211 Michigan St., Santa Monica, Cal. 90401.

Budget Films, 4590 Santa Monica Blvd., Los Angeles, Cal. 90029.

Canyon Cinema Co-op, Industrial Center Bldg., Sausalito, Cal. 94965.

Carousel Films, 1501 Broadway, New York, N.Y. 10036.

Cathedral Films, 1921 W. Alameda Ave., Burbank, Cal. 91505.

CBS-TV, 383 Madison Ave., New York, N.Y. 10017.

CCM Films, 866 Third Ave., New York, N.Y. 10022.

Cellar Door Cinema, 56 Merian St., Lexington, Mass. 02173.

Center Cinema Co-op, % Columbia College, 540 N. Lake Shore Dr., Chicago, Ill. 60611.

Children's Television Workshop, 1 Lincoln Plaza, New York, N.Y.

Churchill Films, 662 N. Robertson, Beverly Hills, Cal.

Cine-Craft Co., 1720 N.W. Marshall, Portland, Ore. 97209.

Cinema Femina, 250 W. 57th St., New York, N.Y. 10019.

Cinema Five, 595 Madison Ave., New York, N.Y. 10002.

Cinema Services, Inc., 915 Broadway, New York, N.Y. 10010.

Columbia Cinematheque, 711 Fifth Ave., New York, N.Y. 10022.

Contemporary Films/McGraw Hill, 1221 Ave. of the Americas, New York, N.Y. 10020.

Princeton Rd., Hightstown, N.J. 08520.

828 Custer Ave., Evanston, Ill. 60202.

1714 Stockton, San Francisco, Cal. 94133.

Coronet Films, 65 E.S. Water St., Chicago, Ill. 60601.

Creative Film Society, 7237 Canby, Reseda, Cal. 91335.

Cyclops Films, 1697 Broadway, New York, N.Y. 10019.

Downech Films, 179 Van Buren St., Newark, N.J. 07107.

Educational Film Association, 17 W. 60th St., New York, N.Y. 10023.

Extension Media Center, University of California at Berkeley, Cal. 94720.

Femedia, 2286 Great Highway, San Francisco, Cal. 94116.

Film Images, 17 W. 60th St., New York, N.Y. 10023.

Film-Makers' Cooperative, 175 Lexington Ave., New York, N.Y. 10016.

Films, Incorporated, 161 Massachusetts Ave., Boston, Mass. 02115.

98 W. Jackson St., Hayward, Cal. 94554.

1144 Wilmette, Wilmette, Ill. 60091.

277 Pharr Rd., N.E., Atlanta, Ga. 30305.

FMG Productions, 49 E. 86th St., New York, N.Y. 10028.

Funky Films, 3847 22nd St., San Francisco, Cal. 94114.

Genesis Films, 1040 N. Las Palmas, Hollywood, Cal. 90038.

Grove Press, 53 E. 11th St., New York, N.Y. 10003.

Impact Films, 144 Bleecker St., New York, N.Y. 10012.

Indiana University Audio-Visual Center, Bloomington, Ind. 47401.

International Film Bureau, 332 S. Michigan Ave., Chicago, Ill. 60604.

International Film Foundation, 475 Fifth Ave., New York, N.Y. 10017.

IQ Films, 689 Fifth Ave., New York, N.Y. 10022.

Janus Films, 745 Fifth Ave., New York, N.Y. 10022.

Jason Films, 2621 Palisade Ave., Riverdale, N.Y. 10643.

Los Angeles Film Co-op, 1834 Canyon Rd., Los Angeles, Cal. 90038.

Macmillan Audio Brandon Films, 34 MacQueston Parkway So., Mt. Vernon, N.Y. 10550.

Magus Films, 777 Third Ave., New York, N.Y. 10017.

Media Plus, Inc., 60 Riverside Dr., New York, N.Y. 10024.

Multi Media Resource Center, 340 Jones St., Box 439, San Francisco, Cal. 94102.

Museum of Modern Art, Circulation Department, 11 W. 53rd St., New York, N.Y. 10019.

National Film Board of Canada, Suite 819, 680 Fifth Ave., New York, N.Y. 10019.

New Day Films, P.O. Box 315, Franklin Lakes, N.J. 07417.

New Line Cinema, 121 University Pl., New York, N.Y. 10003.

New Yorker Films, 43 W. 61st St., New York, N.Y. 10023.

Odeon Films, 22 W. 48th St., New York, N.Y. 10036.

Pacific Film Archive, 2625 Durant Ave., Berkeley, Cal. 94704.

Pandora Films, 200 Riverside Dr., New York, N.Y. 10025.

Perennial Education Inc., 1825 Willow Rd., P.O. Box 236, Northfield, Ill. 60093.

Perspective Films, 369 W. Erie St., Chicago, Ill. 60610.

Peter Rosen Productions, 630 Ninth Ave., New York, N.Y. 10036.

Phoenix Films, 470 Park Ave. So., New York,'N.Y. 10016.

Pictura Films, 43 W. 16th St., New York, N.Y. 10011.

Planned Parenthood World Population 810 Seventh Ave., New York, N.Y. 10019.

Polymorph Films, 331 Newbury St., Boston, Mass. 02115.

Pyramid Films, Box 1048, Santa Monica, Cal. 90406.

Quest Productions, 630 Ninth Ave., New York, N.Y. 10036.

Radim Films, 17 W. 60th St., New York, N.Y. 10023.

Ramsgate Films, 704 Santa Monica Blvd., Santa Monica, Cal. 90401.

Serious Business Co., 1927 Marin Ave., Berkeley, Cal. 94707.

Sterling Educational Films, Box 9497, Universal City, Los Angeles, Cal. 91608.

Sussex Films, 29 Washington Sq. W., New York, N.Y. 10011.

Texture Films, 1600 Broadway, New York, N.Y. 10019.

Third World Cinema Group, 244 W. 27th St., New York, N.Y. 10001.

Third World Newsreel, 26 W. 20th St., New York, N.Y. 10011.

Thunderbird Film Enterprises, 421 Court St., Reno, Nev. 89501.

Time-Life Films, 43 W. 16th St., New York, N.Y. 10011

Tricontinental Film Center, 333 Sixth Ave., New York, N.Y. 10014.

   1034 Lake St., Oak Park, Ill. 60301.

   P.O. Box 4430, Berkeley, Cal. 94704.

Twin Cities Women's Film Collective, % Darlene Marvy, 3555 Hamilton Ave., Wayzata, Minn. 55391.

Twyman Films, 329 Salem Ave., Dayton, O. 45401.

UA 16 (United Artists), 729 Seventh Ave., New York, N.Y. 10019.

UNICEF, United Nations, New York, N.Y.

United World Films, 1445 Park Ave., New York, N.Y. 10029.

Universal, 445 Park Ave., New York, N.Y. 10022.

Universal Kinetic, 155 Universal City Plaza, Universal City, Cal. 91608.

University Christian Movement, 1145 Massachusetts Ave., Cambridge, Mass. 02138.

University of California, Extension Media Center, Berkeley, Cal. 94720.

Valley Women's Center, 200 Main St., Northampton, Mass. 01060.

Video Nursing, 2834 Central St., Evanston, Ill. 60201.

Vision Quest and Insight Exchange, 389 Ethel Ave., Mill Valley, Cal. 94941.

   7715 N. Sheridan Rd., Chicago, Ill. 60626.

   P.O. Box 206, Lawrenceville, N.J. 08648.

Visual Resources, 1 Lincoln Plaza, New York, N.Y. 10023.

Walter Reade Organization—16 Division, 241 E. 34th St., New York, N.Y. 10016.

Warner Brothers/Seven Arts, Non-Theatrical Division, 4000 Warner Blvd., Burbank, Cal. 91505.

Wolper Productions, 555 Madison Ave., New York, N.Y. 10022.

Women Make Movies, 257 W. 19th St., New York, N.Y. 10011.

Women's Film Co-op, % Valley Women's Center, 200 Main St., Northampton, Mass. 01060.

Xerox Corporation, Advertising Division, Box 1540, Rochester, N.Y. 14600.

Yellow Ball Workshop, 62 Tarbell Ave., Lexington, Mass. 02173.

Youth Film Distribution Center, 43 W. 16th St., New York, N.Y. 10011.

Zipporah Films, 54 Lewis Wharf, Cambridge, Mass. 02110.

From Mai Zetterling's *The Girls*.

Bibliography

General Reference

BOUSSINOT, ROGER, ed. *L'Encyclopédie du cinéma*. Paris: Bordas, 1967.

CASERTA, GINO, and FERRAU, ALESSANDRO, eds. *Annuario del Cinema italiano*. Rome: Cinedizioni, 1967.

COWIE, PETER, ed. *International Film Guide* (annual). New York: A.S. Barnes and Co., 1964-1972.

Film Daily Yearbook, The. New York: Film Daily, 1929-1968.

HALLIWELL, LESLIE. *The Filmgoer's Companion*. New York: Hill & Wang, 1966 (rev. eds., 1967, 1970). New York: Avon (paperback), 1971.

International Motion Picture Almanac (annual). New York: Quigley Publications, 1933-1972.

LEONARD, HAROLD, ed. *The Film Index: A Bibliography*. Vol. I: The Film as Art. New York: H.W. Wilson, 1941. New York: Arno Press (reprint), 1970.

MANVELL, ROGER, gen. ed. (Lewis Jacobs, American ed.) *The International Encyclopedia of Film*. New York: Crown Publishers, 1972.

Motion Pictures: Catalogue of Copyright Entries. Washington, D.C.: Copyright Office, Library of Congress, 1942-1969.

MUNDEN, KENNETH W., ed. *The American Film Institute Catalogue, Feature Films 1921-1930*. New York and London: R.R. Bowker, 1971.

New York Times Film Reviews 1913-1968 and Index. 6 vols. New York: The New York Times and Arno Press, 1970.

Picturegoer's Who's Who and Encyclopedia. London: Odhams Press, 1933.

SADOUL, GEORGES. *Dictionnaire des cinéastes*. Paris: Microcosme/Editions du Seuil, 1965. Translated, edited, and updated by Peter Morris as: Sadoul, Georges. *Dictionary of Film Makers*. Berkeley-Los Angeles: University of California Press, 1972.

SCHUSTER, MEL, *Motion Picture Directors: A Bibliography of Magazine and Periodical Articles*. Metuchen, N. J.: Scarecrow Press, 1971.

Who Wrote the Movie? Los Angeles: The Academy of Motion Picture Arts and Sciences and the Writers Guild of America, West, 1970.

Film Histories

BALCON, MICHAEL, et al. *Twenty Years of British Films, 1925-1945.* London: Falcon Press, 1947.

BAXTER, JOHN. *Hollywood in the Thirties.* London: A. Zwemmer Ltd., and New York: A.S. Barnes and Co., 1968. New York: Paperback Library (paperback), 1970. Also included in: Cowie, Peter, ed. *Hollywood, 1920-1970.* Cranbury, N.J.: A.S. Barnes and Co.

BROWNLOW, KEVIN. *The Parade's Gone By.* New York: A.A. Knopf, 1968. New York: Ballantine (paperback), 1969.

DICKINSON, THOROLD, and DE LA ROCHE, CATHERINE, eds. *Soviet Cinema.* London: Falcon Press, 1948.

FORD, CHARLES. *Femmes cinéastes, ou Le Triomphe de la volonté.* Paris: Denoël/Gonthier, 1972.

HARDY, FORSYTH. *Scandinavian Film.* London: Falcon Press, 1952.

HASKELL, MOLLY, *From Reverence to Rape: The Treatment of Women in the Movies.* New York: Holt, Rinehart and Winston, 1974.

HIBBIN, NINA. *Eastern Europe: An Illustrated Guide.* London: A. Zwemmer, Ltd., and New York: A.S. Barnes and Co., 1969.

HUMPHREY, ELEANORE. "The Creative Woman in Motion Picture Production." Unpublished master's thesis. Los Angeles: University of Southern California, August, 1970.

JACOBS, LEWIS. *The Documentary Tradition: From Nanook to Woodstock.* New York: Hopkinson & Blake, 1971.

———. *The Emergence of Film Art.* New York: Hopkinson & Blake, 1969.

———. *The Rise of the American Film.* New York: Harcourt, Brace, 1939 (and 1955). New ed., New York: Teachers College Press, 1968.

JEANNE, RENE, and FORD, CHARLES. *Histoire encyclopédique du cinéma.* 5 vols. Vol. 1, Paris: Robert Laffont, 1947. Vols. 2-5, Paris, S.E.D.E., 1952-1965.

JOHNSTON, CLAIRE, ed., *Notes on Women's Cinema.* London: Society for Education in Film and Television, 1973.

KAUFFMANN, STANLEY, with HENSTELL, BRUCE, *American Film Criticism, from the Beginnings to Citizen Kane,* New York: Liveright, 1972.

KNIGHT, ARTHUR. *The Liveliest Art.* New York: Macmillan, 1957. New York: New American Library (paperback), 1959.

LEYDA, JAY. *Dianying—Electric Shadows.* Cambridge, Mass.: MIT Press, 1972.

———. *Films Beget Films.* New York: Hill & Wang, 1964 and 1970 (paperback).

———. *Kino: A History of Russian and Soviet Film.* New York: Macmillan, 1949 (and 1960). New York: Collier (paperback), 1973.

MELLEN, JOAN, *Women and Their Sexuality in the New Film.* New York: Horizon Press, 1974.

POWDERMAKER, HORTENSE. *Hollywood, The Dream Factory.* Boston: Little, Brown & Co., 1950.

PRATT, GEORGE C., *Spellbound in Darkness: a History of the Silent Film.* Greenwich, Conn.: N. Y. Graphic Society, Ltd., 1973.

RAMSAYE, TERRY, *A Million and One Nights.* New York: Simon & Schuster, 1964.

RENAN, SHELDON. *An Introduction to the American Underground Film.* New York: E.P. Dutton, 1967.

ROBINSON, DAVID. *Hollywood in the Twenties.* London: A. Zwemmer, Ltd., and New York: A.S. Barnes, 1968. Also included in: Cowie, Peter, ed. *Hollywood, 1920-1970.* Cranbury, N.J.: A.S. Barnes & Co., 1973.

ROSEN, MARJORIE, *Popcorn Venus: Women, Movies and the American Dream.* New York: Coward, McCann and Georghegan, 1973.

ROSTEN, LEO C. *Hollywood: The Movie Colony, the Movie Makers.* New York: Harcourt, Brace, 1941. New York: Arno Press (reprint), 1970.

ROTHA, PAUL. *The Film Till Now.* New York: Twayne, 1960.

SADOUL, GEORGES. *The Cinema in the Arab Countries.* Beirut and London: Interarab Centre of Cinema and Television, 1966.

———. *French Film.* London: Falcon Press, 1953.

SARRIS, ANDREW. *The American Cinema: Directors and Directions, 1929-1968.* New York: E.P. Dutton, 1968.

TALBOT, DANIEL, ed. *Film.* New York: Simon & Schuster, 1959. Berkeley-Los Angeles: University of California Press (paperback).

Books by Women in Film

ARVIDSON, LINDA (Mrs. D.W. Griffith). *When the Movies Were Young.* New York: E.P. Dutton, 1925. New York: Dover (paperback), 1969.

COFFEE, LENORE, *Recollections of a Hollywood Screenwriter.* New York: Macmillan, 1972.

DEREN, MAYA. *An Anagram of Idea, Art Form and Film.* Yonkers, N.Y.: Alicat Book Shop Press, 1945.

GISH, LILLIAN, with PINCHOT, ANN. *Lillian Gish: The Movies, Mr. Griffith and Me.* Englewood Cliffs, N.J.: Prentice-Hall, 1969.

LOOS, ANITA. *A Girl Like I.* New York: Viking, 1966.

———, and EMERSON, JOHN. *Breaking into the Movies.* New York: James A. McCann Co., 1921.

PICKFORD, MARY. *Sunshine and Shadow: The Autobiography of Mary Pickford.* New York: Doubleday, 1955.

SONTAG, SUSAN. *Against Interpretation.* New York: Farrar, Straus & Giroux, 1966. New York: Delta (paperback), 1967.

———. *Brother Carl, A Screenplay.* New York: Farrar, Straus & Giroux, 1973.

———. *A Duet for Cannibals.* New York: Noonday Original Screenplays, 1970.

———. *Styles of Radical Will.* New York: Farrar, Straus & Giroux, 1969.

Index

The names below appear in Part One (pages 1 to 144)

Abel, Jeanne, 69, 72
Ackerman, Chantal, 94
Akins, Zöe, 25
Aktasheva, Irina, 94
Alemann, Claudia, 142
Allen, Dede, 74-76
Allen, Jay Presson, 71
Amir, Aziza, 92
Anderson, Sylvia, 69, 72
Andjaparidze, Marija, 137
Angel, Suzanne, 98
Angelou, Maya, 71
Anhalt, Edna, 41
Anhalt, Edward, 41
Appel, Wendy, 85
Archibald, Nancy, 98
Arvele, Ritva, 112
Arzner, Dorothy, 19-24, 26, 28
Asseyev, Tamara, 69
Assis, 92
Audry, Jacqueline, 118-119
Avdeyenko, Yakov, 136
Aviv, Nurith, 126

Bachrach, Doro, 83-86
Bachvarova, Radka, 94
Baker, Jane, 72
Bakkar, Selma, 93
Baldwin, Ruth Ann, 13
Ballantyne, Tanya, 97
Barkhausen, Hans, 139
Barkley, Deanne, 77

Barnes, Bianca, 98
Barriscale, Bessie, 16
Barron, Evelyn, 69
Barskaya, Margarita, 137
Basaglia, Maria, 129
Batchelor, Joy, 108
Bauchens, Anne, 18, 28, 41, 74
Bauer-Adamara, 141
Bebderskaya, N., 137
Bellon, Yannick, 118
Belmont, Vera, 123
Benaceraf, Margot, 131
Bennett, Constance, 27
Benson, Sally, 28
Beranger, Clara, 15
Berg, Gretchen, 85
Bergere, Ouida, 17
Bergholm, Eija-Elina, 112
Berlin, Jeannie, 49, 51
Bezaire, Sara, 98
Bielinska, Helina, 133
Bierling, Lore, 141
Biran, Tova, 126
Blaché, Alice Guy, 2-8, 24, 133
Blaché, Herbert, 3, 6
Blaché, Simone, 3-7
Blyth, Ann, 80
Bocquet, Florence, 54
Bodard, Mag, 123
Boland, Bridget, 72
Boldt, Deborah, 85
Bologna, Joseph, 72

Booth, Margaret, 18-19, 25, 75
Bostan, Elizabeth, 143
Botley, Betty, 72
Boughner, Ruth, 98
Bow, Clara, 16, 20-21
Box, Betty, 111
Box, Joy, 73
Box, Muriel, 109-110, 133
Boyadgieva, Lada, 94
Brackett, Leigh, 71
Brien, Anja, 143
Broyde, Ruth, 125-126
Bruce, Angela, 98
Brumberg, Valentina, 137
Brumberg, Zenajeda, 137
Brunius, Pauline, 134
Bruno-Ruby, Jane, 114
Bryan, Ruth Jennings (later
  known as Ruth Bryan Owen), 13
Bryant, Charles, 15
Brzozowska, Natalia, 133
Burke, Joanne, 76
Burstyn, Ellen, 68-69
Bussi, Solange, 116
Bute, Mary Ellen, 33, 42
Byrne, Bridget, 83

Carl, Renée, 114
Carroll, Diahann, 66
Carroll, Nancy, 21
Carter, Elizabeth, 15
Cash, June, 69
Cavani, Liliana, 126, 128
Cawthorne, Ann, 72-73
Cecchi d'Amico, Suso, 129
Cekalski, Eugeniusz, 132
Cervenkova, Thea, 100
Changar, Myra, 98
Charvein, Denise, 119
Chatterton, Ruth, 20, 22
Chekhova, Olga, 135
Chenier, Louise, 98
Chester, Mrs. George
  Randolph, 13
Chevallay, Annie, 54
Chiang Ching, 99

Chichkova, Ludmilla, 100
Chou En-lai, Madame, 63
Chytilova, Vera, 100-101
Cicogna, Countess Marina, 129
Clarke, Shirley, 42-48
Clifton, Elmer, 37
Coates, Anne V., 41, 74-75
Coffee, Lenore, 17, 25
Cohen, Janelle, 69
Colbert, Claudette, 20, 22
Coleman, Delle, 64
Colfach, Elsa, 135
Colin, Lotte, 72
Collingwood, Monica, 28
Colson-Malleville, Marie, 115
Comandini, Adele, 25
Comden, Betty, 42
Companeez, Nina, 119
Cones, Nancy Ford, 24
Connell, Barbara, 77
Connell, Thelma, 77, 111
Coolidge, Martha, 86
Cooper, Budge, 110
Corrington, Joyce, 72
Cosima, Renée, 119
Costa, Lucile, 119
Craigie, Jill, 110
Cram, Mildred, 25
Crawford, Joan, 22-23
Crawford, Joanna, 72
Croft, Esther, 85
Crothers, Rachel, 16
Crozet, Simone, 119
Cruze, James, 20
Cunard, Grace, 12-13
Cusack, Dymphna, 143

Dai, Alima, 126
Dai, Yona, 126
Daniels, Bebe, 27
Danis, Aimée, 98
Dansereau, Mireille, 97
Dastrée, Anne, 119
Davis, Barbara, 98
Davis, Bea, 77
Dawn, Isabel, 25

Deans, Marjorie, 110
Debi, Arundhati, 125
de Broyer, Lisette, 94
Dee, Frances, 22
Dee, Ruby, 72
de Grasse, Joseph, 12
Delmar, Vina, 25
Delsol, Paule, 119
De Mille, Cecil B., 18
de Mol, Francoise, 94
Denis, Michaela, 111
De Passe, Suzanne, 72
Derain, Lucy, 115
Deren, Maya, 34-35, 42
Desbiens, Francine, 98
Deses, Greta, 94
Deutsch, Helen, 27, 42, 72
Devoyod, Suzanne, 114
Dey, Manju, 124
Didion, Joan, 72
Dillow, Jean Carmen, 111
Dimitri, Michèle, 94
Dinesen, Isak, 73
Di Tursi, Mary, 98
Dix, Beulah Marie, 17
Donner, Vyvyan, 24
Dossick, Jane, 70
Douglas, Pamela, 78-79
Dovzhenko, Alexander, 136
Drabble, Margaret, 72
Drew, Polly, 14
Drew, Sidney, 14
Ducey, Lillian, 13
Dulac, Germaine, 112-115
du Luart, Yolande, 119
Duncan, Alma, 98
Dunn, Marion, 98
Dunne, Irene, 26
Duras, Marguerite, 122

Earhart, Amelia, 62
Eastman, Andrea, 77
Eastman, Carole (also known as
    Adrian Joyce), 73-74
Edwards, Karen, 77
Eglington, J., 98

Eisenstein, Sergei, 135
Eklund, Alice, 135
Elek, Judit, 123
Elliot, Grace, 24
Elmer, Rita, 98
el Nahhas, Hashim, 92
Elnecave, Viviane, 98
Emerald, Connie, 36
Engel, Morris, 39
Elliott, Peggy, 72
Ephron, Henry, 42
Ephron, Phoebe, 42
Epstein, Marie, 115
Evans, Mark, 80

Fairfax, Marion, 15, 17
Falck, Karin, 135
Farnum, Dorothy, 15
Favreau, Michèle, 98
Fazan, Adrienne, 26, 28, 41, 75
Feiffer, Judy, 77
Fellini, Federico, 126
Ferchiou, Sofia, 93
Field, Mary, 108
Fielder, Margaret, 98
Fields, Verna, 76
Findlay, Roberta, 82, 85
Fiore, Joan, 97
Firestone, Elizabeth, 80
Fisher, Lois, 77
Fisher, Nicola, 85
Flack, Luise, 143
Flaherty, Robert, 28
Flanz, Marta, 133
Fletcher, Yvonne, 110
Fonda, Jane, 64
Fontaine, Joan, 38
Ford, Francis, 12-13
Forrest, Sally, 37
Fortier, Monique, 98
Fowler, Marjorie, 28, 74-75
Fox, Beryl, 95-96
Franchina, Sandra, 129
Frank, Harriet, Jr., 71
Franklin, Elsa, 98
Friedman, Yona, 123

Fuller, Loie, 114

Gaffney, Marjorie, 24
Gainey, Celeste, 85
Gardin, W. R., 135
Garson, Arline, 76
Gaskell, Jane, 72
Gates, Eleanor, 25
Gaudard, Lucette, 116
Gaumont, Lèon, 2, 5, 6
Gauntier, Gene (also known as
    Genevieve G. Ligget), 13
Geller, Joyce, 72
Georgi, Katja, 103
Gérard, Jenny, 123
Gervais-L'Heureux, Suzanne, 98
Geyra, Ellida, 125
Gil'ad, Nelly, 126
Gilbert, Nicole, 94
Gilliatt, Penelope, 111
Giroud, Francoise, 123
Gish, Dorothy, 15
Gish, Lillian, 15
Gleckler, Gayle, 73
Glyn, Elinor, 15-16, 108
Gobbi, Anna, 129
Gobeil, Charlotte, 98
Godard, Jean-Luc, 45
Gogoberidze, Lana, 137
Goldscholl, Mildred, 39
Goldscholl, Morton, 39
Gomez-Quinones, Ronda, 77
Goodrich, Frances, 28, 42
Gordon, Ruth, 28
Gottlieb, Linda, 69, 79-80
Gouse-Rénal, Christine, 123
Grafton, Sue, 73
Grand'Ry, Geneviève, 94
Green, Eve, 25
Green, Ingeborg, 39
Grennan, Laurie, 85
Griffith, D. W., 15-16, 18, 20
Grubcheva, Ivanka, 94
Guillemot, Agnes, 122
Guillon, Madelaine, 117
Gurit, Anna, 126

Gyrmathy, Livia, 124

Habeebullah, Shyama, 125
Hafez, Bahija, 92
Hain, Nadine, 54
Hall, Jenni, 72
Hamill, Pete, 62
Hammid, Alexander, 35
Hanalis, Blanche, 73
Hancock, Reba, 69
Harel-Lisztman, Colette, 119
Harrington, Joy, 111
Harrison, Joan, 27, 111
Haskell, Molly, 84
Hayward, Lillie, 27
Hayworth, Rita, 27
Hedmann, Trine, 102
Hein, Birgit, 142
Hein, Wilhelm, 142
Heller, Rosilyn, 77
Hellman, Lillian, 27
Henning-Jensen, Astrid, 101-102
Henry, Gale, 14
Henson, Joan, 98
Hepburn, Katharine, 20, 22
Hernon, Nan, 20
Hesse, Isa, 142
Hill, Emma, 26
Hill, Gladys, 72
Hillel-Erlanger, Irene, 112
Hoffman-Uddgren, Anna, 133-134
Hooper, Joyce, 73
Hoskin, Mai, 98
Hovmand, Annelise, 102
Hsia Kuei-ying, 99
Hubley, Faith, 59-62
Hubley, John, 59-61
Hulin, Sylvia, 119
Hullet, Daniele, 142
Huntington, Joan, 73
Huyck, Willard, 73
Hyams, Nessa, 77

Ingram, Rex, 13
Iribe, Marie-Louise, 115
Ivers, Julia Crawford, 13

Jaffe, Patricia Lewis, 77
Jakubowska, Wanda, 131-132
Jallaud, Sylvia, 123
James, Monique, 77
Jashenko, Elena, 98
John, Barbara, 69
Johnson, Agnes, 15-16
Johnson, Osa, 24-25
Jones, Natalie R., 70
Jong, Erica, 67
Joyce, Adrian (pseudonym for
    Carole Eastman), 73-74
Junge, Winifred, 103

Kaarresalo-Kasari, Eila, 112
Kael, Pauline, 53
Kallen, Lucille, 73
Kaniewska, Maria, 133
Kanin, Fay, 42
Kapf, Elinor, 72
Kaplan, Nelly, 120
Katainen, Elina, 112
Katz, Gloria, 73
Kavalauskas, Maryte, 85
Kehoe, Isobel, 98
Kellogg, Marjorie, 72
Kellogg, Virginia, 28, 42
Kelly, George, 22
Kennedy, Ethyl, 17
Kernochan, Sarah, 67
Kerr, Anita, 77, 79
Kerr-Sokal, Charlotte, 142
Khodatayeva, O., 137
Kiel, Edith, 94
Kingsley, Dorothy, 42, 72
Klausner, Margot, 125
Klein, Bonny, 98
Klein, Judith, 98
Klingman, L. Deborah, 77
Klove, Jane, 72
Knudsen, Mette, 102
Kocheverova, Nadezhda, 137
Konalski, Tadeusz, 132
Krasilovsky, Alexis, 85
Krawicz, Mécislas, 133
Kronish, Amy, 85

Krumbachova, Ester, 101
Kubrick, Stanley, 45
Kunhenn, Dr. Paul, 142

Lake, Veronica, 69
Lambart, Evelyn, 95
Lang, Fritz, 141
Laughlin, Tom, 67-68
Lavallée, Nicole, 98
Lawrence, Viola, 17-18, 25, 28,
    41, 74
Leacock, Richard, 44
Lederberg, Dov, 35
Lee, Joanna, 73
Leenhardt, Yvonne, 117
Lehman, Gladys, 27
Lennart, Isobel, 42, 71
Lenoir, Claudine, 116
Lepeuve, Monique, 123
Lesser, Laura, 77
Levie, Francoise, 94
Levien, Sonya, 25, 42
Leyer, Rhoda, 98
Liprott, Peggy, 98
Littlefield, Nancy, 85
Littlewood, Joan, 111
Lobarsky, Anat, 126
Locke, Jeannine, 98
Loden, Barbara, 42, 54-58
Loos, Anita, 15-16
Lott, Mona, 73
Lovett, Josephine, 16
Lucas, Marcia, 68, 76
Luce, Clare Booth, 28
Lumière brothers, 2, 5
Lupino, Ida, 26, 36-40

Maas, Audrey, 68
Maas, Willard, 35
Mabaouj, Najet, 93
MacDonald, Sally, 98
MacKenzie, Shelagh, 98
MacLaine, Shirley, 62-63
Macrorie, Alma, 28, 41, 74
Madison, Cleo, 13
Maldoror, Sarah, 91-92

Mangini, Cecilia, 129
Manoogian, Betzi, 69
Mansarova, Aida, 137
Marczakowi, Marta, 133
Mariani, Dacia, 129
Marion, Frances, 14-16, 25
Marsh, Mary, 110
Martin, Susan, 69
Mason, Sarah Y., 25
Mathis, June, 16
May, Elaine, 42, 48-52, 58
Mayer, Louis B., 18
Mayo, Nine, 123
Mazzetti, Lorenza, 129
McCord, Vera, 13
McCrea, Bonnie, 54
McDonagh sisters, 143
McKnight, Anna, 18
McLaren, Audrey, 98
McLean, Barbara, 26, 28,
    41, 74-75
McNair, Sue, 72
McPherson, Margaret, 72
McVey, Lucille (also known as
    Polly Drew), 14
Meineche, Annelise, 102
Meliés, George, 4
Menard, Lucie, 98
Menken, Marie, 35, 42
Meredyth, Bess, 16, 25
Meszaros, Marta, 124
Meyer, Muffie, 77
Miller, Julia, 66-67
Milton, Joanna, 69, 72
Minelli, Liza, 74
Misonne, Claude, 93-94
Moinet, Monique, 94
Moise, Mina, 24
Molas, Zet, 100
Montgomery, Robert, 80
Montivier, Monique, 54
Moravia, Alberto, 129
Morgan, Diana, 111
Morra, Irene, 18, 25, 28, 75
Movin, Lisbeth, 102
Mozisova, Bozena, 100

Mulay, Vijaya, 125
Muntcho, Monique, 116
Murfin, Jane, 13-14
Murgatroyd, Susan, 98
Murnau, F. W., 141
Murphy, Julia, 98
Murray, Mary P., 69
Murray, Rita, 69
Musidora (Jeanne Roques), 114
Myers, Carol, 98

Napolean, Jo, 69, 72
Nassiter, Marcia, 77
Nathan, Vivian, 86
Naumberg, Nancy, 24
Navarra, Aimee, 93
Nazimova, 15, 17
Needles, Susan, 85
Negulesco, Jean, 36
Nekes, Dore, 142
Nekes, Werner, 142
Nemeth, Ted, 33
Newman, Eve, 74, 76
Neuer, Joann, 85
Nickel, Gitta, 103-107
Nichols, Mike, 49-50, 74
Nides, Tina, 77
Noguchi, Isamu, 35
Noiseux-Labreque, Lise, 98
Noldan, Svend, 142
Nordstrom, Frances, 13
Normand, Mabel, 15
Nunes, Maxine, 98

Oberon, Merle, 22-23
Oettinger, Nancy, 85
O'Fredericks, Alice, 101
Ogden, Rita, 85
O'Hara, Maureen, 22
Oliver, Suzanne, 98
Olson, Mary, 72
Omatsu, Maryka, 98
Orfyn, Wedad, 92
Orkin, Ruth, 39
Oro, Renee, 131

Pade, Astrid, 102
Pansini, Rose, 114
Paranjpe, Sai, 125
Pard, Yvette, 98
Pardis, Monique, 98
Parent, Gail, 73
Park, Ida May, 12
Parker, Claire, 116
Parker, Francine, 21, 23, 63-64
Parsons, Harriet, 27
Paul, Edna, 77, 85
Paul, Millie, 77
Pedersen, Ann, 85
Pennebaker, Donn, 44
Perla, Brenda, 73
Perry, Eleanor, 70-71
Perry, Margaret, 98
Petelska, Eva, 133
Peters, Brock, 65
Petkanova, Magda, 94
Peyser, Lois, 72
Phillips, Michael, 67
Phillips, Zoe, 69
Pi, Rosario, 143
Pickett, Elizabeth, 12
Pickford, Mary, 14-15
Pilikhina, Margarita, 137
Pilon, Raymonde, 98
Pine, Tina, 65, 70-71
Piper, Anne, 72
Plivova-Simkova, Vera, 137
Poirier, Anne-Claire, 97
Pokras, Barbara, 77
Pollack, Mimi, 135
Poplavskaya, Irina, 137
Porter, Edwin S., 4
Powers, Mala, 37
Pravov, Ivan, 135
Premysler, Francine, 119
Preobrazhenskaya, Olga, 135
Pressman, Lynn, 70
Puchi, Rebecca, 131

Queeny, Mary, 92

Raabeova, Hedvika, 100

Rafelson, Toby, 68
Ralston, Esther, 20
Rascoe, Judith, 73
Rashevskaya, Natalya, 137
Raynal, Jackie, 122
Reals, Nancy, 69
Reenberg, Annelise, 102
Reeves, Theodore, 27-28
Reid, Dorothy Davenport, 40
Reiner, Carl, 50
Reiniger, Lotte, 142
Renoir, Marguerite, 117
Resnais, Alain, 135
Reville, Alma, 107
Revol, Claude, 115
Rhodes, Harriet, 73
Richards, Jean, 98
Richardson, Tony, 50
Riefenstahl, Leni, 137-140
Riggs, Sarah, 72
Riley, Brooks, 85
Riley, Nancy, 98
Robb, Dodi, 98
Roberts, Marguerite, 71
Robinson, Christine, 85
Robson, Mark, 79
Rochlin, Diane, 72
Roland, Rita, 76
Romero, Nancy, 70
Ronnel, Ann, 80
Roos, Lisa, 102
Roosevelt, Leila, 26
Rose, Louisa, 73
Rosen, Marjorie, 24, 71
Rosencrantz, Margareta, 135
Rosenfield, Lois, 70
Roshal, Gregori, 136
Rosher, Charles, 15
Rothman, Marion, 74, 76
Rothman, Stephanie, 42, 58-59
Rozan, Micheline, 69
Rule, Beverly C., 13
Russell, Rosalind, 20, 22, 27, 38-39

Saare, Arla, 98

Sabogal, Ernesto, 131
Sagan, Leontine, 140-141
Samper, Gabriela, 130-131
Samuels, Maxine, 98
Sanders, Helke, 142
Sanders, Marlene, 80-81
Sands, Diana, 65
Sarner, Sylvia, 77
Saunders, Janet, 85
Scandrani, Fatma, 93
Scappettone, Sandra, 72
Schaffer, Jane, 69
Schefer, Mandy, 39
Schlesinger, Riva, 77
Schoenfeld, Bernard C., 42
Schoonmaker, Thelma, 76
Schreiber, Nancy, 85
Schulman, Nina, 70
Schuster, Harry, 57
Scola, Katherine, 25
Scorsese, Martin, 68
Scott, Cynthia, 98
Selznick, Joyce, 65, 69-70
Sewell, Blanche, 18, 25
Shackleton, Allan, 83
Shannon, Kathleen, 95
Shepherd, Cybill, 51
Shepitka, Larissa, 137
Sherman, Alida, 72
Sherman, Vincent, 36
Shigekawa, Joan, 69
Shih, Mei, 99
Shipman, Nell, 14
Shu Shuen, 99
Shub, Esther, 135
Shurey, Dinah, 107
Shyman, Mona, 85
Sidney, Sylvia, 20, 22
Silver, Joan, 72, 80
Silverstein, Helen, 69
Singer, Judith, 72
Sita-Bella, Thérèse, 93
Slesin, Aviva, 63
Smalley, Phillips, 11
Smith, Howard, 67
Sokolowska, Anna, 133

Solntseva, Yulia, 136
Somerset, Pat, 77
Sontag, Susan, 42, 52-54, 120,
  139-140
Sopanen, Jeri, 54
Soray, Türkan, 144
Sorère, Gabrielle, 114
Spencer, Dorothy, 26, 28, 41,
  74-75, 80
Sperling, Karen, 83-86
Spewack, Bella, 25
Spils, Mai, 142
Spring, Sylvia, 97
Stanton, Jane C., 73
Starevich, Irene, 117
Stark, Ray, 19
Stayden, Gail, 70
Steed, Judy, 98
Sten, Anna, 22
Stenback, Kirsten, 102
Stéphane, Nicole, 54, 119-120,
  123
Stewart, Paula, 69
Stone, Andrew, 40
Stone, Virginia, 40, 77
Stonehouse, Ruth, 15
Strandgaard, Charlotte, 102
Straub, Jean-Marie, 142
Strauss, Helen M., 78
Streisand, Barbra, 71
Stroyeva, Vera, 136
Sullivan, C. Gardner, 40
Sutherland, Donald, 64
Sutherland, Efua, 93
Swanson, Gloria, 16
Szemes, Marianne, 124
Szolowski, K., 132

Tanaka, Kinuyo, 130
Tanser, Julia, 85
Tavel, Ronald, 35
Tayer, Elyana, 115
Taylor, Delores, 67-68
Taylor, Renee, 72
Teff, Joyce, 98

Tewkesbury, Joan, 73
Thome, Karen, 142
Thompson, Danielle, 72
Thompson, Margaret, 111
Thorndike, Annelie, 103
Thulin, Ingrid, 135
Titayna, 115
Toeplitz, Jerzy, 132
Tokieda, Toshie, 130
Torres, Joan, 72
Toscano, Carmen, 131
Toscano, Salvador, 131
Toshevas, Nevena, 94
Toukermine, Doris, 98
Touloubieva, Z., 137
Toye, Wendy, 111
Travers, Roxy, 98
Tresgot, Annie, 122
Trevor, Claire, 37
Trintignant, Nadine
    Marquand, 122
Troyanova, I., 137
Tual, Denise, 118-119
Tuchock, Wanda, 15
Tully, May, 13
Turner, Helene, 26
Trylova, Hermina, 100

Ulitskaya, Olga, 137
Ulrych, Lucy, 123
Ursianu, Malvina, 143
Uszycka, Walentyna, 133

Valentino, Rudolph, 16, 20
Vandal, Marion, 116
Van Dongen, Helen, 28
Van Dyke, Willard, 44-45
Van Heyningen, Judy, 85
Van Stolk, Mary, 98
Van Upp, Virginia, 25-27
Varda, Agnès, 120-121
Vas, Judit, 124
Vedrès, Nicole, 117-118
Vergez-Tricom, 119
Vertov, Dziga, 135
Viby, Marguerite, 102
Vidor, Charles, 26-27, 36

Viel, Marguerite, 115
Virginia, Barbara, 144
von Harbou, Thea, 141
von Prauheim, Rosa, 142

Wagner, Mamie, 18
Wali, Mustafa, 92
Wang Ping, 99
Warren, Eda, 18, 25, 75
Watson, Patricia, 98
Watts, Alan, 47-48
Waugh, Evelyn, 50
Webb, Mildred, 13
Weber, Lois, 11-12, 24, 28
Weed, Marlene, 72
Wegener, Else, 141
Weidman, Joan, 64
Weill, Claudia, 63
Weinstein, Hannah, 65-66
Weintraub, Sandy, 68
Weissova, Lenka, 100
Wertmuller, Lina, 126-128
West, Mae, 25
White, Deanna, 98
White, Gloria, 98
Whitlin, Ray, 131
Wieland, Joyce, 97
Wigmore, Donna-Lou, 98
Wilson, Elsie Jane, 13
Wilson, Margery, 13
Winsloe, Christa, 140
Winston, Helen, 111
Wohl, Stanislaw, 132
Wolfe, Fanny (Fanchon), 26
Wolff, Ruth, 73
Woods, Lotta, 17
Wright, Else Gress, 102

Yeomans, Mary, 77
Yoresh, Abigail, 126
Young, Clara Kimball, 16
Young, Collier, 37

Zerzyski, Jerzy, 132
Zetterling, Mai, 133-134
Zheljazkova, Binka, 94
Zwerin, Charlotte, 69, 76

THE AUTHOR

Sharon Smith, who is a native of Santa Monica, began her research for this book while studying for a master's degree at the University of Southern California. She completed the book four years later amid the trials of renovating a 150-year-old farmhouse she and her husband found near the village of Canaan in central Maine. Her next book will be about the ordeal of restoring an old farmhouse and coping with Maine winters.